Dynamic Testing

The goal of this book is to present and evaluate the concept of dynamic testing. Unlike "static" tests, such as the SAT or IQ tests, dynamic tests emphasize learning potential rather than past learning accomplishments. The book opens with a theoretical framework of abilities as forms of developing expertise. It continues with an introduction to dynamic testing and then a capsule history of dynamic testing. The book also reviews the approaches of Feuerstein and Budoff and other diverse approaches to dynamic testing. Drs. Sternberg and Grigorenko present their own three-pronged approach to dynamic testing along with two case studies from their own research in which dynamic testing was utilized. The authors conclude that dynamic testing has enormous potential that has not yet been fully tapped.

Robert J. Sternberg is IBM Professor of Psychology and Education in the Department of Psychology and Director of the Center for the Psychology of Abilities, Competencies, and Expertise (PACE Center) at Yale University. He has won a number of awards, most recently the James McKeen Cattell Award of the American Psychological Society, the Palmer O. Johnson Award of the American Educational Research Association, and the Distinguished Lifetime Contribution Award of the Connecticut Psychological Association.

Elena L. Grigorenko is Associate Professor of Psychology at Moscow State University and Research Scientist and Deputy Director of the PACE Center at Yale University. She has published more than 100 books and articles and is Associate Editor of *Contemporary Psychology*.

DYNAMIC TESTING

*The Nature and Measurement of
Learning Potential*

Robert J. Sternberg
Yale University

Elena L. Grigorenko
Yale University
Moscow State University

CAMBRIDGE
UNIVERSITY PRESS

PUBLISHED BY THE PRESS SYNDICATE OF THE UNIVERSITY OF CAMBRIDGE
The Pitt Building, Trumpington Street, Cambridge, United Kingdom

CAMBRIDGE UNIVERSITY PRESS
The Edinburgh Building, Cambridge CB2 2RU, UK
40 West 20th Street, New York, NY 10011-4211, USA
10 Stamford Road, Oakleigh, VIC 3166, Australia
Ruiz de Alarcón 13, 28014 Madrid, Spain
Dock House, The Waterfront, Cape Town 8001, South Africa

http://www.cambridge.org

First published 2002

Printed in the United States of America

Typeface Palatino 10/13 pt.   *System* QuarkXPress [AG]

A catalog record for this book is available from the British Library.

Library of Congress Cataloging in Publication data
Sternberg, Robert J.
Dynamic testing : the nature and measurement of learning potential / Robert J.
Sternberg, Elena L. Grigorenko.
p.   cm.
Includes bibliographical references and index.
ISBN 0-521-77128-5 – ISBN 0-521-77814-x (pb.)
1. Learning ability – testing. 2. Intelligence tests – Evaluation. 3. Transfer of training.
I. Grigorenko, Elena. II. Title.
LB1134 .S74 2001
153.9′4–dc21   2001025402

ISBN 0 521 77128 5 hardback
ISBN 0 521 77814 x paperback

Contents

Preface

Each year, millions of tests are given to children and adults in the United States. The number of tests given in the world is probably in the billions. Almost all of these are what are called *static tests*, meaning that the examiner presents items, either one at a time or all at once, and each examinee is asked to respond to these items successively, without feedback or intervention of any kind. At some point in time after the administration of the test is over, each examinee typically receives the only feedback he or she will get: a report on a score or set of scores. By that time, the examinee is likely studying for one or more future tests.

Lev Vygotsky in the Soviet Union and later Reuven Feuerstein in Israel developed the foundation for and proposed an alternative to this traditional form of static testing. The alternative they proposed is usually called *dynamic testing*. In this form of testing, each examinee receives one or more items, as in static testing. But rather than the score's being based simply on performance on the initial presentations of these items, the score is based on a system that takes into account the results of an intervention. In this intervention, the examiner teaches the examinee how to perform better on individual items or on the test as a whole. The final score may be a learning score representing the difference between pretest (before learning) and posttest (after learning) scores, or it may be the score on the posttest considered alone.

Although the rationales of Vygotsky and Feuerstein for such testing used slightly different terminology, they were nevertheless surprisingly similar. Vygotsky proposed dynamic testing as a means of measuring what he referred to as a *zone of proximal development (ZPD)*, or the zone between an individual's independent and guided performance. The motivating idea was that a dynamic test would measure a person's ability to profit from guidance and thereby provide insight into that person's ZPD. The more the individual could profit from guidance and thereby improve an initial score, the greater the ZPD was proposed to be. Feuerstein viewed dynamic testing as a way to measure an individual's ability to profit from mediation. Feuerstein suggested that learning could be either direct (as typically goes on in a classroom) or mediated. Whereas static classroom tests might measure direct learning, a dynamic test administered by a trained examiner might measure the ability to profit from what Feuerstein referred to as *mediated learning experience (MLE)*. Feuerstein was particularly impressed with the results of dynamic testing on children who had been labeled mentally retarded and children who were from nontraditional ethnic backgrounds. Many of these children who looked to be delayed in development on traditional measures performed much better in the context of a dynamic-testing environment.

Since the proposals of Vygotsky and Feuerstein, many studies have been carried out to test the value of dynamic testing. Our book reviews these studies and the accompanying theories and methodologies. The book originated in an article (Grigorenko & Sternberg 1998), but goes well beyond the article in its coverage, analysis, and currency.

The main thesis of this book is that dynamic testing is a wonderful idea whose implementations for the most part have been less than fully satisfactory. If a hard-headed empiricist were to judge the literature on the basis of the large majority of the work published so far, the empiricist probably would conclude that dynamic testing promises somewhat more, perhaps substantially more, than it delivers. If, however, one were to judge dynamic testing on the basis of the most encouraging work conducted so far, one would come to a very different conclusion, namely, that it is an approach with enormous promise that is already starting to be realized. Thus, we strongly believe in and support use of the construct.

We had five main motivations for writing this book:

First, we believe and our data have shown, as have the data of others, that dynamic testing has a major contribution to make to the testing of both children and adults. We believe that it can provide all of the information furnished by static tests and more.

Second, most psychologists and educators, even those in the testing field, are only minimally acquainted with the concepts of dynamic testing and the examples of dynamic tests that have been created to date. This book serves as a text to inform psychologists and educators about dynamic-testing concepts.

Third, many educators have recognized the need to combine instruction and assessment – to view them as integrated rather than as separated. But these educators have not always been clear on how this integration can be accomplished. Dynamic testing provides a natural vehicle for such integration. Indeed, such integration is a necessary result of using dynamic testing.

Fourth, in some societies, including but not limited to the United States, testing rules. People's success and failure in the society are largely, although certainly not exclusively, determined by results of tests. People who do not test well lose opportunities – with regard to grouping in schools, college admissions, admissions to graduate and professional schools, and financial aid. We believe that a major problem is not with the use of tests per se, but with the kinds of tests being used. Conclusions are being drawn that go way beyond the inferences that properly should be drawn from the test scores. We believe that dynamic tests possess the potential to make information gleaned from tests more valid and more useful.

Finally, although test development is ongoing in many parts of the world, we believe that the direction this development is taking is far less than optimal. Testing organizations often throw large amounts of money into cosmetic changes in tests, such as changes in vehicles of delivery (e.g., converting paper-and-pencil tests to computerized tests). Instead, or at least in addition, we believe these organizations should be investing in the creation of a new generation of tests. These tests would differ not only in minor ways from what we now have, but rather, in fundamental ways. Dynamic tests provide one important direction for such research and development efforts.

We believe that there is a wide range of potential audiences for this book. These audiences cover a variety of fields.

First and foremost are psychologists who are already interested in dynamic testing. There are a number of organizations worldwide with such an interest, with many members who will find this book useful in updating themselves about the most recent developments in dynamic testing.

Second, we believe the book should be of interest to psychologists and educators who are interested in measurement and assessment issues. Because the methods can be applied to education more broadly defined, the book should be of equal interest to all educational and school psychologists.

Third, we believe the book should be of interest to developmental, cognitive, clinical, and counseling psychologists who have an interest in understanding and assessing cognitive abilities. Our book is oriented not only toward improving assessment but also toward understanding cognitive functioning, an interest of people in all of these fields.

Fourth, we believe the book will be of interest to individuals in the field of special education. Much of the use of dynamic testing has been in this field and has been oriented toward showing skills in children who do not ordinarily show their skills well in traditional static assessments.

Finally, the book can be used as a text for students who are interested in the topic of dynamic testing. Students or others who want to learn about dynamic testing in a systematic and easy-to-understand way will find our book useful for this purpose.

The authors of this book have wide-ranging backgrounds relevant to dynamic testing. Robert J. Sternberg is IBM Professor of Psychology and Education in the Department of Psychology at Yale University and Director of the Center for the Psychology of Abilities, Competencies, and Expertise at Yale. He received a Ph.D. in psychology from Stanford University. He is the author of roughly 800 articles, books, and book chapters in the field of psychology. His specialties are in intelligence, creativity, wisdom, and related higher-cognitive abilities. Sternberg is past editor of *Psychological Bulletin* and editor of *Contemporary Psychology*. He is a Fellow of the American Academy of Arts and Sciences, American Association for the Advancement of Science, American Psychological Association, and American Psychological Society. He is president or past president of four divisions of the APA. He has won numerous awards, including two awards from the American Psychological Association, one award from the American Psychological Society, and four awards from the American Educational Research Association. Sternberg has worked with several major testing organizations as both a consultant and an external researcher. He has received honorary doctorates from four universities. Dr. Sternberg is known, in particular, for his ability theories, including the theory of abilities as forms of developing expertise.

Elena L. Grigorenko is Research Scientist in the Department of Psychology and Child Study Center at Yale University and Associate Professor of Psychology at Moscow State University. She is also Deputy Director of the Center for the Psychology of Abilities, Competencies, and Expertise at Yale. She received a Ph.D. in psychology from Moscow State University and a Ph.D. in both psychology and genetics from Yale. She is the author of roughly 100 books and articles in the fields of psychology and genetics. Grigorenko was educated at Moscow State by colleagues, students, and students of students of Vygotsky (such as Bluma

Zeigarnik, Sergei Smirnov, Ludmila Obukhova, and Valerii Petukhov) and is senior author of an article on "Dynamic Testing" published in the *Psychological Bulletin* (Grigorenko & Sternberg 1998). Due to her background in multivariate statistics, Grigorenko is especially interested in issues related to the analysis of the data generated by dynamic testing instruments. Moroever, she also has been involved in a number of studies in diverse cultures, such as ones in Tanzania, Kenya, Zambia, the Gambia, India, and Russia, and she has observed the power of dynamic assessment in variable cultural contexts.

Preparation of this book was supported under the Javits Act Program (Grant No. R206R000001) as administered by the Office of Educational Research and Improvement, U.S. Department of Education, and by the National Science Foundation (Grant No. REC-9979843). Grantees undertaking such projects are encouraged to express freely their professional judgment. This book, therefore, does not necessarily represent the position or policies of the National Science Foundation, Office of Educational Research and Improvement, or the U.S. Department of Education, and no official endorsement should be inferred.

PART ONE

THEORETICAL FRAMEWORK

In this part of the book, we present the theoretical framework for our analysis of dynamic testing, a framework that views abilities as forms of developing expertise. According to this framework, abilities are malleable and flexible rather than fixed. Hence a form of measurement is needed for abilities that takes their malleability and flexibility into account.

CHAPTER ONE

Abilities as Forms of Developing Expertise

The conventional view of abilities is that they represent relatively stable attributes of individuals that develop as an interaction between heredity and environment. Factor analysis and related techniques then can be used on tests of intelligence to determine the structure of intellectual abilities, as illustrated by the massive analysis of Carroll (1993).

The argument of this chapter, advancing that of Sternberg (1998a, 1999b), is that this view of what abilities are and of what ability tests measure may be incorrect. An alternative view is that of abilities as developing expertise and of ability tests as measuring an aspect – typically a limited aspect – of developing expertise. Developing expertise is defined here as the ongoing process of the acquisition and consolidation of a set of skills needed for a high level of mastery in one or more domains of life performance. Good performance on ability tests requires a certain kind of expertise, and to the extent this expertise overlaps with the expertise required by schooling or by the work place, there will be a correlation between the tests and performance in school or in the work place. But such correlations represent no intrinsic relation between abilities and other kinds of performance, but instead represent overlaps in the kinds of expertise needed to perform well under different kinds of circumstances.

There is nothing privileged about ability tests. One could as easily use, say, academic achievement to predict intelligence-related scores. For example, it is as simple to use the SAT-II (a measure of achievement) to predict the SAT-I (a measure once called the Scholastic Assessment Test and formerly called the Scholastic Aptitude Test) as vice versa, and of course, the levels of prediction will be the same. Both tests measure achievement, although the kinds of achievements they measure are different.

According to this view, although ability tests may have temporal priority relative to various criteria in their administration (i.e., ability tests are administered first, and later, criterion indices of performance, such as grades or achievement test scores, are collected), they have no psychological priority. All of the various kinds of assessments are of the same kind psychologically. What distinguishes ability tests from other kinds of assessments is how the ability tests are used (usually predictively) rather than what they measure. There is no qualitative distinction among the various kinds of assessments. All tests measure various kinds of developing expertise.

Conventional tests of intelligence and related abilities measure achievement that individuals should have accomplished several years back (see also Anastasi & Urbina 1997). Tests such as vocabulary, reading comprehension, verbal analogies, arithmetic problem solving, and the like, are all, in part, tests of achievement. Even abstract-reasoning tests measure achievement in dealing with geometric symbols, skills taught in Western schools (Laboratory of Comparative Human Cognition 1982). One might as well use academic performance to predict ability-test scores. The problem regarding the traditional model is not in its statement of a correlation between ability tests and other forms of achievement but in its proposal of a causal relation whereby the tests reflect a construct that is somehow causal of, rather than merely temporally antecedent to, later success. The developing-expertise view in no way rules out the contribution of genetic factors as a source of individual differences in who will be able to develop a given amount of expertise. Many human attributes, including intelligence, reflect the covariation and interaction of genetic and environmental factors. But the contribution of genes to an individual's intelligence cannot be directly measured or even directly estimated. Rather, what is measured is a portion of what is expressed, namely, manifestations of developing expertise, the kind of expertise that potentially leads to reflective practitioners in a variety of fields (Schon 1983). This approach to measurement has been used explicitly by Royer, Carlo, Durfresne, and Mestre (1996), who have shown that it is possible to develop measurements of reading skill reflecting varying levels of developing expertise. In such assessments, outcome measures reflect not simply quantitative assessments of skill, but qualitative differences in the types of developing expertise that have emerged (e.g., ability to understand technical text material, ability to draw inferences from this material, or ability to draw out "big ideas" in technical text).

According to this view, measures of abilities *should* be correlated with later success, because both measures of abilities and various measures of success require developing expertise of related types. For example, both typically require what are sometimes referred to as *metacomponents* of thinking: recognition of problems, definition of problems, formulation of strategies to solve problems, representation of information, allocation of resources, and monitoring and evaluation of problem solutions (Sternberg 1985). These skills develop as results of gene-environment covariation and interaction. If we wish to call them *intelligence,* that is certainly fine, so long as we recognize that what we are calling intelligence is a form of developing expertise.

A major goal of work under the point of view presented here is to integrate the study of intelligence and related abilities (see reviews in Sternberg 1990, 1994b, 2000) with the study of expertise (Chi, Glaser, & Farr 1988; Ericsson 1996; Ericsson & Smith 1991; Hoffman 1992). These literatures, typically viewed as distinct, are here viewed as ultimately involved with the same psychological mechanisms.

The Specifics of the Developing-Expertise Model

The specifics of the developing-expertise model are shown in Figure 1.1. At the heart of the model is the notion of *developing expertise* – that individuals are constantly in a process of developing expertise when they work within a given domain. They may and do, of course, differ in rate and asymptote of development. The main constraint in achieving expertise is not some fixed prior level of capacity, but purposeful engagement involving direct instruction, active participation, role modeling, and reward.

Elements of the Model

The model of developing expertise has six key elements (although certainly they do not constitute an exhaustive list of elements in the development of expertise): metacognitive skills, learning skills, thinking skills, knowledge, motivation, and expertise. Although it is convenient to separate these six elements, they are fully interactive, as shown in the figure. They influence each other, both directly and indirectly. For example, learning leads to knowledge, but knowledge facilitates further learning.

1. *Metacognitive skills.* Metacognitive skills (or metacomponents, see Sternberg 1985) refer to people's understanding and control of

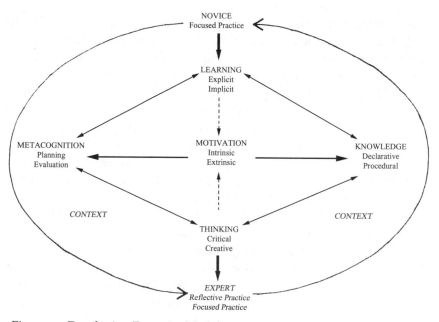

Figure 1.1 Developing Expertise Model

their own cognition. For example, such skills would encompass
what an individual knows about writing papers or solving arithmetic word problems, both with regard to the steps that are involved and with regard to how these steps can be executed effectively. Seven metacognitive skills are particularly important:
problem recognition, problem definition, problem representation,
strategy formulation, resource allocation, monitoring of problem
solving, and evaluation of problem solving (Sternberg 1985, 1986).
All of these skills are modifiable (Sternberg 1986, 1988; Sternberg
& Grigorenko 2000; Sternberg & Spear-Swerling 1996).

2. *Learning skills.* Learning skills (knowledge-acquisition components) are essential to the model (Sternberg 1985, 1986), although
they are certainly not the only learning skills that individuals use.
Learning skills are sometimes divided into explicit and implicit
ones. Explicit learning is what occurs when we make an effort to
learn; implicit learning is what occurs when we pick up information incidentally, without any systematic effort. Examples of learning skills are selective encoding, which involves distinguishing
relevant from irrelevant information; selective combination,
which involves putting together the relevant information; and se-

lective comparison, which involves relating new information to information already stored in memory (Sternberg 1985).

3. *Thinking skills.* There are three main kinds of thinking skills (or performance components) that individuals need to master (Sternberg 1985, 1986, 1994a). It is important to note that these are sets of, rather than individual, thinking skills. Critical (analytical) thinking skills include analyzing, critiquing, judging, evaluating, comparing and contrasting, and assessing. Creative thinking skills include creating, discovering, inventing, imagining, supposing, and hypothesizing. Practical thinking skills include applying, using, utilizing, and practicing (Sternberg 1997a). They are the first step in the translation of thought into real-world action.

4. *Knowledge.* There are two main kinds of knowledge that are relevant in academic situations. Declarative knowledge is of facts, concepts, principles, laws, and the like. It is "knowing that." Procedural knowledge is of procedures and strategies. It is "knowing how." Of particular importance is procedural tacit knowledge, which involves knowing how the system functions in which one is operating (Sternberg et al. 2000; Sternberg & Horvath 1999; Sternberg et al. 1995).

5. *Motivation.* One can distinguish among several different kinds of motivation. A first kind of motivation is achievement motivation (McClelland 1985; McClelland et al. 1976). People who are high in achievement motivation seek moderate challenges and risks. They are attracted to tasks that are neither very easy nor very hard. They are strivers – constantly trying to better themselves and their accomplishments. A second kind of motivation is competence (self-efficacy) motivation, which refers to persons' beliefs in their own ability to solve the problem at hand (Bandura 1977, 1996). Experts need to develop a sense of their own efficacy to solve difficult tasks in their domain of expertise. This kind of self-efficacy can result both from intrinsic and extrinsic rewards (Amabile 1996; Sternberg & Lubart 1996). Of course, other kinds of motivation are important, too. Indeed, motivation is perhaps the indispensable element needed for school success. Without it, the student never even tries to learn.

6. *Context.* All of the elements discussed above are characteristics of the learner. Returning to the issues raised at the beginning of this document, a problem with conventional tests is that they assume that individuals operate in a more or less decontextualized envi-

ronment. A test score is interpreted largely in terms of the individual's internal attributes. But a test measures much more, and the assumption of a fixed or uniform context across test-takers is not realistic. Contextual factors that can affect test performance include native language, emphasis of test on speedy performance, importance to the test taker of success on the test, and familiarity with the kinds of material on the test.

These elements are, to a large extent, domain specific. The development of expertise in one area does not necessarily lead to the development of expertise in another area, although there may be some transfer, depending upon the relationship of the areas, a point that has been made with regard to intelligence by others as well (e.g., Gardner 1983, 1999).

In the theory of successful intelligence (Sternberg 1985, 1997a, 1998b, 1999c), intelligence is viewed as having three aspects: analytical, creative, and practical. Our research suggests that the development of expertise in one creative domain (Sternberg & Lubart 1995, 1996) or one practical domain (Sternberg et al. 1995) shows modest correlations with the development of expertise in other such domains. Psychometric research suggests more domain generality for the analytical domain (Jensen 1998). Moreover, people can show analytical, creative, or practical expertise in one domain without showing all three of these kinds of expertise, or even two of the three.

Interactions of Elements

The novice works toward expertise through deliberate practice. But this practice requires the interaction of all six of the key elements. At the center, driving the elements, is motivation. Without it, the elements remain inert. Eventually, one reaches a kind of expertise, at which one becomes a reflective practitioner of a certain set of skills. But expertise occurs at many levels. The expert first-year graduate or law student, for example, is still a far cry from the expert professional. People thus cycle through many times, on the way to successively higher levels of expertise. They do so through the elements in the figure.

Motivation drives metacognitive skills, which in turn activate learning and thinking skills, which then provide feedback to the metacognitive skills, enabling one's level of expertise to increase (see also Sternberg 1985). The declarative and procedural knowledge acquired through the extension of the thinking and learning skills also results in these skills being used more effectively in the future.

All of these processes are affected by, and can in turn affect, the context in which they operate. For example, if a learning experience is in English but the learner has only limited English proficiency, his or her learning will be inferior to that of someone with more advanced English-language skills. Or if material is presented orally to someone who is a better visual learner, that individual's performance will be reduced.

How does this model of developing expertise relate to the construct of intelligence?

The g Factor and the Structure of Abilities

Some intelligence theorists point to the stability of the alleged general (g) factor of human intelligence as evidence for the existence of some kind of stable and overriding structure of human intelligence. But the existence of a g factor may reflect little more than an interaction between whatever latent (and not directly measurable) abilities individuals may have and the kinds of expertise that are developed in school. With different forms of schooling, g could be made either stronger or weaker. In effect, Western forms and related forms of schooling may, in part, create the g phenomenon by providing a kind of schooling that teaches in conjunction the various kinds of skills measured by tests of intellectual abilities.

This point of view is related to, but different from, that typically associated with the theory of crystallized and fluid intelligence (Cattell 1971; Horn 1994). In that theory, fluid ability is viewed as an ability to acquire and reason with information, whereas crystallized ability is viewed as the information so acquired. According to this view, schooling primarily develops crystallized ability, based in part upon the fluid ability the individual brings to bear upon school-like tasks. In the theory proposed here, however, both fluid and crystallized ability are roughly equally susceptible to development through schooling or other means societies create for developing expertise. One could argue that the greater validity of the position presented here is shown by the near-ubiquitous Flynn effect (Flynn 1987; Neisser 1998), which documents massive gains in IQ around the world throughout most of the twentieth century. The effect must be due to environment, because large genetic changes worldwide in such a short time frame are virtually impossible. Interestingly, gains are substantially larger in fluid abilities than in crystallized abilities, suggesting that fluid abilities are likely to be as susceptible as or probably more susceptible than crystallized abilities to environmental influences. Clearly, the notion of fluid abilities as some basic genetic potential one brings into the world, whose development is expressed in crystallized abilities, does not work.

Suppose, for example, that children were selected from an early age to be schooled for a certain trade. Throughout most of human history, this is in fact the way most children were schooled. Boys, at least, were apprenticed at an early age to a master who would teach them a trade. There was no point in their learning skills that would be irrelevant to their lives.

To bring the example into the present, imagine that we decided, from an early age, that certain students would study English (or some other native language) to develop language expertise; other students would study mathematics to develop their mathematical expertise. Still other students might specialize in developing spatial expertise to be used in flying airplanes or doing shop work or whatever. Instead of specialization beginning at the university level, it would begin from the age of first schooling.

These students then would be given an omnibus test of intelligence or any broad-ranging measure of intelligence. There would be no general factor because people schooled in one form of expertise would not have been schooled in others. One can imagine even negative correlations between subscores on the so-called intelligence test. The reason for the negative correlations would be that developing expertise in one area might preclude developing expertise in another because of the form of schooling.

Lest this tale sound far-fetched, we hasten to add that it is a true tale of what is happening now in some places. In the United States and most of the developed world, of course, schooling takes a fairly standard course. But this standard course and the value placed upon it are not uniform across the world. And we should not fall into the ethnocentric trap of believing that the way Western schooling works is the way all schooling should work (e.g., Serpell 1993).

In a collaborative study among children near Kisumu, Kenya (Sternberg et al. 2001; see also Sternberg & Grigorenko 1997), we devised a test of practical intelligence that measures informal knowledge for an important aspect of adaptation to the environment in rural Kenya, namely, knowledge of the identities and use of natural herbal medicines that could be used to combat illnesses. The children use this informal knowledge an average of once a week in treating themselves or suggesting treatments to other children, so this knowledge is a routine part of their everyday existence. By *informal knowledge,* we are referring to kinds of knowledge not taught in schools and not assessed on tests given in the schools. It is essentially the same as tacit knowledge.

The idea of our research was that children who knew what these medicines were, what they were used for, and how they should be dosed would be in a position better to adapt to their environments than would children without this informal knowledge. We do not know how many, if any, of these medicines actually work, but from the standpoint of measuring practical intelligence in a given culture, the important thing is that the people in Kenya believe that the medicines work. For that matter, it is not always clear how effective are the medicines used in the Western world.

We found substantial individual differences in the tacit knowledge of like-aged and -schooled children about these natural herbal medicines. More important, however, was the correlation between scores on this test and scores on an English-language vocabulary test (the Mill Hill), a Dholuo equivalent (Dholuo is the community and home language), and the Raven Coloured Progressive Matrices. We found significantly *negative* correlations between our test and the English-language vocabulary test. Correlations of our test with the other tests were in the same direction, but not significant. The better children did on the test of indigenous tacit knowledge, the worse they did on the test of vocabulary used in school, and vice versa. Why might we have obtained such a finding?

Based on ethnographic observation, we believe a possible reason is that parents in the village may emphasize either a more indigenous or a more Western education. Some parents (and their children) see little value to school. They do not see how success in school connects with the future of children who will spend their whole lives in a village, where they do not believe they need the expertise the school teaches. Other parents and children seem to see Western schooling as of value in itself or potentially as a ticket out of the confines of the village. The parents thus tend to emphasize one type of education or the other for their children, with corresponding results. The kinds of developing expertise the families value differ, and so therefore do scores on the tests. From this point of view, the intercorrelational structure of tests tells us nothing intrinsic about the structure of intelligence per se, but rather, something about the way abilities as developing forms of expertise structure themselves in interaction with the demands of the environment.

Nuñes (1994) has reported related findings based on a series of studies she conducted in Brazil (see also Ceci & Roazzi 1994). Street children's adaptive intelligence is tested to the limit by their ability to form and successfully run a street business. If they fail to run such a business successfully, they risk either starvation or death at the hands of death squads should they resort to stealing. Nuñes and her collaborators have found that the same children who are doing the mathematics needed for running a successful street business cannot well do the same types of mathematics problems presented in an abstract, paper-and-pencil format.

From a conventional-abilities standpoint, this result is puzzling. From a developing-expertise standpoint, it is not. Street children grow up in an environment that fosters the development of practical but not academic mathematical skills. We know that even conventional academic kinds of expertise often fail to show transfer (e.g., Gick & Holyoak 1980). It is scarcely surprising, then, that there would be little transfer here. The street children have developed the kinds of practical arithmetical expertise they need for survival and even success, but they will get no credit for these skills when they take a conventional abilities test.

It also seems likely that if the scales were reversed, and privileged children who do well on conventional ability tests or in school were forced out on the street, many of them would not survive long. Indeed, in the ghettoes of urban America, many children and adults who, for one reason or another end up on the street, in fact barely survive or do not make it at all.

Jean Lave (1989) has reported similar findings with Berkeley housewives shopping in supermarkets. There just is no correlation between their ability to do the mathematics needed for comparison shopping and their scores on conventional paper-and-pencil tests of comparable mathematical skills. And Ceci and Liker (1986) found, similarly, that expert handicappers at racetracks generally had only average IQs. There was no correlation between the complexity of the mathematical model they used in handicapping and their scores on conventional tests. In each case, important kinds of developing expertise for life were not adequately reflected by the kinds of developing expertise measured by the conventional ability tests.

One could argue that these results merely reflect the fact that the problem that these studies raise is not with conventional theories of abilities, but with the tests that are loosely based on these theories: These tests do not measure street math, but more abstracted forms of mathematical thinking. But psychometric theories, we would argue, deal with a similarly abstracted general factor. The abstracted tests follow largely from the abstracted theoretical constructs. In fact, our research has shown that tests of practical intelligence generally do not correlate with scores on these abstracted tests (e.g., Sternberg et al. 2000; Sternberg et al. 1995).

The problem with the conventional model of abilities does not just apply in what to us are exotic cultures or exotic occupations. In a collaborative study with Michel Ferrari and Pamela Clinkenbeard (Sternberg et al. 1996; Sternberg et al. 1999), high school students were tested for their analytical, creative, and practical abilities via multiple-choice and essay items. The multiple-choice items were divided into three content domains: verbal, quantitative, and figural pictures. Students' scores were factor analyzed and then later correlated with their performance in a college-level, introductory psychology course.

We found that when students were tested not only for analytical abilities, but for creative and practical abilities, too (as follows from the model of successful intelligence, Sternberg 1985, 1997a), the strong general factor that tends to result from multiple-ability tests becomes much weaker. Of course, there is always some general factor when one factor analyzes but does not rotate the factor solution, but the general factor was weak, and of course disappeared with a varimax rotation. We also found that all of the analytical, creative, and practical abilities predicted performance in the introductory psychology course (which itself was taught analytically, creatively, or practically, with assessments to match). Moreover, although the students who were identified as high analytical were the traditional population – primarily white, middle- to upper middle-class, and well educated – the students who were identified as high creative or high practical were much more diverse in all of these attributes. Most important, students whose instruction better matched their triarchic pattern of abilities outperformed those students whose instruction more poorly matched their triarchic pattern of abilities.

Thus, conventional tests may unduly favor a small segment of the population by virtue of the narrow kind of developing expertise they measure. When one measures a broader range of developing expertise, the results look quite different (Sternberg, Castejón, et al. 2001). Moreover, the broader range of expertise includes kinds of skills that will be important in the world of work and in the world of the family.

Analytical, creative, and practical abilities, as measured by our tests or anyone else's, are simply forms of developing expertise. All are useful in various kinds of life tasks. But conventional tests may unfairly disadvantage those students who do not do well in a fairly narrow range of kinds of expertise. By expanding the range of developing expertise we measure, we discover that many children not now identified as able have, in fact, developed important kinds of expertise. The abilities conventional tests measure are important for school and life performance, but they are not the only abilities that matter.

Teaching in a way that departs from notions of abilities based on a general factor also pays dividends. In a recent set of studies, we have shown that generally lower-socioeconomic-class third-grade and generally middle-class eighth-grade students who are taught social studies (a unit in communities) or science (a unit on psychology) for successful intelligence (analytical, creative, and practical, as well as for memory) outperform students who are taught just for analytical (critical) thinking or just for memory (Sternberg, Torff, & Grigorenko 1998a, 1998b). The students taught "triarchically" outperform the other students not only on performance assessments that look at analytical, creative, and practical kinds of achievements, but even on tests that measure straight memory (multiple-choice tests already being used in the courses). None of this is to say that analytical abilities are not important in school and life – obviously, they are. Rather, what our data suggest is that other types of abilities – creative and practical ones – are important as well and that students need to learn how to use all three kinds of abilities together.

Thus, teaching students in a way that takes into account their more highly developed expertise and also enables them to develop other kinds of expertise results in superior learning outcomes, regardless of how these learning outcomes are measured. The children taught in a way that enables them to use kinds of expertise other than memory actually remember better, on average, than do children taught for memory.

We have also done studies in which we have measured informal procedural knowledge in children and adults. We have done such studies with business managers, college professors, elementary-school students, salespeople, college students, and general populations. This important aspect of practical intelligence, in study after study, has been found to be uncorrelated with academic intelligence as measured by conventional tests, in a variety of populations, occupations, and at a variety of age levels (Sternberg et al. 2000; Sternberg et al. 1995). Moreover, the tests predict job performance as well as or better than do tests of IQ. The lack of correlation of the two kinds of ability tests suggests that the best prediction of job performance will result when both academic and practical intelligence tests are used as predictors. Most recently, we have developed a test of common sense for the work place – for example, how to handle oneself in a job interview – that predicts self-ratings of common sense but not self-ratings of various kinds of academic abilities (Sternberg & Grigorenko 1998).

Although the kinds of informal procedural expertise we measure in these tests do not correlate with academic expertise, they do correlate across work domains. For example, we found that subscores (for managing oneself, managing others, and managing tasks) on measures of informal procedural knowledge are correlated with each other and that scores on the test for academic psychology are moderately correlated with scores on the test for business managers (Sternberg et al. 2000; Sternberg et al. 1995). So the kinds of developing expertise that matter in the world of work may show certain correlations with each other that are not shown with the kinds of developing expertise that matter in the world of the school.

It is even possible to use these kinds of tests to predict effectiveness in leadership. Studies of military leaders showed that tests of informal knowledge for military leaders predicted the effectiveness of these leaders, whereas conventional tests of intelligence did not. We also found that although the test for managers was significantly correlated with the test for military leaders, only the latter test predicted superiors' ratings of leadership effectiveness (Sternberg et al. 2000).

Both conventional academic tests and our tests of practical intelligence measure forms of developing expertise that matter in school and on the job. The two kinds of tests are not qualitatively distinct in that they measure "formed," or developed, knowledge and skills. The reason the correlations are essentially null is that the kinds of developing expertise they measure are quite different. The people who are good at abstract, academic kinds of expertise are often people who have not emphasized learning practical, everyday kinds of expertise, and vice versa, as we found in our Kenya study. Indeed, children who grow up in challenging environments such as the inner city may need to develop practical over academic expertise as a matter of survival. As in Kenya, this practical expertise may better predict their survival than do academic kinds of expertise. The same applies in business, where tacit knowledge about how to perform on the job is as likely or more likely to lead to job success than is the academic expertise that in school seems so important.

The practical kinds of expertise matter in school, too. In a study at Yale, Wendy Williams and Robert Sternberg (cited in Sternberg, Wagner, & Okagaki 1993) found that a test of tacit knowledge for college predicted grade-point average as well as did an academic-ability test. But a test of tacit knowledge for college life better predicted adjustment to the college environment than did the academic test.

Taking Tests

Developing expertise applies not only to the constructs measured by conventional intelligence tests, but also to the very act of taking the tests.

Sometimes the expertise children learn that is relevant for in-school tests may actually hurt them on conventional ability tests. In one example, we studied the development of children's analogical reasoning in a country day school where teachers taught in English in the morning and in Hebrew in the afternoon (Sternberg & Rifkin 1979). We found a number of second-grade students who got no problems right on our test. They would have seemed, on the surface, to be rather stupid. We discovered the reason why, however. We had tested in the afternoon, and in the afternoon, the children always read in Hebrew. So they read our problems from right to left, and got them all wrong. The expertise that served them so well in their normal environment utterly failed them on the test.

Our sample was of upper middle-class children who, in a year or two, would know better. But imagine what happens with other children in less supportive environments who develop kinds of expertise that may serve them well in their family or community lives or even school life, but not on the tests. They will appear to be stupid rather than lacking the kinds of expertise the tests measure.

Patricia Greenfield (1997) has done a number of studies in a variety of cultures and found that the kinds of test-taking expertise assumed to be universal in the United States and other Western countries are by no means universal. She found, for example, that children in Mayan cultures (and probably in other highly collectivist cultures as well) were puzzled when they were not allowed to collaborate with parents or others on test questions. In the United States, of course, such collaboration would be viewed as cheating. But in a collectivist culture, someone who had not developed this kind of collaborative expertise, and, moreover, someone who did not use it, would be perceived as lacking important adaptive skills (see also Laboratory of Comparative Human Cognition 1982).

CONCLUSION

Thus, we have argued in this chapter that ability tests measure developing expertise. Tests can be created that favor the kinds of developing expertise formed in any kind of cultural or subcultural milieu. Those who have created conventional tests of abilities have tended to value the kinds of skills most valued by Western schools. This system of valuing is understandable, given that Binet and Simon (1905) first developed intelligence tests for the purpose of predicting school performance. Moreover, these skills are important in school and in life. But in the modern world, the conception of abilities as fixed or even as predetermined is an anachronism. Moreover, our research and that of others (reviewed more extensively in Sternberg 1997a) shows that the set of abilities assessed by conventional tests measures only a small portion of the kinds of developing expertise relevant for life success. It is for this reason that conventional tests predict only about 10 percent of individual-difference variation in various measures of success in adult life (Herrnstein & Murray 1994).

Not all cultures value equally the kinds of expertise measured by these tests. In a study comparing Latino, Asian, and Anglo subcultures in California, for example, we found that Latino parents valued social kinds of expertise as more important to intelligence than did Asian and Anglo parents, who more valued cognitive kinds of expertise (Okagaki & Sternberg 1993). Predictably, teachers also more valued cognitive kinds of expertise, with the result that the Anglo and Asian children would be expected to do better in school, and did. Of course, cognitive expertise matters in school and in life, but so does social expertise. Both need to be taught in the school and the home to all children. This latter kind of expertise may become even more important in the work place. Until we expand our notions of abilities, and recognize that when we measure them, we are measuring developing forms of expertise, we will risk consigning many potentially excellent contributors to our society to bleak futures. We will also be potentially overvaluing students with expertise for success in a certain kind of schooling, but not necessarily with equal expertise for success later in life.

The best way to measure developing expertise, we believe, is not through static but rather through dynamic tests. Indeed, dynamic tests were created explicitly to measure developmental potential. We consider the nature of dynamic tests in the next part.

PART TWO

THE NATURE OF DYNAMIC TESTING

In this second part of the book, we introduce the notion of dynamic testing and provide a capsule history of the concept of dynamic testing. Our goal is to prepare the reader for an understanding of modern approaches to dynamic testing, which are considered in Part Three.

CHAPTER TWO

An Introduction to Dynamic Testing

During the course of their lives, many people will, at some time or another, have taken a conventional test of cognitive skills. Such tests include IQ tests, as well as other tests that measure some mix of abilities and achievements, which often cannot be distinguished clearly, in any case. Such tests would include O-level and A-level tests (created in the United Kingdom), or SATs, ACTs, GREs, LSATs, and many other tests (created in the United States).

LATENT CAPACITIES AND DEVELOPED ABILITIES

Conventional tests of cognitive skills attempt to quantify developed abilities. If, as we argue in Chapter 1, abilities are always forms of developing expertise (and thus never fully developed), then a measure of developed abilities must be incomplete. For example, these tests might measure a person's ability to retrieve meanings of words. A typical test item of this type might be to define the word *absolution*. Or the tests might measure the person's ability to complete series of numbers, given what the person (a) knows about numbers, (b) the person's ability to infer relations between these numbers, and (c) the person's ability to hold the numbers in working memory. A typical test item might ask what number comes next in the following series: 1, 4, 9, 16, ?

Thus, conventional tests measure latent capacity only as it is realized in performance, which, in turn, is affected by many variables, such as amount of education, test-wiseness skills, parental support, and so on. For example, someone with more education will be at an advantage in knowing the meaning of a word or in recognizing a series of perfect squares. Someone with more test-wiseness skills will have techniques available for increasing the probability of responding correctly. For example, such a person may not know what *absolution* is, but know that *to absolve* means to clear of blame, and thereby infer what *absolution* might mean.

These tests measure some unknown mix of abilities that have fully developed and abilities that are not yet fully developed. The extent to which the abilities can develop will depend, in turn, on both latent capacity and the kind of instruction one receives that will help one to develop this latent capacity. Sometimes, the term *ability* is used to refer to a developed latent *capacity*. For example, children brought up in upper middle-class households in pricey suburbs are likely to have the educational opportunities that will allow them to make the most – or almost the most – of the latent capacities they have. They are thus likely to score relatively higher on tests of developed abilities. In contrast, children brought up in lower-class households in urban slums are much less likely to have the educational opportunities that will allow them to capitalize fully on their latent capacities. They are therefore likely to score relatively lower on tests of developed abilities.

Often, we may wish we could know the extent to which developed abilities reflect latent capacities and the extent to which they reflect developed abilities. In other words, to what extent does a score on a test reflect what a person can do, given the opportunities he or she has had, and to what extent does it reflect what the person could do, given ideal or nearly ideal opportunities in life. We also may wish to know the difference between the developed abilities and the latent capacities – to what extent do the developed abilities fully reflect the latent capacities? In other words, we may wish to understand the difference between latent capacities and developed abilities.

Consider an example. Alberto and Javier, hypothetical children, have both grown up in Caracas, Venezuela. Suppose, for the sake of argument, they were born with nearly identical latent capacities. Differences between them will begin to emerge very quickly as a result of their different social classes.

Alberto is a child of the upper class and has had extensive and intensive educational opportunities since his birth. He went to an expensive preschool that provided him with basic literacy skills, and then he went to a series of exclusive private schools that spared no expense in educating him. As a first-year university student, he is fully literate and now has a vocabulary well in excess of 100,000 words. He is knowledgeable about mathematics through calculus, and is also knowledgeable about many other subjects, such as science and history. He speaks English as well as Spanish, both of which help him get along in the world and pre-pare for an intended career in international finance.

Javier is a child of the lower class who has grown up in a rancho in the slums surrounding Caracas. A rancho is a usually illegally con-structed dwelling of stone, metal, and whatever elements happen to be lying around that is placed on the ground with no real foundation. A se-vere storm or even a fairly mild earthquake can be enough to demolish it. There is no running water in the rancho, and the electricity is illegally stolen from power lines. The electricity supports only a few electric lights and a television. Javier had no preschooling and his parents, who are semiliterate, cannot help him develop literacy skills. Javier went to an elementary school on the outskirts of Caracas, but the school had few books or even desks. The schooling was uninteresting and unmotivat-ing. Because Javier was on the streets trying to earn money any way he could from an early age, he did not spend much time at school, and by grade five he had dropped out. He was underage for dropping out, but no one was going to make any fuss.

It would make very little difference what conventional test of abilities or achievements Alberto and Javier might take. Alberto would probably outscore Javier by a substantial margin. There would be no way of know-ing that the two children were born with nearly equal capacities. It cer-tainly would be of theoretical interest to have a test that would show that Alberto and Javier had roughly equal capacities. It also would be of prac-tical use: Javier is someone who, with proper educational interventions, might develop into a citizen with useful literacy skills who could make as much of a difference to the society as might Alberto. But how might we obtain information regarding the two boys' underlying capacities, and how these capacities differ from their developed abilities?

DEFINING DYNAMIC TESTING AND COMPARING IT TO STATIC TESTING

Dynamic testing has been proposed as a way of uncovering this infor-mation. What is dynamic testing? Dynamic testing is testing plus an in-structional intervention. In a conventional test, sometimes called a *static test*, individuals receive a set of test items and solve these items with lit-tle or no feedback. Often, giving feedback is viewed as a source of error of measurement and therefore as something to be avoided at all costs. In a *dynamic test*, individuals receive a set of test items with explicit in-struction (Lidz 1987, 1997; Wiedl, Guthke, & Wingenfeld 1995). Some of the main approaches to dynamic testing are shown in Table 2.1.

Table 2.1. *Dynamic Testing Approaches*

Approach	Method	Target Population	Format	Context of Testing (nature of the task)	Outcome (goal)	Focus (orientation)	Predictive Power
The theory of structural cognitive modifiability (Feuerstein and colleagues)	Learning Potential Testing Device	All individuals who can use modification	Test – mediate – test	Artificial (outside the context of school program)	Structural cognitive changes	Child-driven	Not well established
Learning potential testing (Budoff and colleagues)	Test-centered coaching	Children who have experienced school failure (low-IQ, low-achieving students)	Formal pretest – standardized training/coaching – formal posttest	Artificial (outside the context of school program); Abstract reasoning problems (mostly nonverbal)	Improved test performance	Task-driven	Fairly high
Testing via Learning and Transfer (*Graduated prompt*	Hinting procedure	Scholastically weak students	Pretest (level-of-performance information) – initial mediated	With the exception of usage of traditional tests, testing is	A Measure of Zone of Proximal Development	Task-driven	Not established

approach) (Campione & Brown)			learning – static maintenance and transfer testing – mediated maintenance and transfer	situated within specific domains			Fairly high for individuals with IQ below average
Lerntest approach (Learning potential testing)	German Learning Potential Tests (Guthke and colleagues)	Mentally retarded children and adults with brain disorders	(1) pretest-training-post-test (long-term) and (2) train-within-test paradigm (short term)	Psychometrically oriented approach where testing is situated within specific domains	Records of learning gain	Task-oriented	Fairly high for individuals with IQ below average
	Dutch Learning Potential Test for minority groups (Heesels and Hamers)	Children of ethnic minorities	Train-within-test paradigm	Psychometrically oriented approach where testing is situated within specific domains	Extent to which children benefit from help	Task-oriented	The test appears to be a moderate predictor of school achievement, but not a better predictor than a static intelligence test

(continued)

Table 2.1 *(continued)*

Approach	Method	Target Population	Format	Context of Testing (nature of the task)	Outcome (goal)	Focus (orientation)	Predictive Power
Testing-the-limits approach	Teach-to-the-limit approach (Carson and Wiedl)	Normal, mentally retarded, and children with learning disabilities	Multiple conditions (varying amount of verbalization and feedback)	Testing is situated within specific domains	Improved test performance	Task-driven	No better than IQ in terms of prediction of school achievement, but is predictive of adaptive learning styles
Information-processing framework	Swanson-Cognitive Processing Test (S-CPT)	Children with learning disabilities	Test – teach – test	Artificial (working memory tasks)	Indicator of processing potential	Task-driven	Appears to be fairly high for learning-disabled children, especially the group of slow learners

Two Common Formats for Dynamic Testing

There are two common formats for dynamic tests. The first format is that the instruction may be sandwiched between a pretest and a posttest. The second format is that the instruction may be in response to the examinee's solution to each test item. Note that they are not the only possible formats, just the two most commonly used ones. We shall use two terms of our own invention to describe these two formats: the *sandwich format* and the *cake format*.

In the first format, examinees take a pretest, which is essentially equivalent to a static test. After they complete the pretest, they are given instruction in the skills measured by the pretest. The instruction may be given in an individual or a group setting. If it is in an individual setting, it may or may not be individualized to reflect a particular examinee's strengths and weaknesses. If it is individualized, then the amount as well as the type of feedback can be individualized. If it is in a group setting, then the instruction typically is the same for all examinees. After instruction, the examinees are tested again on a posttest. The posttest is typically an alternate form of the pretest, although less commonly, it may be exactly the same test. For convenience, this format will be referred to as the *sandwich format.* In individual-testing settings, the exact contents of the sandwich (type of instruction) as well as its thickness (amount of instruction) can be varied to suit the individual. In group-testing settings, the contents and thickness of the sandwich are typically uniform.

In the second format, which is always done individually, examinees are given instruction item by item. An examinee is given an item to solve. If he or she solves it correctly, then the next item will be presented. But if the examinee does not solve the item correctly, he or she is given a graded series of hints. The hints are designed to make the solution successively more nearly apparent. The examiner then determines how many and what kinds of hints the examinee needs in order to solve the item correctly. Instruction continues until the examinee is successful, at which time the next item is presented. The successive hints are presented like successive layers of icing on a cake. For convenience, this format will be referred to as the *cake format.* In the cake format, the number of layers of the cake is almost always varied (i.e., the amount of feedback depends on how quickly the examinee is able to use the format to reach a correct solution). The contents of the layers, however (i.e., the type of feedback), may or may not be constant. Most often, they are constant: The number of hints varies across examinees, but not the content of them.

Differences between Static and Dynamic Testing

There are three major differences between the static and dynamic paradigms. The differences are best viewed as ones of emphasis rather than of dichotomous differences. A static test can have dynamic elements, just as a dynamic test can have static elements.

The first difference regards the respective roles of static states versus dynamic processes. *Static testing* emphasizes products formed as a result of preexisting skills, whereas *dynamic testing* emphasizes quantification of the psychological processes involved in learning and change. In other words, static testing taps more into a developed state, whereas dynamic testing taps more into a developing process. In both of the formats of dynamic testing described here, the examiner is able to assess how the problem-solving process develops as a result of instruction. In the sandwich format of dynamic testing, the instruction is given all at once between the pretest and the posttest. In the cake format of dynamic testing, the instruction is given in graded layers after each test item, as needed. Static testing typically does not allow the examiner to draw such inferences.

The second difference regards the role of feedback. In *static testing*, an examiner presents a graded sequence of problems and the test-taker responds to each of the problems. There is no feedback from examiner to test-taker regarding quality of performance. In *dynamic testing*, feedback is given, either explicitly or implicitly.

The type of feedback depends on which kind of dynamic testing is used. In the sandwich format, the feedback may be explicit if the testing is individual, but will probably be implicit if the testing is in a group. The instruction sandwiched between the pretest and the posttest gives each examinee an opportunity to see which skills he or she has mastered and which skills he or she has not mastered. But in a group-testing situation, the examiner will not be able explicitly to tell each examinee about these skills. In an individual-testing situation with the sandwich format, it will be possible to provide explicit feedback, should the examiner decide to give it.

In the cake format, the examiner presents a sequence of progressively more challenging tasks; but after the presentation of each task, the examiner gives the test-taker feedback, continuing with this feedback in successive iterations until the examinee either solves the problem or gives up. Testing thus joins with instruction, and the test-taker's ability to learn is quantified while she or he learns.

The third difference between static and dynamic testing pertains to the quality of the examiner–examinee relationship. In static testing, the examiner attempts to be as neutral and as uninvolved as possible toward the examinee. The examiner wants to have good rapport, but nothing more. Involvement beyond good rapport risks the introduction of error of measurement. In dynamic testing, the test situation and the type of examiner–examinee relationship are modified from the one-way traditional setting of the conventional psychometric approach to form a two-way-interactive relationship between the examiner and the examinee.

In individual dynamic testing, this tester–testee interaction is individualized for each child: The conventional attitude of neutrality is thus replaced by an atmosphere of teaching and helping. In group dynamic testing using the sandwich format, the examiner is still helpful, although at a group rather than an individual level. The examiner is giving instruction in order to help the examinees improve on the posttest. As in the individual-testing format, he or she is anything but neutral.

Thus, dynamic testing is based on the link between testing and intervention and examines the processes of learning as well as its products. By embedding learning in evaluation, dynamic testing assumes that the examinee can start at the "zero (or almost zero) point" of having certain developed skills to be tested, and that teaching will provide all the necessary information for mastery of the tested skills. In other words, what is tested is not just previously acquired skills, but the capacity to master, apply, and reapply skills taught in the dynamic-testing situation. This view of the testing procedure underlies the use of the term, *test of learning potential,* which is often applied to dynamic testing.

How Successful Is Dynamic Testing?

If dynamic testing is successful, then it is also revolutionary. We at last have a way to reduce the effects of all the environmental variables that can color performance and hence distort estimates of latent capacity. Dynamic testing may give us a means to quantify a person's true potential for growth, from wherever he or she may happen to be cognitively at any one moment. Does dynamic testing deliver on its promise? And if it does not yet quite deliver, what needs to be done so that it will? These are among the questions addressed in this book.

The idea of quantifying the learning potential underlying the processes and products of learning initially appeared perhaps to be in the realm of wishful thinking. Wouldn't it be nice if we were equipped to quantify someone's potential rather than actualized abilities, something developing and modifiable rather than something developed and perhaps even fixed? Wouldn't it be nice if we could test people's ability to learn new things rather than just their ability to demonstrate the knowledge they have already acquired? But these goals seemed more like pie in the sky than like potentially realizable outcomes.

In our interpretation, dynamic testing is part of a larger process referred to as dynamic assessment; testing and assessment here are not synonyms. Dynamic testing, along with other types of evaluations (e.g., observations and judgments, Salvia & Ysseldyke 1981), is only one of many procedures used in assessment. Assessment might involve, in addition to testing, interviews, projects and performances of various kinds, and other forms of evaluation. This view of dynamic testing justifies our somewhat restricted conception of the tester–testee interaction. Because we define our undertaking as an attempt to review *dynamic testing* (and not all of dynamic assessment), we, correspondingly, limit ourselves to a narrowly conceived interpretation of the tester–testee interaction. Broadly defined, dynamic assessment is naturally linked with intervention. In essence, the goal of dynamic assessment is to intervene and to change. The goal of dynamic testing, however, is much more modest – it is to see whether and how the participant will change if an opportunity is provided. As mentioned above, in some approaches to dynamic testing, the tester–testee interaction component is limited to providing simple feedback, whereas in others, this interactive link exceeds simple feedback boundaries and takes the form of targeted intervention. It is also important to note that, in this review, we limit ourselves to commentaries only on those approaches that identify themselves as dynamic-testing approaches, although there is an ongoing discussion in the literature that the term *dynamic assessment* should be replaced by the term *learning assessment* and thus become a component of a much larger field (Snow 1990).

As we shall see, multiple attempts to quantify learning potential and to transform the construct of dynamic testing into a set of robust psychological diagnostic tools have not produced consistent results. Nevertheless, the idea of dynamic testing is so appealing that, despite its relatively sparse empirical validation, it has been widely discussed and fairly widely used. A number of procedures have been developed for testing its validity (Carlson & Wiedl 1992b, in press).

The scientific community, especially in the fields of psychology and education, has paid insufficient attention to dynamic testing. There are several reasons behind this lack of attention.

The first reason is the relative lack of published empirical data on the reliability and validity of dynamic testing. Without an adequate database, scholars and educators find themselves unable adequately to evaluate a procedure, and thus may be inclined not to pay much attention to it.

The second reason is, for some approaches, insufficient detail in the presentation of methods – which has made replication difficult. There have been only a handful of reviews of dynamic-testing studies published in peer-reviewed journals (e.g., Day et al. 1997; Elliott 1993; Grigorenko & Sternberg 1998; Jitendra & Kameenui 1993; Laughon 1990; Missiuna & Samuels 1988). Most of these studies focus on the educational and clinical applicability of dynamic testing, rather than on the underlying psychological models and hard empirical data yielded by such testing.

The third reason is the novelty of dynamic testing. The constructs are not familiar and do not fit well with what psychologists and educators learn about testing during the years they are in training. These professionals may therefore be inclined to ignore dynamic testing because it does not fit well into their prototype of what testing is and should be about.

This book attempts to fill in the gap created by the relative lack of refereed empirical work in the field. The book summarizes much (although certainly not all) of the current literature on dynamic testing. It discusses the achievements and limitations of various approaches that have attempted to measure people's learning potential. It also proposes a three-pronged approach to testing learning potential.

Although we are at times critical of dynamic testing, our goal is not to drive a stake through the heart of dynamic testing. On the contrary, we endorse the concept, and are attempting to construct dynamic tests ourselves, as described later. But we are concerned with the paucity of evidentiary support for the utility of many of the operationalizations of the construct that have been proposed to date.

CONCLUSION: THE NEED FOR DYNAMIC TESTING

Russian psychologist Sergei Rubinstein (1946) wrote that in order for an educator to evaluate students' ability to learn, the educator needs to teach students something and then to observe their learning. People draw conclusions about other people's ability to learn – their learning potential – all the time. Experts in different fields are able to predict the future performance of novices by first giving the novices a chance to

participate in professional activities and then evaluating their performance while they are learning. When a professor starts working with a
student on research, the first step is usually some kind of informal
pretest on the student's understanding of the problem to be solved. Usually the student, who has just started working on the problem, does not
know much. Therefore, the professor suggests ideas, appropriate readings, and issues on which to concentrate. After a series of subsequent
visits and discussions based on the learned material, the professor has
enough information to make a preliminary judgment about the learning potential of the student. Similarly, an experienced car mechanic, trying to train apprentices in the garage, gradually involves them in the operation and lets them handle more and more difficult tasks, observing
and correcting the novices' performance. In this way, the expert evalu-
ates the ability of the novice to learn.

This kind of implicit prediction of a novice's future achievement,
based on learning during an apprenticeship, occurs frequently in everyday life. Now picture a test that measures the ability to learn something
new. For example, a person is about to make a career decision. He takes
two tests in different fields, let us say, in biology and psychology. The
tests are designed in such a way that initially they assess his unassisted
performance. Then they measure his performance while working on
problems with experts in each field. Each expert is equally effective as
a teacher. Finally, the experts measure his individual performance when
he is retested. He does equally well on the pretests, but he has learned
much more successfully while working with the biology expert than
with the psychology expert. Thus, his posttest biology performance is
significantly better than his posttest psychology performance.

These results might be interpreted as suggesting that the field of biology perhaps will be more promising for the person – that he can better realize his potential in this field. Thus, the test provides results that
predict to some degree his future performance in the field. Or picture a
child whose parents are recent immigrants to a new culture. Irrespec-
tive of his or her knowledge of English, if this child is given a conventional test that is not traditional to his or her culture, the child is most
likely going to demonstrate a fairly low level of performance. On the
other hand, if the same child is given a chance to be reevaluated after
the test-specific intervention, his or her performance might be drastically different.

One of the most important applications of dynamic testing has been
in work with disadvantaged children who have performed exception-

ally poorly on conventional static tests (e.g., Feuerstein, Rand, & Hoffman 1979). The category *disadvantaged* (or, sometimes, *challenged*) *students,* in contrast to *advantaged* (*nonchallenged*) *students,* is used to refer to a large class of pupils viewed as having reduced learning opportunities. This reduction can be due to deficient previous education, lack of match in previous and current cultural and educational practices, or apparent learning disability or mental deficiency. The claim that these students should be tested dynamically is motivated by the belief that dynamic testing in its proper application can help reduce educational inequalities by providing what are seen as more compassionate, fair, and equitable means for assessing students' learning capacities. For disadvantaged children, quantifying their learning in action, with the assistance of and under the supervision of an adult, might be the only way to evaluate their true level of functioning.

The idea of developing a methodological paradigm that goes beyond the measurement of developed abilities and that quantifies the potential that will be a main force in students' learning is an extraordinarily appealing idea to scientists and laypeople alike. A number of synonymous or nearly synonymous concepts, traditionally unified under the name "dynamic testing/assessment" (e.g., interactive testing/assessment, process testing/assessment, measuring the zone of proximal development, assisted testing/assessment, and tests of learning potential), have been suggested for this paradigm. This book will explore these concepts.

CHAPTER THREE

A Capsule History of Dynamic Testing

Although the concept of dynamic testing has been heavily researched only during the last two decades, the theoretical foundations for this methodology were laid some time ago. For example, the creator of static testing, as we know it today, Alfred Binet (1909), advocated process assessment. He did not suggest or devise an instrument suitable for such an assessment, however. Thorndike (1924) argued for the necessity of measuring the "ability to learn" as part of intelligence. Buckingham (1921) suggested that the best measure of intelligence is one that takes into account either the rate at which learning takes place or the products of learning, or both. Penrose (1934) wrote that "the ideal test in the study of mental deficiency would be one which investigates the ability to learn" (p. 49). Dearborn (1921) and DeWeerdt (1927) believed there was a need for tests involving and measuring actual learning and practice, rather than just their results. André Rey (1934) suggested testing educability, and to this end he constructed some 400 tests. Rey's name is perhaps appropriate (*rey* means *king* in Spanish), because Rey is truly the king of the field of dynamic testing: Many of the tests used today by Feuerstein and others, originated with Rey. In the form Rey proposed them, however, most of the tests were of a static nature.

A German psychologist, Kern (1930), also attempted to conceptualize the measurement of learning ability. Kern criticized the psychometric tests of the times, stating that initial inhibitions frequently distort the results of the first testing session. What really should be a predictor of future success, according to Kern, is capacity for learning. Kern conducted an experiment in which intelligence tests were administered repeatedly for several weeks. He found a significant shift in the rank order of his test-takers from the beginning of the training period to the fifth testing session, after which ranks remained fairly stable. He concluded that one-shot testing does not provide enough information for developing an adequate prognosis and might, in fact, lead to incorrect conclusions.

Credit for introducing the concept of dynamic testing to modern psychology is usually given to Lev Vygotsky (1934/1962). Actually, it is arguable who deserves credit for the modern concept of dynamic testing. Some research, such as that of Brown (e.g., Brown et al. 1992; Brown & Ferrara 1985; Campione & Brown 1987; Palincsar, Brown, & Campione 1991) and Guthke (e.g., Guthke 1992) was directly derived from Vygotsky's theory (see Lidz 1987), whereas other work (e.g., that of Feuerstein et al. 1979) is presented as of independent origin (Kozulin & Falik 1995), although it appears to be closely related to Vygotsky's earlier work and also, as mentioned above, to work of Rey.

Whatever their antecedents, we formulate our analyses here on the conceptual rather than the historical antecedents of various approaches, and therefore attempt to cluster research on the basis of theoretical and methodological dimensions. We do, however, assign historical priority to Vygotsky, whose theory appears to have been the first systematic, if incomplete, theory of dynamic testing. Many of the implications of the theory, however, were worked out not by Vygotsky himself, but by his followers (e.g., Ginzburg 1981; Vlasova 1972).

The theoretical background for dynamic testing was established and the first experimental investigations were conducted in the 1930s and 1940s (e.g., Kern 1930; Vygotsky 1934/1962). But extensive professional attention began to be devoted to this methodology only in the 1960s and 1970s, during a time of severe criticism of static testing. This interest led to intensive research in Israel (Feuerstein et al. 1979) and in the United States (Brown, & French 1979; Budoff 1975; Carlson 1992; Lidz 1987, 1991) on learning ability and dynamic testing. The renaissance of interest was probably most directly due to the work of Feuerstein, and to a lesser extent, of Budoff.

This reestablished interest in dynamic testing has been attributed to the development of certain societal needs and to the formation of more mixed and even critical professional opinion on the usefulness of static testing (Grigorenko & Sternberg 1998; Tzuriel & Haywood 1992). With regard of societal needs, researchers recognized the desirability of (a) more nearly culture-fair tests that could be used in work with immigrants for the purpose of integrating them into society, (b) tests that would be useful for comparing results obtained in culturally diverse populations, (c) developmental tests appropriate for testing of individuals with deprived educational experiences, and (d) the measurement of learning potential as distinct from what has been learned, regardless of the culture, population, or social group of a tested individual. Such measurement is especially attractive when one considers the relatively modest to moderate forecasting power of most static ability tests for many predictive purposes (e.g., Sternberg 1996, 1999c; Sternberg et al. 2000).

Historically, the use of the term *dynamic testing* involves multiple senses.

First, dynamic testing can provide a basis for teaching and developing cognitive skills (Lidz, 1997). In this context, teaching is a form of intervention, and school evaluations are forms of pre- and posttests. Whole pedagogical programs have been designed so that teaching would extend the child's ability by gradually expanding his or her skills to learn to work independently. Such programs may be consummated through interactions with caregivers (e.g., Tzuriel in press-a) and through societal institutions such as schools (e.g., Davydov 1986; M. R. Jensen, Robinson-Zañartu, & M. L. Jensen 1992; Kalmykova 1975; Klein 1987; Newman, Griffin, & Cole 1989; Talyzina 1995).

Second, the concept of dynamic testing provides methodologies for the testing of learning potential. Indeed, dynamic testing has come to be explored in a wide variety of testing contexts, including testing of the abilities of (a) job candidates (Coker 1990; Downs 1985; Robertson & Mindel 1980); (b) children in social-learning situations (Zimmermann, cited in Guthke 1993); (c) children with mental retardation and other developmental disabilities (e.g., Ashman 1985, 1992; Jepsen 2000; Molina & Perez 1993; Paour 1992); (d) patients with brain damage (Baltes, Kühl, & Sowarka 1992) and with various types of sensory as well as language handicaps (Keane, Tannenbaum, & Krapf 1992; Peña 1996; Peña & Gillam 2000); (e) aging individuals (Fernandez-Ballesteros et al. 1997; Kliegl & Baltes 1987; Kliegl, Smith, & Baltes 1989); (f) candidates for undergraduate admissions (Shochet 1992); (g) college students and adults (Barr & Samuels 1988; Samuels 2000; Samuels & Scholten 1993); (g) children exhibiting learning difficulties (e.g., Brownell, Mellard, & Deshler 1993; Gerber, D. Semmel, & M. Semmel 1994; Peña, Quinn, & Iglesias 1992; Samuels, Tzuriel, & Malloy-Miller 1989); (h) gifted disadvantaged pupils (Bolig & Day 1993; Borland & Wright 1994; Hickson & Skuy 1990; Kirschenbaum 1998); (i) immigrants to different cultures (Gutierrez-Clellen, Peña, & Quinn 1995; Kozulin 1998; Tzuriel & Kaufman 2000) and culturally diverse students (Coxhead & Gupta 1988; Hamers, Hessles, & Van Luit 1991; Hamers, Hessels, & Pennings 1996; Hessels

1996, 1997, 2000; Luther, Cole, & Gamlin 1996; Peña in press; Robinson-Zañartu & Sloan Aganza 2000); (j) foreign-language learners (Frawley & Lantolf 1985); (k) penitentiary inmates (Silverman & Waksman 1992); and (l) preschoolers (Day et al. 1997; Lidz 2000; Olswang, & Bain 1996; Spector 1992), including even infants and toddlers (Kahn 2000). Of course, there have been other uses of dynamic testing as well.

Third, dynamic testing is a sociopolitical concept that can serve sociopolitical or cultural goals. For example, dynamic testing had a long history in the former USSR. Static testing was prohibited by state decree in 1936 because its goal, according to the Communist Party officials of that time, was to label children as deficient by estimating the current status of their abilities and without considering their future potential. Consequently, for a number of decades, dynamic testing was virtually the only paradigm accepted in psychology and remedial education in the countries of the former Soviet bloc (e.g., Grigorenko 1998; Guthke, Beckman, & Dobat 1997; Klein 1987). When the concept of cognitive testing was used, it was assumed to be in the context of dynamic testing. Dynamic testing was viewed as opening up the world for the child, whereas static testing was viewed as closing it.

What are the most influential approaches to dynamic testing, and how are they related? We consider this question next.

THEORIES UNDERLYING DYNAMIC TESTING

The First Operationalization: Vygotsky, his Followers, and his Interpreters

We start our discussion with a description of the work of Lev Vygotsky, because Vygotsky's writings provide the context for contemporary approaches to dynamic testing (Kozulin, 1990; Lidz 1995; Lidz & Elliott 2000; Rutland & Campbell 1996). The ideas of Vygotsky that are relevant to dynamic testing appeared in the context of his theory of higher mental functions (Vygotsky 1931/1983).

One of the major concepts of this theory is that of the zone of proximal development (ZPD). One of Vygotsky's followers and colleagues, Leont'ev, in his discussions with Bronfenbrenner (cited in Bronfenbrenner 1977), summarized the meaning of this concept by saying that it tries "to discover not how the child came to be what it is, but how it can become what it not yet is" (p. 528). Thus, the ZPD reflects development itself: It is not what one is, but what one can become; it is not what has developed, but what is developing. The ZPD is a construct that exists neither within the individual nor within the social context. It exists only in the interaction between the individual and his or her social context, because it exists only in the individual's social interaction and is created by this interaction. The developmental, interactive, and forward-looking nature of the ZPD resulted in its becoming one of the ideas of Vygotsky that has received the most attention in the West.

According to Newman and Holzman (1993), the popularity of the ZPD is due to the fact that it (a) lends itself well to contemporary interests in social cognition and classroom interaction, (b) delves into the essence of learning and development, and (c) is an expression of the individual-in-society. The construct thus meets a number of needs of contemporary psychological and educational theorizing.

The concept of the ZPD is epistemologically complex and is neither fully described nor fully researched in Vygotsky's work (Ginzburg 1981). Vygotsky discussed the multiple implications of the ZPD in the context of (a) mature versus maturing cognitive functions, (b) learning versus development, (c) the discrepancy between what the child can do independently versus in collaboration with others (adults and peers), and (d) the types of activities in which the ZPD is most likely to manifest itself. Below, we will briefly sketch each of these implications.

In developing the idea of mature versus maturing cognitive function, Vygotsky (1987) wrote:

> The state of development is never defined only by what has matured. If gardeners decide only to evaluate the mature or harvested fruits of the apple tree, they cannot determine the state of their orchards. Maturing trees must also be taken into consideration. Psychologists must not limit their analysis to functions that have matured. They must consider those that are in the process of maturing. If they are to evaluate fully the state of the child's development, psychologists must consider not only the actual level of development but the zone of proximal development. (pp. 208–209)

One can assess these maturing cognitive functions by setting up a collaborative effort between a child and others (adults or more capable peers) to provide a basis for estimating the discrepancy between what the child can do independently and what he or she can do with the help of others. In this context, the ZPD is viewed by Vygotsky as the distance between a child's "actual developmental level as determined by independent problem solving" and the higher level of "potential development as determined through problem solving under adult guidance or in collaboration with more capable peers" (Vygotsky 1978, p. 86).

Vygotsky (1987) also wrote about the ZPD in the context of studying the relations between learning and development. Instruction is useful when it moves ahead of development and when it impels or wakens a whole series of functions that are in a stage of maturation and thus still lie in the zone of proximal development rather than having been actualized already. The instruction must move ahead of development enough so as to pull the child forward, but not so much that the child is unable to profit from it.

The type of activity in which the ZPD is most likely to appear, according to Vygotsky (1978), is in play. In play, a child always behaves beyond his average age, above his daily behavior; in play it is as though he were "a head taller than himself" (Vygotsky 1978, p. 102). McLane (1990) developed this idea, saying that play encourages the player to act as if he or she were already competent in the activity under consideration. Thus, he suggests, when children are learning how to write, their playing with the processes and forms of writing may result in a sense of "ownership" of this complex cultural activity, making them feel like they are writers long before they have the needed skills and knowledge to produce mature, culturally appropriate, and fully conventional writing.

It is important to note that, in contrast to the well-elaborated and grounded theoretical representation of the ZPD by Vygotsky, experimental validation of the construct is very scarce. Vygotsky did not conduct any systematic empirical validation of the ZPD, nor did his immediate followers and colleagues. Thus, in the 1930s, this concept gained theoretical grounding, but sorely needed compelling experimental validation.

Vygotsky's theoretical account of the ZPD and its various implications has spawned research in many countries, among them, Russia (e.g., Davydov 1986; Rubtsov 1981; Vlasova 1972), Germany (e.g., Guthke 1993), the Netherlands (van Geert 1998, 2000), and the United States (e.g., Rogoff & Wertsch 1984). Two main lines of contemporary interpretation of Vygotsky's ZPD can be pointed out. One has to do with its sociological–pedagogical aspect, and the other with an individualized means to improve the testing of a child's mental functioning (Wertsch & Tulviste 1992).

Sociological–Pedagogical Interpretation of the ZPD

In the context of its sociological–pedagogical aspect, the ZPD is viewed as a dynamic region of sensitivity to learning cultural skills that is created by more experienced members of the culture, has distinct historical and cultural qualities, and determines a child's learning and development within a given culture (Newman & Holzman 1993; Rogoff 1990). The research capitalizing on this aspect of the ZPD is variegated, with respect to target populations of students, teaching methods, and the results that have been obtained. Its style often tends to be qualitative rather than quantitative. Moreover, much of the work has been conducted at the conceptual level or at the level of descriptive analysis, making it difficult to conduct an evaluation of relevant empirical findings. What relevant literature there is can be classified into clusters.

One relatively small cluster of literature presents a broad interpretation of the ZPD as the main mechanism of vertical transmission (from adults to children) of cultural knowledge (Cole 1985). Such understanding of the ZPD, according to Cole, is applicable to anthropological–psychological studies of socialization in different cultures. Moll and Greenberg (1990) illustrated this idea by utilizing the concept of ZPD in their study of the means by which young children of the Mexican community in Arizona master knowledge about household maintenance, and showed that the initial steps of mastery are carried out in joint activities of children and adult housekeepers.

The second cluster includes studies on the pedagogical implications of the ZPD. In this context, the ZPD is viewed as being of such great importance that users of the ZPD see its manifestation in instructional settings as essential to good teaching. They believe that teaching should involve assisting performance through the ZPD (Tharp & Gallimore 1988). From this point of view, teaching is interpreted as a kind of negotiation between teacher and student in which the teacher provides instruction that helps students take on additional responsibility for managing their own learning through activity (Cole 1985). Teachers constantly "test the waters" (Wertsch 1991) to see whether their students are ready to move to a new level of self-regulation. When students fail the test, teachers return to instruction that requires less developed thinking on the part of the students.

There have been a number of attempts to design teaching programs based on the concept of the ZPD. For example, Hedegaard (1990) conducted a study in which she and her colleagues implemented the concept of the ZPD in a three-year curriculum for school subjects (biology, history, and geography) in Danish school classrooms of third- to fifth-graders. Similarly, McNamee and her colleagues utilized the concept of the ZPD in devising programs to develop literacy in both preschoolers and children with learning disabilities (McNamee 1990; McNamee et al.

1985). Bodrova and Leong (1996) pulled together examples of and activities relevant to ZPD-based strategies of teaching and learning, all of which were developed and tested in different subject areas and at different stages of schooling.

In yet another educational use of the ZPD, Newman, Griffin, and Cole (1989) extended the pedagogical notion of the ZPD and renamed it "the construction zone," referring to it as the zone between the thoughts of two people, a shared activity in the frame of which interpsychological (shared mental) processes can take place. Cognitive change does not occur in a closed, determined system. Rather, the child's cognitive system opens up in the "construction zone," in which the shared activity of constructing new (or advancing old) cognitive functions takes place. Cognitive tasks are first constructed in the interaction between expert and novice, and later, in the novice's independent activity. Initially, the novice not only lacks the skills necessary to carry out the tasks independently, but also, and more importantly, does not understand the goal toward which a given situation is directed. Thus, in their school program, Newman, Griffin, and Cole ensured that teaching took place in a Vygotskian manner, whereby children were introduced to a given task so that the goal and the procedure were simultaneously internalized in the course of the interaction. Generalizing from their school-based experiences, they suggested that the concept of the ZPD refers to an interactive system within which people work on a problem that at least one of them could not solve effectively on his or her own. Thus, in their interpretation, the ZPD is a more general phenomenon, observed when two or more people with unequal expertise are jointly accomplishing a goal.

In Russia, this type of broad interpretation of the ZPD as a "place" in which development stimulated by learning takes place, led to the formulation of the theory of systematic formation of mental actions and concepts (Gal'perin 1966). In the context of this theory, teaching is viewed as a psychological experiment, the goal of which is to bring the student to a new, higher level of development. By conducting teaching as an experiment, that is, by determining the dependent (outcome) and the independent (treatment) variables in teaching, the researchers view teaching as the way systematically to influence and continually to monitor the child's cognitive and educational progress. The teaching is conducted in six steps (for details, see Haenen 1996; van Geert 1987): (1) the motivational stage (preliminary introduction of the action to the learner and mobilization of the learning motive), (2) the orienting stage (con-

uction of the orienting, schematic basis of the action), (3) the materialized stage (mastering the action using material or materialized objects), (4) the stage of overt speech (mastering the action by speaking the
steps out loud), (5) the stage of covert speech (mastering the action by
"speaking to oneself"), and (6) the mental stage (transferring the action
to the mental level or internalizing the steps necessary to the action). For
example, to explain addition/subtraction, the teacher first tries to moti-
vate students to master this action (stage 1), then gives the learners a
whole set of orienting elements to guide them in the execution of the action – for example, explains what subtraction does and what components it includes (stage 2) – and then, using the subject matter as the basis for teaching, provides the student with a means to master the
operation using mediating tools, such as objects, drawings, and pictures
(stage 3). Then, at the fourth stage, the children are taught to execute the
action without any direct links to mediating tools by verbalizing the
steps of subtraction that they originally learned by manipulating real
objects. Similarly, at the fifth stage, the action is still verbalized, but the
learners are encouraged to whisper to themselves instead of speaking
aloud. Eventually, whispering disappears, and the action "moves" en-
tirely into the mind. Now the children can add and subtract mentally;
that is, the function has been taught and mastered.

The followers of this approach state that their intention is not to in-
stall in the child a developmental stage or level, but rather, gradually to
help the child move on to the next, higher stage of development (Talyzina 1995). Gal'perin's theory has never been implemented in the form of
a complete curriculum but has been applied in many subject-specific areas (e.g., reading and arithmetic [El'konin 1960] and math [Obukhova
1972; Salmina & Kolmogorova 1980]). A number of monographs (e.g.,
Talyzina 1995) have presented mostly qualitative data indicating significant gains in children's school achievement when they were taught by
Gal'perin's method, but no robust quantitative validity data have yet
been presented.

Yet another Vygotsky-based Russian school program was developed
by the group of Davydov in three Russian schools. Davydov (1986) com-
bined Leont'ev's theory of activity and Vygotsky's ideas about the relationship between development and learning to create a theoretical approach that he called "developing teaching." The general principles of
this approach were used in the Russian, biology, mathematics, arts, and
physics curricula in the elementary grades of Moscow School 91 and
Khar'kov Schools 4 and 17 (see Dmitriev 1997; Kozulin 1984). The core

of the program was the belief that students should master general reasoning (as a method of scientific analysis) in a given subject domain, and
that such mastery later would enable them to solve domain-specific concrete problems. Mastery of reasoning, according to Davydov (1986), is
possible even by the age of six or seven if the child is engaged in an appropriate and carefully orchestrated learning activity. Thus, the task of
educators and psychologists is to design special reasoning-targeted
learning-activity scenarios and to lead students through the process of
mastering new concepts by guiding them from the abstract to the concrete – from the most general relationship characteristic of the mastered
concept to its concrete, empirical manifestation. The main task of teaching is to ensure the identification of the concept and its representation
in a symbolic form, indicating the formation of a corresponding abstraction. Moreover, the teacher should lead the student through the ex-
ploration of the links between the abstraction and its various empirical
manifestations and the established links between the original abstraction and abstractions of the second order.

All of these teacher-guided activities are conducted in the child's zone
of proximal development, and at the end point of the process, the original abstractions become concrete concepts, which are assumed to help
students solve any empirical problem pertaining to a given subject. For
example, the formation of the concept of real numbers is based on the
child's mastery of the concept of quantity. The first-grade math course
of School 91 starts with the introduction of the concept of quantity
through the concepts of *equal to*, *more than*, and *less than*. These concepts
are given initially in their abstract form by means of letter formulas (e.g.,
$a = b, a > b, b < a, a + c > b$). At the next stage, the teacher introduces real-
world comparisons and gives children problems comparing the lengths
and weights of different objects. The teacher thereby ensures the establishment of a link between the real-world object and the children's ability to "translate" the quantity relationships into abstract forms (e.g., if
the weight of one object is a and the weight of the other object is b, then
$a > b$). At the next step, the children are expected to discover that immediate comparison often is not feasible and that they therefore have to
find a mediating quantity that can be measured in relation to the two
objects that are being compared (e.g., if $a > c$ and $c > b$, then $a > b$). Thus,
the concept of mediation is introduced. The next stage involves the mastery of the concept of relation (e.g., if $A/c = K$ and $b < c$, then $A/b > K$).
The last stage of this section of the math curriculum is the mastery of
the concepts of *discrete* and *continuous*. It is assumed that the mastery

of the four concepts of *quantity, mediation, relation,* and *discrete* versus *continuous* results in the mastery of the concept of real numbers. The curriculum includes sets of detailed practices and learning exercises based on Davydov's theory of learning activity. All of these activities are performed together with the teacher, that is, in the spectrum of the children's ZPD.

The 15-year-long intervention study showed significant positive differences in the short- and long-term academic achievements of students enrolled in the experimental program when compared with control students (Davydov 1986). Moreover, related studies that investigated the development of general cognitive functions in experimental versus control students showed significant differences in metacognitive development, as well as in the development of imagination, thinking, memory, and self-regulatory processes (*Razvitie psikhiki shkol'nikov v protsesse uchebnoi deiatel'nosti,* 1983). Though probably the best-validated ZPD-based pedagogical program, Davydov's curricula are yet to be scrutinized by means of large-scale longitudinal analyses as well as by other independent researchers.

In general, the research conducted to date has not produced convincing quantitative empirical data to support the broad claim that ZPD-based teaching results in better educational and cognitive outcomes than do other forms of teaching. Of course, we cannot ignore observed group differences in performance on logic games (with students from the experimental teaching group generalizing rules of the game significantly better – Davydov, Pushkin, & Pushkina 1972) and we cannot dismiss students' overall positive affect and happiness, which have been reported on numerous occasions by many of the investigators mentioned above (see, e.g., Davydov 1986; Newman et al. 1989). But (usually unquantified) feelings of happiness do not necessarily translate into better school or life achievements. Unfortunately, most of the approaches have lacked hard data from carefully controlled studies regarding gains in achievement. Moreover, a very small proportion of these studies have been published in refereed journals; most of the accounts of the programs come from somewhat loose descriptions in monographs and book chapters, where not much attention has been paid to quantitative aspects of the work in general and to program evaluation in particular. Such limited availability of quantitative information inevitably raises questions regarding various biases in available studies, such as how samples were obtained, how and what statistics were applied, and whether there were adequate controls. In addition, to our knowledge, independent evaluations of the approaches described above have been scarce.

The ZPD as an Individualized Means of Improving Testing

The ZPD can be viewed as a means to improve testing of individual mental functioning. Within this framework, cognitive skills are taught initially in the external "space" formed between the teacher and the student and then are internalized by the student so that they become a part of the child's own personal repertoire (Das & Conway 1992; Levina 1968). In some cases, this methodology has been used with children diagnosed as having learning disabilities or mental retardation (Gerber 2000; Gerber et al. 1994; Schlatter & Büchel 2000). For example, in Russia, this aspect of Vygotsky's ideas took the form of research developments in Soviet defectology (the term used in Soviet psychology to signify research on handicapped children; see Grigorenko 1998). Soviet defectology considered the responsiveness of children to prompts as a crucial basis for separating mentally and educationally retarded from normal children (e.g., Vlasova & Pevsner 1971). Many Russian remediational programs are based on the ideas of the ZPD and the careful monitoring of the intervention within the ZPD (e.g., Goncharova 1990; Goncharova, Akshonina, & Zarechnova 1990; Nikolaeva 1995; Pozhilenko 1995; Spirova & Litvinova 1988). In the United States, this notion of the ZPD as a means to improve testing in order to maximize the effectiveness of teaching has been used in intervention programs such as "reciprocal teaching" (Palincsar & Brown 1984, 1988) and in the context of information-integration theory (Das, Kirby, & Jarman 1979), in which teaching is highly individualized and targeted at minimizing the difference between assisted and nonassisted performance.

CONCLUSION

The ZPD provides a way to create "competence before performance" (Cazden 1981). It is this perspective on the ZPD that has formed the basis for the development of the dynamic/interactive testing paradigm that is discussed in detail in the following sections.

Thus, Vygotsky's approach launched research in two major directions: One has studied social methods of transmitting knowledge (including pedagogy), and the other has dealt with enhancing and improving the quantification of individual cognitive functioning. Subsequent developments of Vygotsky's original ideas have modified initial concepts and methodologies, but all these later interpreters took off from Vygotsky's work as the main launching point for their research.

The boundary lines between the two perspectives (teaching-oriented and individual-testing-oriented) are somewhat artificial. These two subfields of dynamic testing have never been completely independent of one another. Quite on the contrary, researchers have crossed these boundaries and extended the work developed in one perspective into the other perspective as well (e.g., educational applications of Feuerstein's ideas by Jensen et al. 1992). Dynamic testing has been used for close to three decades with the goals of both testing and educating, largely in the context of working with children and adolescents with social deprivation, mental retardation, and learning disabilities. Recently, however, there have been more and more attempts to apply these ideas to regular school settings (for a review, see Haywood & Tzuriel 1992).

The bulk of the remainder of the book is devoted to the second perspective on dynamic testing that arose from Vygotsky's work – namely, the individual-testing-oriented perspective.

PART THREE

LEADING MODERN APPROACHES TO DYNAMIC TESTING

The third part of the book describes what we believe to be the leading approaches to individually oriented dynamic testing. Our descriptions of these approaches focus on a number of aspects, including (a) method of testing, (b) target population, (c) format of testing, (d) nature of testing materials, (e) outcome measures, and (f) predictive power of the approach. Of course, it is not possible to describe and evaluate every approach that has been used.

In order to provide adequate sampling, we will review selected paradigms, representative of the four major clusters of dynamic testing approaches. Expanding on Haywood's (1997) three-cluster classification (a–c), we point out one more group of approaches to dynamic testing (d). The clusters are: (a) metacognitive intervention targeted at teaching generalizable concepts and principles (e.g., Feuerstein's mediated learning, Hurtig's experimental learning, Paour's induction of learning structures), (b) learning within the test (e.g., Guthke's learning test; Brown's graduated prompts approach), (c) restructuring the test situation (e.g., Budoff's training tests, Carlson & Wiedl's optimization of test administration, and Haywood's "enriched input"), and (d) training a single cognitive function (e.g., Swanson's working memory battery, Spector's test of phonemic awareness, Peña's test of narrative performance).

We use a four-point profile to evaluate the empirical data collected through these approaches:

(1) *Comparative Informativeness.* This dimension indicates various qualities of the discussed method (e.g., its differentiating properties, its psychometric characteristics, and the quality and informativeness of the obtained data). The underlying question here is whether the given methodological paradigm contributes any new

information over and above that obtained with conventional measures.

(2) *Power of Prediction.* This dimension pertains to the relationship between the information collected and the criteria used to assess validity. The underlying question is how successfully the new methodology predicts performance in a designated population for a given set of criteria.

(3) *Degree of Efficiency (time and effort invested, taking into account the uniqueness of information obtained).* This dimension reflects how much effort a proposed test or testing procedure requires for its administration as compared with conventional testing and the uniqueness of the information obtained. The underlying issue is the extent to which using the new method takes more (or less) effort when compared with traditional static methods, given the unique nature of the information obtained from the new method.

(4) *Robustness of Results.* This dimension indicates how robust the obtained findings are. The underlying question is whether the results have been shown to be replicable across studies and research groups.

We have to admit that our evaluations of the different approaches are not necessarily equivalent, either in depth or critical analysis. As is often the case, the better developed the approach, the more the data that are available; and the more the work that has been put into a given approach, the easier it is to find flaws and identify questionable practices. The approaches we will review have different publication frequencies, ranging from dozens (e.g., Feuerstein and colleagues) to a few (e.g., the Russian defectological tradition) publications. We have tried to review most of the published material on dynamic testing; however, much of the relevant work has been presented orally or is in preparation for publication. We start our review with the leading approach to dynamic testing, the approach of Feuerstein and colleagues.

CHAPTER FOUR

The Approach of Feuerstein

One of most noteworthy and fully articulated contributions to the field of dynamic testing has been that made by Reuven Feuerstein and his colleagues (e.g., Feuerstein et al. 1979; Feuerstein et al. 1980; Feuerstein et al. 1987), who developed the *Learning Potential Assessment Device* (LPAD) as a dynamic-testing instrument (for a brief description of the LPAD, see R. Feuerstein, R. Feuerstein, & Gross, in press). The LPAD is characterized as a method for assessing the potential of children, adolescents, and adults for growth in specific cognitive processes, wherein the children are first guided by exposure to problems and processes of thought and subsequently are guided by their own independent efforts (Feuerstein et al. 1985). Compared with static testing measures, the LPAD changes the practice of testing in four major areas – namely, the structure of the instruments, the nature of the test situation, the orientation to process, and the interpretation of results (Feuerstein, Rand, & Rynders 1988). The specific instruments constituting the LPAD battery include verbal and nonverbal tasks targeted at specific skills, such as analogical and numerical reasoning, categorization, and memory strategies.

THE APPROACH OF FEUERSTEIN AND HIS COLLEAGUES

The Theory of the LPAD

In order to understand any of Reuven Feuerstein's thinking, one needs to understand his basic premise – that intelligence is modifiable, and quite drastically so. Feuerstein has made good on this assumption: He has taken retarded performers and effected quite substantial increases in their level of functioning. Feuerstein has used the term *retarded performer* rather than *retarded person*. Feuerstein has believed that it is the performance, not the person, that is retarded and hence that the retardation can be mitigated by improving the performance. But he cannot be viewed as a behaviorist. He has argued that structural changes are possible in the organism through interventions such as his own program of Instrumental Enrichment.

The key concept in Feuerstein's conception of intelligence and its development is mediated learning experience (MLE). Mediated learning experience is the way in which stimuli emitted by the environment are transformed by a "mediating" agent, usually a parent, sibling, or other caregiver. This mediating agent, guided by his intentions, culture, and emotional investment, selects and organizes the world of stimuli for the child. The mediator selects the stimuli that are most appropriate and then frames, filters, and schedules them; he determines the appearance or disappearance of certain stimuli and ignores others. Through this process of mediation, the cognitive structure of the child is affected. The child acquires behavior patterns and learning sets, which in turn become important ingredients of his capacity to become modified through direct exposure to stimuli. (Feuerstein et al. 1980, p. 16)

Feuerstein has argued that the two main ways to attain modification of cognitive structure are direct exposure to stimuli and MLE, but that it is MLE that will enable the individual effectively to use direct exposure to stimulation. Thus, in mediating the environment for the child, the parent or teacher not only teaches the child important knowledge and skills but also develops in that child the capacity to profit from the environment without mediation. To Feuerstein, therefore, MLE is the critical ingredient in cognitive development and in differentiating people who perform better or worse in cognitive tasks. Clearly, Feuerstein's notion of MLE is similar to Vygotsky's concept of internalization, although Feuerstein has emphasized less the social environment as a whole and more the influence of one-on-one interaction, especially of the mother with a child. The difference, however, is one of degree rather than one of kind.

Feuerstein has suggested that MLE has several components. First is the selection of stimuli. The caregiver selects those stimuli that he or she believes will profit the child. Second is scheduling of stimuli. It is not enough just to pick out the right stimuli. The caregiver needs to schedule the presentation of stimuli so that the child will be able to learn from them in an optimal way. Third is anticipation. The child needs to be taught to anticipate certain outcomes as a result of certain actions. A fourth component is imitation. One of the most powerful tools of MLE is the provision of models that the child can imitate. A fifth component is the provision of specific stimuli. Feuerstein has noted that such stimuli are usually culturally determined and that the child's attention is consistently directed toward the stimuli. A sixth component is repetition and variation. Feuerstein, like Vygotsky, has recognized that children do not internalize what they observe right away. Repetition and variation are necessary for full internalization to take place. Internalization also can be facilitated by learning to solve problems across various problem domains (e.g., verbal and abstract symbolic – see Karpov & Gindis 2000). A seventh component is the transmission of the past and the representation of the future. The child learns what has been true in the past and what he or she can expect of the future. And the last component is comparative behavior, by which the child learns to see how things are similar and different.

Feuerstein has suggested that MLE can occur either through the intervention of a particular individual, such as the parent, or through general cultural transmission. Children who are culturally deprived – who have inadequate exposure to their own culture – will tend to receive inadequate MLE. Note that, for Feuerstein, cultural deprivation is not in terms of a mainstream or host culture, but in terms of the culture of the child and his family. Feuerstein has suggested that there are two main sources of lack of MLE: the nature of the individual's environment and the condition of an individual at a given point in his or her development. With respect to environmental determinants, Feuerstein has suggested several determinants that can lead to lack of MLE: breakdown in cultural transmission, poverty, ideology, inadequate parent–child relationship, and pathological conditions of parents. With respect to conditions of the child, he has noted as well several sources of lack of absorption of MLE: autism, constitutional factors (such as hyperactivity), and emotional disturbance. Feuerstein has proposed a number of deficient cognitive functions that can result from a lack of MLE, as well as other sources. He has not claimed completeness for his list, but merely that the functions he has listed are ones that he has found deficient time and again. The functions he has described fit into four categories: impairments in cognition at the input phase, impairments in cognition at the elaborational phase, impairments in cognition at the output phase, and affective motivational factors. We will not attempt to list all of the functions Feuerstein has described but, rather, some representative ones.

Impairments affecting the input phase include unplanned, impulsive, and unsystematic exploratory behavior; lack of, or impaired, receptive verbal tools and concepts affecting discrimination; lack of, or impaired, spatial orientation, including the lack of stable systems of reference that impair the organization of space; and lack of, or impaired, capacity for considering two sources of information at once, reflected in dealing with data in a piecemeal fashion rather than as a unit of organized facts. Examples of impaired cognitive functions affecting the elaborational phase include inadequacy in experiencing the existence of an actual problem and subsequently defining it; inability to select relevant, as opposed to irrelevant, cues in defining a problem; narrowness of the mental field; and lack of, or impaired, strategies for hypothesis testing. Examples of impaired cognitive functions affecting the output phase include egocentric communicational modalities; trial-and-error responses; lack of, or impaired, verbal tools for communicating adequately elaborated responses; and impulsive acting-out behavior, affecting the nature of the communication process. Feuerstein has not explicitly characterized the affective and motivational factors that can adversely affect cognitive processes; he merely has stated that they exist.

Feuerstein has suggested that mental acts can be analyzed, categorized, and ordered via a cognitive map involving seven parameters. In this respect, one is reminded of geographic metaphors and particularly of Guttman's (1965) approach to understanding intelligence in terms of facets. The parameters of the cognitive map are content, operations, modality (e.g., figurative, numerical, verbal), phase (input, elaboration, output), level of complexity, level of abstraction, and level of efficiency. The idea of the cognitive map, again, is to fit mental performances into some unified framework.

To conclude, Feuerstein, like Vygotsky, has argued for the importance of socialization for intelligence and its development. The key construct of Feuerstein's theory, MLE, may be viewed as the process by which Vygotsky's internalization takes place. The two theories are thus largely compatible.

Instrumentation

The 15 instruments in the LPAD battery are designed to challenge a participant to utilize (or to form and then utilize) different cognitive operations (e.g., serialization, classification) in different cognitive domains (i.e., numeric, verbal, logico-deductive, figural). Most of the tests are based on (or are) standardized psychometric instruments, which are used in dynamic, mediational modes. For example, the LPAD directly utilizes the Raven Colored and Standard Progressive Matrices and the Rey-Osterreith Complex Figure Test. Other instruments (e.g., Set Variations I and II, the Organizer, the Representational Stencil Design Test) were developed for the LPAD specifically but are either based on or are modifications of older existing instruments (e.g., the LPAD Stencil Test is an adaptation of the Grace Arthur Stencil Test). Participants' time is not limited, but their response time is registered.

A limited selection of the total battery of tests is usually administered. The number of tests used with a given participant, as well as the time of testing, vary widely depending on the individual profile of the participant and the amount of mediation (Kozulin & Falik 1995).

We consider some key features of this approach in the following sections.

Target Population

Initially the LPAD was developed as a testing device for work with low-achieving children. Feuerstein started developing his theory at a point in time when Israeli society was struggling to integrate minorities and immigrants from all over the world into its culture (Feuerstein & Krasilowsky 1972; Tzuriel 1992). Throughout 20 years of research, the LPAD has been utilized in case studies involving children with severe handicaps having discouraging prognoses on static IQ measures (Feuerstein et al. 1988; R. Feuerstein, R. Feuerstein, & Schur in press), as well as in work with special-needs children (e.g., Keane & Kretschmer 1987) and educationally deprived children, such as immigrants in Israel (Kaniel, Tzuriel et al. 1991).

Later, however, Feuerstein redefined the target population of his instrument to include almost everyone. This expansion appears to have been justified only weakly. It might be assumed that an expansion of such magnitude would be supported by empirical evidence suggesting that the proposed instrument has proven itself to be appropriate for the newly designated population. However, the extended population has never been clearly specified. Moreover, a lack of criterion-related validity studies convincingly demonstrating the predictive power of the LPAD (see below) places the enterprise in doubt.

The Goal

In contrast to other approaches with more modest aspirations, Feuerstein's approach allegedly takes advantage of the modifiability of the individual's cognitive structure. The test assesses the level of modifiability, and then subsequent intervention can be used to induce, promote, and strengthen the degree of modification obtained. Thus, the goal is not a concrete, specific change but rather a global modification of a somewhat loosely defined set of cognitive structures. Cognitive modifiability is viewed as a type of ability, distinct from conventional intelligence, to self-modify cognitive functioning and adapt to changing demands. Thus, the stated goal of this approach is to evaluate the individual's ability to profit from instruction and subsequently to modify his or her own cognitive functioning. The goal of the LPAD is to ferment change in old cognitive structures and even to introduce new structures. Feuerstein has stated that evaluation and remediation should take place simultaneously.

The Model

The LPAD is rooted in Feuerstein's concept of mediated learning experience (MLE), an interactional process in which an adult interposes himself or herself between the child and the task and modifies both the task (by adjusting frequency, order, complexity, and context) and the child (by arousing him or her to a higher level of curiosity and to a level at which structural cognitive changes can occur). For example, an adult who explains to a child what is happening in a television show is mediating the show for the child. Mediated learning experience can be contrasted with direct instruction, which teaches children facts or procedures directly rather than attempting to teaching indirectly through mediation of experience.

The concept of MLE is ideologically quite close to some of Vygotsky's concepts. MLE highlights the role of adults or older children as catalysts in younger children's mastery of both declarative and procedural knowledge. However, in its broader interpretation, any interaction can be viewed as MLE if it meets a set of criteria among which are the mediator's intention to change the child and the generalizability of the projected change beyond the precipitating situation. According to Feuerstein, everybody experiences MLE. What is important, however, is that inadequate MLE leads to inadequate cognitive development (Haywood 1997). This belief might very well have served as the basis for Feuerstein's redefinition of the target population – everybody has a chance of experiencing inadequate MLE, so everybody has a chance of having some cognitive functions developed inadequately. Correspondingly, everybody can benefit from modification.

To implement his paradigm, Feuerstein has eschewed the use of conventional standardized tests. Nevertheless, he has assembled tests that are similar and in some cases identical to those found in conventional test batteries. He has argued for a flexible, individualized, and highly interactive format of testing. The LPAD model encompasses three dimensions crucial for the testing of learning potential: (a) modality of presentation, (b) novelty/complexity, and (c) operations required for task solution. Different subtests of the LPAD vary on which of these dimensions they assess. Together, the device covers various combinations of values on the three dimensions. The tests are administered in a specially designed *test situation* that is intended to be a flexible, individualized, and intensely interactive three-way (task–examinee–examiner) process.

In the LPAD paradigm, the examiner has a very important role. The examiner not only has to detect failures, but also has to find the best way to remedy them. In order to anchor the examiner's activity and to help him or her approach each child effectively, the concept of a cognitive map has been developed. The cognitive map is a heuristic representation proposed to analyze both cognitive tasks and corresponding mental acts. The cognitive map is composed of seven parameters (content, modality, phase, operation, level of complexity, level of abstraction, and level of efficiency). The function of the cognitive map is to "map" the cognitive deficit and pinpoint the directions that instruction should take.

The administration of the LPAD is thought to be of special value to the child because it provides an MLE by creating a ZPD. In this interaction, affect plays a crucial role. The neutral unresponsive attitude of the examinee that characterizes static-testing situations is expected to reinforce the child's already negative self-image. Even the provision of simple positive feedback is not seen as a sufficient counterbalance to the child's negative self-image. In administering the LPAD, the examiner is expected to behave as a good teacher who is responsive to the examinee in a variety of ways (e.g., giving and asking for explanations, selecting examples and control tasks, and monitoring progress).

The LPAD is designed to evaluate how modifiable the child's cognitive structures are and where the child's cognitive deficits lie. The LPAD-based evaluation is expected to reveal what must be done in an intervention in order to provide a situation in which the mediated learning experience can take place. The outcome of the MLE is the active production of new, adequate cognitive structures. This is where, according to Haywood (1997), the crucial difference between static and dynamic tests lie: Whereas static tests accurately and reliably point to deficient cognitive functions, dynamic tests point to what can be done to overcome these deficiencies and thereby defeat the prediction of static tests that otherwise – were there no dynamic testing followed by intervention – might have proved correct.

In contrast to other dynamic-testing approaches, Feuerstein's approach does not assume that the administration of the LPAD will result in deep structural changes in the participant's cognitive structures. The transient changes produced and observed in the participant during the administration of the LPAD provide a professional with an idea of what type and how much intervention will be needed to yield the desired deep structural changes. The quality of the child's response to mediated learning experiences is operationalized by the concept of *structural cognitive modifiability* (Feuerstein et al. 1985).

The LPAD is, by design, tightly linked to intervention and is distinct from traditional static testing. Feuerstein et al. (1979) have emphasized four principal differences between the LPAD and the conventional static testing approach: (a) the LPAD tasks are designed to teach and assess cognitive changes rather than to measure the individual's status relative to his or her peers; (b) the LPAD is oriented toward process rather than toward product; (c) the LPAD's testing situation provides an interactive-dynamic approach rather than a standard formal approach; and (d) the interpretation of results on the LPAD focuses on the peaks of individual performance, attempts to locate origins of success and failure, and assesses the changes possible through cognitive modifiability. Specific sampling of learning potential is done in different domains, taking into account the quality and the amount of intervention.

Thus, the model of Feuerstein is an elaborate one with the concept of cognitive modifiability at its center. Some researchers have suggested what they believe to be two limitations of the model.

First, researchers (e.g., Frisby & Braden 1992) have pointed out the vagueness and imprecision of the theoretical terminology utilized by Feuerstein. In close analyses, it appears that semantic fields of different concepts overlap, lack exactness, and suggest undemonstrated causal links. For example, it has been argued (Feuerstein & Rand 1974; Feuerstein et al. 1979) that the proximal cause of individual differences in cognitive performance is lifetime exposure to MLE. The support for this claim is drawn from studies that showed improvement in cognitive performance after mediated learning had been experienced (Feuerstein et al. 1979). However, an individual's response to a specific treatment in a specific situation does not necessarily imply causality outside the context of that situation. In other words, even a convincing demonstration of the fact that an individual's performance has improved after experiencing mediated learning does not mean that the initial low performance was caused by a lack of mediated experience. For example, a drug might be used to activate the pituitary gland and increase height, but the fact that the drug serves this function does not mean that the drug is responsible for individual differences in height over people's lifetimes. Solid controls are needed to draw any strong conclusions at all.

Second, there is a certain degree of discrepancy between the elaborateness of the conceptual model and the fairly meager usage of these constructs within the framework of empirical research actually conducted with the LPAD. The ultimate test of Feuerstein's approach is in improvements in academic performance. The results of the studies addressing this question are mixed (see Bradley 1983; Bransford et al. 1985; Frisby & Braden 1992, for reviews and analyses; see also Missiuna & Samuels 1989). Here we will briefly analyze some of the studies conducted within this framework.

Empirical Findings

Feuerstein's approach has been adopted by many psychologists and educational professionals. Despite large amounts of published material, however, the empirical findings are somewhat difficult to evaluate because very few of these studies have been published as original empirical reports in peer-reviewed journals. Most of them have been presented in book chapters or as papers delivered at meetings. Therefore, it is difficult (and sometimes impossible) to ascertain such important data as sample size, F-values, p-values, and magnitudes of effects. Consequently, this review is by no means complete, and our conclusions are open to modification pursuant to new or more detailed data. We will structure our analyses using the four-point profile we proposed for evaluating the empirical findings. Some of the points we make will be illustrated with selected studies.

Comparative Quality

Internal consistency and test–retest reliability of the LPAD have been assessed within a static mode. As such, reliability coefficients of the group-administered LPAD range between .70 and .95 (Rand & Kaniel 1987; Tzuriel & Feuerstein 1992; Wingenfeld, as presented in Frisby &

Braden 1992), thus falling within an acceptable range. These coefficients, however, are no surprise, due to the fact that the LPAD components, when administered statically, are conventional tests themselves. What is a challenge to the individually administered LPAD is the registered low inter-rater reliabilities that are obtained when different observers evaluate the types and severity of cognitive deficiencies exhibited by a child (Samuels et al. 1989; Vaught & Haywood 1990). Specifically, in one study, the estimates of inter-rater agreement on deficient cognitive functions rating scales ranged from 31.0% to 97.1%, with the median of 65.7% (Tzuriel & Samuels 2000). These low inter-rater reliabilities render the results suspect, as they might reflect more of the observers' than the child's characteristics.

Despite vast amounts of data accumulated by proponents of the LPAD in various studies, very little attention has been given to questions of either construct or criterion validity. Regarding the construct validity of the LPAD, factor-analytic studies (traditionally employed for establishing internal construct validity) have not been published, so there is no evidence that the structure of the LPAD corresponds to the major parameters of the proposed cognitive map.

Many validity studies have compared the effectiveness of different types of mediation on test performance (e.g., Burns et al. 1987; Missiuna & Samuels 1989). One of the more recent, as well as comprehensive and elaborately designed, studies is that of Tzuriel and Feuerstein (1992). The goal of this study was to compare the performance of advantaged and disadvantaged children in grades four to nine (total $N = 1394$) on the Raven's Standard Progressive Matrices (RSPM) to their performance on a group-administered subtest of the LPAD based on selected matrices from the individual version of the test (the Set Variations-II subtest of the LPAD) under different amounts of mediation. The group administration of the LPAD involved four stages, namely, demonstration, test, learning, and retest. All stages of test administration were conducted by the same experimenter.

In this study, the experimenter varied the amount of teaching (high, low, and no teaching) provided at the LPAD intervention stage. The RSPM problems were administered twice – before and two weeks after the intervention. According to the authors' interpretation, the results showed that (a) LPAD performance was predicted by RSPM scores; (b) children perform significantly better on the LPAD after intervention than at pretest; (c) children who received higher levels of teaching performed better; (d) disadvantaged children performed worse than did advantaged children, but with more teaching, the difference in performance was smaller; and (e) the gain acquired during the intervention remained for two weeks and was detectable with the RSPM problems when they were readministered two weeks after the intervention.

Our closer inspection of the employed statistical procedures, however, revealed a number of possibly troublesome details that might have influenced the final outcomes. These drawbacks in the design challenge the conclusions regarding the impact of the LPAD intervention.

First, there were two different designs in one study. The first design, within which the comparison of the RSPM scores on pre- and posttest at different levels of teaching was carried out, included a control group (the no-teaching group), whereas the second design, allowing for comparison of the LPAD Set Variations' performance at different levels of teaching, did not have a control group (i.e., the comparison was carried out only in high- versus low-teaching). The authors present this circumstance as a logical feature of the design – the set variations are where the teaching is carried out, so there is implicitly, according to the authors, no possibility for a control group.

However, let us draw an analogy. Suppose the effect of training on singing ability were studied. The participants were students from two different groups: The first group consisted of participants who took music lessons, and the second group consisted of participants who did not. At the pretest, participants were asked to sing a song they had never heard before. Their performance was recorded as their initial level of ability. Then participants were randomly assigned to different groups: (a) a group to which five singing lessons were given, (b) a group to which one singing lesson was given, and (c) a group to which no lessons were given. The teaching was targeted at the test song. A week later the training participants were asked to sing the same song again. When researchers analyzed the data, they took into account the quality of music schooling and the initial performance of the song.

Virtually any psychologist familiar with the abilities literature would agree that this singing example manifests an aptitude-by-treatment interaction (ATI) design. Similarly, we would argue that the Tzuriel-Feuerstein study is an example of a typical ATI design. The study would have been more relevant to the field of dynamic testing if the researchers had used a measure of learning potential for all groups and incorporated this index into their models. If such an index remained significant over and above the effect of initial performance, and if the children in the no-teaching condition (whose learning potential was controlled for) gained less, then the findings would have been novel. Otherwise, the results, showing that more teaching leads to better outcomes and that students who demonstrate lower levels of performance at the baseline gain more from targeted teaching, appear to be less than novel. Moreover, there was no control for any other (non-LPAD-relevant) type of instruction. It might be that the disadvantaged students were more sensitive to any kind of instruction, and thus that their learning gain might have been greater than the gain of advantaged students, who were at a higher level to begin with. Regression effects also could have accounted for the results.

Second, there is a statistical problem with the presented results due to the fact that most of the analyses presented include two highly correlated variables reflecting the initial level of performance: (1) a continuous variable–RSPM-initial and (2) the level of performance, specified as low, medium, or high on the basis of the very same pretest RSPM scores. The inclusion of these two highly correlated variables in the analyses results in multicollinearity (or, possibly, even singularity), causing logical and statistical problems. Moreover, the correlation itself is artificially inflated due to its part–whole nature.

Finally, the data analyses did not explore the practice effects that occur in RSPM performance simply as a result of taking the test twice. We have explored the data (as presented in Tzuriel & Feuerstein 1992, pp. 194–195) on percentage gains in correct answers on the RSPM posttest compared to the pretest for children in grades four–six and seven–nine. Under the assumption that the standard deviation within different teaching groups is at least as high as the one calculated from the means of different subtypes of the groups, we compared the total group means for the high-, low-, and no-teaching groups; there was no significant difference among the gains under the three conditions. This finding suggests that any speculations regarding the effects of teaching are not warranted unless the variance in improvement due to the second test administration is taken into account.

In summary, strictly speaking, none of these findings are dynamic-testing specific. In essence, all they suggest is that if students are test-specifically trained (the more the better), then their post-training performance will improve. Similar results have been obtained with the test–train–retest paradigm using static tests (e.g., Throne & Farb 1978). Moreover, other researchers have observed significant spontaneous practice effects in performance on static tests in cultures where these tests are not commonly used (Ombrédane, Robayer, & Plumail 1956; Serpell 1993).

As noted earlier, the Tzuriel-Feuerstein study (1992) is prototypical of many other studies that have been conducted earlier and with different samples. The main goals of these studies are to show that (a) the performance on the dynamically administered tests is higher on posttest than on pretest, (b) more mediation results in more improvement, and (c) disadvantaged students tend to benefit more from dynamically administered tests than do advantaged students.

A number of studies, conducted within this framework, were strongly influenced by Feuerstein's work but utilized different instruments and populations. For example, Lidz (1991) gave the Preschool Learning Assessment Device (PLAD, Lidz & Thomas 1987) to a group of Head Start children. The PLAD is a modification of the LPAD, based on Feuerstein's approach and Luria's (1973) methodology (Naglieri & Das 1988), and is targeted at three- to five-year-old children. The comparison was to a matched group that was exposed to the same pre- and posttest materials but did not undergo the cognitive intervention that is usually a component of the PLAD. In other words, similar to other studies in the field, the design included a no-intervention control group (to rule out practice effects) but no "placebo" group for teaching. The researchers found that mediated children showed greater gains than did control children, who showed no change. In another study (Reinharth 1989, cited in Lidz 1991), the PLAD was administered to a group of developmentally delayed children. The comparison was also to members of a matched group who were not trained. Once again, the mediated group showed greater cognitive gains. Follow-up testing a week later documented an increase in performance of the experimental group. In addition, using another application of the LPAD for preschoolers (the Children's Analogical Thinking Modifiability Test, CATM, Tzuriel 1997b; Tzuriel & Klein 1985, 1987), Tzuriel and Klein (1985) conducted a study comparing the performances of advantaged, disadvantaged, special education, and mentally retarded children. All four groups performed better (as shown by the absolute values; no variability measure was presented) on the dynamic test, the CATM, than on a static test, the Raven's Colored Progressive Matrices (RCPM, Raven 1956). For example, the disadvantaged children answered 64% of the CATM problems correctly as compared with 44% of the RCPM items. A similar pattern of results regarding the children's performance on static and dynamic tests was found in a study of hearing (66% on the CATM versus 42% on the RCPM) and deaf (54% on the CATM versus 39% on the RCPM) children (Tzuriel & Caspi 1992) and in case studies (e.g., Haywood & Menal 1992; Kaniel & Tzuriel 1992; Katz & Bucholz 1984; Tzuriel 1998, 2000). In addition, the CATM and the Complex Figure Test have been used to show the effectiveness of enrollment in a cognitive early education program in Israel, Bright Start (Tzuriel et al. 1998; Tzuriel et al. 1999). The results showed higher improvements in the Bright Start group both on static tests' indicators and on dynamic tests' change scores. Thus, one after another, the studies address the question of how much better the mediated performance and the posttest performance are when they are compared with pretest performance in different groups and across different conditions. Other validity-related issues are not dealt with.

Researchers have addressed the issue of the external validity of some of the LPAD components, modified for young children. For example, the effectiveness of the mediation approach (Feuerstein et al. 1979) and that of the "graduated-prompts" procedure (Brown & French 1979) in assessing independent and transfer task performance were compared in a number of studies conducted by the Vanderbilt group (Burns 1991; Declos et al. 1992; Vye et al. 1987). In the graduated-prompts approach, one gives examinees successive clues to help them solved failed items, continuing until the examinees are able to solve the items they have failed.

In Burns's (1991) study, 127 4- to 6-year-olds were divided into three groups: mediation, graduated prompts, and static testing groups. The comparisons were made for children's independent performances on the task they had been trained on and on a transfer task. The independent performance was better for dynamically assessed children for both mediational and hinting approaches when compared with static procedures. Moreover, the mediational group did better than did the hinted group. The transfer performance was better for mediated children, but there were no differences between the hinting and the static procedures. Thus, it appears that the data support the usefulness of the mediational approaches. The authors speculated, however, that the graduated prompting procedure might be more relevant to school experiences and thus could be more predictive of children's performance than the mediation approach.

There are two worrisome aspects of this study. First, there was no control group for the effect of teaching per se. As in the Tzuriel-Feuerstein study, the assumption was made that the no-treatment group could be used as a control group; the question, however, remains – if there is no control for the fact of teaching or simply interacting continuously with the tester and getting used to him or her, how do we know that the effects of intervention are not mostly due to teaching per se? To rule out the effect of teaching, some kind of placebo control is needed. Second, the magnitudes of the reported effects were quite low; taking into account the fact that multivariate models were not tested and that the obtained p-values were not corrected for multiple comparisons, the published p-values of .01 might not hold under proper reanalyses. These findings, however, were supported by the results from two other studies conducted by the same group (Burns et al. 1987; Burns et al. 1992). Thus, even though the magnitudes of the observed effects are not strong, their consistency across the Vanderbilt group studies suggests their durable nature.

Another important index of criterion validity of the LPAD would be a study that could demonstrate correlations between the device and changes in academic achievement. We are not aware of any studies that have directly investigated this issue.

Another important type of validity is treatment validity. This type of validity refers to the extent to which an individual's test scores can be used to detect the kind of instruction that will be most effective for that individual. In other words, based on the belief that the LPAD should lead directly to intervention, it is expected that the device should be able to predict differential responses of the assessed children to instruction, and to address the issue of *aptitude–treatment interactions.* However, beyond the observation that students of lower ability tend to benefit more from mediation than do students of higher ability, the LPAD-based studies do not address this question. For example, in the Tzuriel-Feuerstein study described above, the highest posttest gains were demonstrated by the initially low-performance group followed by the medium- and high-performance groups, with the larger magnitude of effect for the higher-intensity teaching condition. However, these findings have not been translated into intervention recommendations. They also may be due in part or wholly to regression effects.

Concluding this section, we want to pose a number specific questions pertaining to the design of the studies and the magnitudes of the obtained effects. One issue relates to the fact that the LPAD and its variants represent not a single test, but rather a collection of tests. Mean differences between pre- and posttest scores on different tests are not adjusted for multiple comparisons. This apparent oversight in failing to control for Type I error (the error of rejecting the null hypothesis when it is actually true) results in the probability levels of these tests being much higher than the 0.05 level claimed. Just by chance, some of these statistical tests would be expected to be significant. Another problem that appears to be relevant to most of the studies mentioned above centers around the power of the statistical tests used. With degrees of freedom (df) of $1/1375$ (e.g., Tzuriel & Feuerstein 1992), the power to produce statistical significance is large, even if the difference between the means is quite small and possibly trivial in a practical sense. Thus, researchers conducting large-scale studies need to formulate a priori hypotheses regarding the magnitude of differences between means that they believe a priori to be practically and psychologically important. If such estimates are not made a priori, it is often assumed that the differences should at least exceed the standard error of the measurement for a given test (Salvia, as cited in Bradley 1983). Bradley (1983) conducted a scrupulous analysis of the mean differences obtained by Feuerstein et al. (1979) and found that none of the reported mean differences even approached the standard-error-of-measurement criterion.

Power of Prediction

It seems reasonable to assume that if a child's cognitive processing has been modified and presumably strengthened by training, then there should be effects of these modifications on school performance. Feuerstein and his colleagues have argued against the use of school achievement as a criterion for the evaluation of the predictive validity of dynamic instruments (see Feuerstein et al. 1979). Feuerstein has suggested concentrating instead on "changes in the functioning of the individual following the intervention characteristic of the dynamic assessment," (1979, p. 326), but it would be desirable to have some clearly specified and important criterion that is external to the tests whose validity is being evaluated. As of today, the "target of prediction" of dynamic testing is not clear. According to Tzuriel (1992), in order to predict cognitive modifiability, an intervention should be carried out first with the goal of actualizing the potential diagnosed by a dynamic test. Following Feuerstein's argument, Tzuriel has argued that automatic transfer from test results to school achievements cannot be assumed. To reiterate, in order to validate and verify results of dynamic testing, a complex intervention should be carried out first. In other words, in this approach, testing and intervention are linked together: Initially, testing is done for the sake of devising appropriate interventions; then, intervention is carried out to validate the test results; then, once again, more testing is undertaken to identify the next round of intervention, and so on.

A criterion-validation study with clearly formulated external criteria was, however, conducted by Shochet (1992), who studied the role of dynamic testing in predicting the success of 104 advantaged and 52 disadvantaged undergraduate students in South Africa. The criterion measures were number of credits and grade-point average at the end of the first year. Using scores on the Deductive Reasoning Test (DRT, Verster 1973) administered both statically and dynamically, Shochet obtained three scores: (a) manifest intellectual functioning (as measured by a statically administered DRT), (b) potential intellectual functioning (as measured by a dynamically administered DRT), and (c) modifiability (as measured by the difference between scores on the statically and dynamically administered DRT). Based on the modifiability score (c), the sample of disadvantaged students was divided into two groups of greater or lesser cognitive modifiability. The results revealed significant differences for the beginning versus the end of the school year in the prediction of the criterion measures among the less modifiable students as compared with no differential prediction among the more modifiable students. Shochet found that the less modifiable students' scores on the DRT administered statically at the beginning of the academic year correlated significantly with both number of credits and grade-point average ($r = .55$, $p < .01$ and $r = .50$, $p < .01$, respectively), whereas the DRT scores of more highly modifiable students did not correlate with the criterion measures. Shochet concluded that static tests might be not only unreliable but also unfair when applied to highly cognitively modifiable individuals.

The Shochet study has a number of methodological drawbacks, among which are a relatively small sample size of disadvantaged students ($N = 52$), a limited sampling of abilities measured (only deduction), and ambiguity of the cutoff point between more and less modifiable students. However, this is the only study that has anchored (even if, perhaps, weakly) Feuerstein's paradigm to a criterion measure. Many researchers, when they did not find any evidence for criterion validity, have used the phrase "As expected . . ." (e.g., Haywood & Arbitman-Smith 1981, p.134), stating after the fact that the changes one might get either could not be observed yet or the time period had passed in which changes could have been observed. These equivocations led Bradley (1983) to question how many failures to find evidence for the paradigm's criterion validity would need to be accumulated before the researchers would admit that Feuerstein's measures have questionable predictive power.

Effort Invested in Training and Administration

It has been stated many times that LPAD-based testing requires more skill and greater investment of time from both examiner and examinee than does static testing. On average, according to Tzuriel (1995), if a complete 15-subtest version of the LPAD is administered, a one-participant investment may take about 10 hours. Vye et al. (1987, p.330) effectively described the demands of such testing: "His [Feuerstein's] extended assessment can last from a number of hours to several days." To justify such an investment, one should be confident that the results of the testing will be sufficiently worthwhile for both examiner and examinee. Of course, most of the practitioners use only reduced versions of the LPAD, combining its components with other approaches. Moreover, group-administered versions of the LPAD save considerable time by testing many children simultaneously. However, as has been stated by the developers of the group version of the LPAD, the group testing is only a first step of the process and, in many cases, is expected to be followed by the more refined and time consuming individual LPAD testing (Rand & Kaniel 1987).

An extremely important aspect of dynamic testing concerns teachers' perceptions of the evaluated children. Using their brief-form modification of Feuerstein's Stencil Design Test, Delclos, Burns, and Kulewicz (1987) investigated the effects that viewing dynamic testing situations had on teachers' expectations of handicapped children as learners. Videotapes of two children, one evaluated across the sequence static test – static test – dynamic test, and the other evaluated across the sequence static test – dynamic test, were shown to 60 teachers randomly divided into two groups, each of which viewed one of the children. Even though the teachers did not notice the difference in the children's involvement in static versus dynamic tests, both task-specific and general competencies were viewed as much higher when the children were evaluated dynamically rather than statically. In other words, seeing the children in the context of dynamic testing raised the teachers' expectations. It is interesting to note that Hoy (1983, as cited in Delclos et al. 1992) did not show any such effect when written reports of dynamic and static testing were compared.   Moreover, researchers found that, for programming purposes, standard psychological reports were rated as significantly more useful than LPAD reports (Hoy & Retish 1984). This finding was not supported, however, in the study carried out by Delclos, Burns, and Vye (1993). These researchers found that the perceptions of the psychological reports depended on a number of factors, among which was the individual profile of the evaluated child and the familiarity of the teachers with relevant psychological theories. In combination, these results suggest that, although teachers' perception of children's competencies might be influenced by both observing children's actual performances on dynamic testing and reading about the results, this influence is mediated by many factors.

The LPAD lower age boundary is 10, so that the dynamic testing of younger children is conducted either with CATM or PLAD. Each test requires approximately 90 to 120 minutes.

The LPAD is designed as a clinical procedure. This fact has been viewed as a justification for saying that the device is not a standardized or normative tool, and consequently, that scoring involves clinical judgment and inference (Lidz 1991). As for the LPAD administration, the issue of variability among testers in the administration of the LPAD (or similar instruments) has been raised by a number of researchers (Jitendra & Kameenui 1993). For example, using a sample of 32 children evaluated by five testers, Burns (1996) showed that overall tester/clinician behavior correlated with task performance. (For some reason, the researchers decided to match the children on their pretest scores rather than to keep the pretest score as a covariate.) For example, the tester's behavior, such as asking two-choice rule-goal questions, correlated 0.62 ($p < .01$) with the child's correct nonverbal response. The comparison between the testers was carried out for two testers only. This decision considerably reduced the sample size, and, consequently, the statistical power. No performance differences, but some behavior differences, were found. In other words, the tester–test-taker behavioral exchange varied among different pairs of testers and children, but the children's performance outcome did not vary within the groups of the two testers ($N = 10$ and $N = 7$). This study certainly raises a very interesting methodological question, but, unfortunately, it does not have enough power to answer this question one way or the other. In other words, some behavioral differences in response to testers' behaviors were registered, but the question of whether or not these differences are linked to differences in performance remains open.

As one can imagine, the scoring of the LPAD is a complex process, involving mapping the obtained data back to the model and making subjective conclusions about such dimensions of the test as phase of the mental act (i.e., input, elaboration, or output), level of abstraction (i.e., conceptual distance between the object and the mental operations required), and five more dimensions that seem somewhat abstract and vague. Perhaps this vagueness is why the mastery of scoring requires extensive and potentially expensive residential training sponsored by the Feuerstein groups and why scoring reliabilities are nevertheless variable (Haywood & Wingenfeld 1992).

The LPAD methodology seems to be effective in work with handicapped children and adolescents (e.g., Feuerstein et al. 1979) for differentiating populations of underachievers much more finely than do conventional tests. The device may also serve as a basis for remediation programs and for conducting individual evaluations of handicapped children.

A different situation arises when the LPAD is administered to mainstream children. No strong validation data have yet been provided that adequately support the claim that the information obtained via the LPAD has more predictive power than do scores from conventional tests. As Blagg (1991) noted, it is somewhat paradoxical that, although Feuerstein has rejected IQ tests as predictors of learning potential, he still has referred to changes in IQ scores observed after the mediation as major evidence to support the application of the LPAD (e.g., Feuerstein et al. 1979). Given the similarity of content, mediation may in effect be doing nothing more than teaching to the tests. At this point, we just cannot be sure.

Robustness of Results

Studies of the LPAD are probably more numerous in the field of dynamic testing than are studies of alternative dynamic measures. However, quite a few of these studies have what appear to be limitations.

First, consider the theoretical basis of this approach. In describing drawbacks of the LPAD, Büchel and Scharnhorst (1993) pointed to what they believe to be the lack of explicitly and unequivocally defined concepts, the uncontrolled use of ill-defined concepts, the overlapping subcomponents of the theory, and the incorporation of heterogeneous "description-languages" belonging to different types of theories. We suggest a somewhat different formulation of the problem: The vagueness of the concepts underlying Mediated Learning and Cognitive Modifiability theory renders operationalization difficult, with validation of these concepts even more so. For example, it is not clear how the "transcendent nature of intervention," which is one of the characteristics of mediated learning experience, translates into valid cognitive performance outcomes that are related to school or other activities.

This criticism, however, might not be totally fair. There are researchers who have been able to overcome, at least in part, the vagueness of the MLE-related concepts. For example, Lidz (1991) has attempted to operationalize MLE by modifying and reinterpreting some MLE components and placing them on a scale. However, empirical research on the MLE at this time is limited and has been carried out primarily in the context of parent–child interactions (e.g., Tzuriel 1997a, in press; Tzuriel & Weiss 1998). The goals of this research are (a) to define characteristics of parent–child interactions that are linked to various components of MLE; (b) to describe the methods for accomplishing MLE; and (c) to investigate the effect of MLE on children's cognitive modifiability.

Second, at the level of methodology, the LPAD does not fulfill a number of requisites. One is standardization (in test administration, analysis, and interpretation of results). A second is reliability. The LPAD and its modifications have weak test-retest reliability (Büchel & Scharnhorst 1993) and are supported by virtually no data addressing the issue of the reliability of change. Moreover, most of the studies that have been done use less than ideal statistical analysis, failing to use multivariate research designs and not controlling for numbers of comparisons in significance testing.

Any dynamic testing procedure, especially one as interactive as Feuerstein's, may result in both temporary and lasting changes in the child's cognition. Even though, as we have mentioned earlier, the LPAD does not have as its goal providing MLE that might result in durable changes, there have been a few reports noting that the group-administered LPAD may have different consequences from the individually administered one. We need a better sense of what the changes are and how long they last.

Third, this approach requires a substantial investment of time and money in training. The assumed ability of the mediator to respond to any slight change in an examinee requires a fairly high level of professionalism, and, like any demanding requirement, limits the applicability and availability of competent administration of the instrument.

In sum, Feuerstein's work is an example of a well-intentioned paradigm that very much needs convincing empirical validation. The principles and ideas developed by Feuerstein and his followers have had major implications for the field of dynamic testing and have facilitated the development of new approaches to testing. The field of dynamic testing is indebted to Feuerstein for his pioneering and path-making efforts. He placed his work in a comprehensive psychological and philosophical framework; he articulated the societal need for alternative approaches to testing; he initiated practical movement away from conventional testing; and he created an elaborate theory and a corresponding methodology. Feuerstein's work is ambitious, both in terms of its attempt to cover a wide range of populations and in the cognitive functions it addresses. Because of this global approach, finer details such as the psychometric properties of the instruments, adequate statistical approaches to data analysis, and precision in making inferential statements in interpreting the data do not appear to have been at the center of attention. Moreover, Feuerstein and his colleagues openly state their preferences. Thus, in response to criticism, the first line of defense is traditionally based on the societal and philosophical aspects of the approach, rather than on the accumulated psychometric and experimental data (e.g., Tzuriel 1992). Feuerstein's approach has provoked more research than any other dynamic testing approach. It also has spawned several approaches that lean heavily on it conceptually. One such approach is the MindLadder approach.

THE MINDLADDER APPROACH

The MindLadder approach of Jensen (1992, 1998, 2000) builds upon Feuerstein's theory, especially with regard to the theory of mediated learning experience, to propose a new model for dynamic assessment. The model is referred to as one of *mediated constructivism,* and it distinguishes among three kinds of functions: intellective functions, nonintellective functions, and performance functions. Examples of intellective functions are reception (such as attention and exploratory behavior), transformation (such as mental representation and planning), and communication (such as verbal tools and self-regulation). Examples of nonintellective functions are motives and needs (such as need for feelings of competence and need for novelty) and personality attributes (such as desire for approval and curiosity). Examples of performance functions are rapidity and precision as well as habit formation. To our knowledge, there is no firm empirical evidence of the validity of this particular theoretical taxonomy.

The model is based on five characteristics of mediated learning expe-

rience (MLE) to develop construction of knowledge. These five characteristics are

1. *Intentionality–reciprocity* – a bond is formed between the mediator
   and the learner.
2. *Transcendence* – the learner develops a new mode of cognitive
   functioning.
3. *Mediation of meaning* – a need is created within the learner to develop a new mode of functioning.
4. *Mediated regulation of behavior* – a new mode of cognitive functioning is placed within the broader sequence of mental acts.
5. *Mediation of a feeling of competence* – learners are motivated to function in new and unfamiliar as well as difficult ways.

An interesting innovation associated with the MindLadder Project is
its collection and analysis of the process data accumulated during dynamic instruction and assessment in a computerized form, utilizing the
knowledge assembly workstation (CAMET). The CAMET software uses
equivalent strings of items so that the analyses of change over time are
conducted on a within-subject basis using parametric tests with cus-
tomary p-values. The workstation utilizes a multimedia environment,
on-line encyclopedias, and a variety of learning materials that are
brought into the assessment process interactively, depending on students' processing needs (Jensen 1998).

In addition, several instruments have been created for dynamic assessment (e.g., Student Learning Profile, SLP-75). There is some tentative evidence for the efficacy of the instruments, but much more extensive research would be needed in order fully to assess the
instrumentation.

CONCLUSION

The utility of Feuerstein's LPAD has yet to be demonstrated adequately.
Although there are many studies of the instrument, their results are
equivocal, and many of them lack sufficient controls and other forms of
methodological rigor to permit reliable conclusions. The approach
seems to have some promise for retarded performers, at least, but more
rigorous quantification and psychometric analysis are needed in order
to ascertain just how great this promise is. At approximately the same

time as Feuerstein's approach was developed, a number of other different approaches grew out of different traditions. Responding in part to the methodological limitations apparent in Feuerstein's work (see, for example, Budoff's criticisms of Feuerstein for lack of standardization of the training segment, as cited in Lidz 1991) and partially driven by their own ideas to improve the psychometric properties of the instruments in the field, researchers have attempted to design paradigms that would maintain the flexibility of dynamic testing but simultaneously introduce into the testing situation more demonstrably reliable and valid measures. Among the attempts to standardize both methodology and interpretation are the approaches of Budoff, Campione and Brown, Guthke, and Carlson and Wiedl.

CHAPTER FIVE

The Approach of Budoff

Budoff has developed a different approach to measuring learning potential. This chapter offers an analysis of this approach.

THE APPROACH

Budoff conducted a number of empirical studies that were both interesting and important to the field. He did not, however, develop a unified theoretical basis for his work. Therefore, we discuss, first, the main characteristics of his framework and, second, the empirical findings obtained by Budoff and his collaborators.

The Framework

Target Population

Budoff (1968) based his work on the assumption that some educable disadvantaged children (e.g., educable mentally handicapped and children from impoverished environments) are more capable of learning than their conventional test results would suggest. The hypothesis was that if children are given the opportunity to learn how to solve a problem through organized, specialized instructions, at least some disadvantaged students will demonstrate improved performance beyond that predicted by ability tests. Thus, the *target population* is a broadly defined population of disadvantaged low-IQ students, which includes underachievers, children with learning disabilities, immigrants, and others.

Ideologically, Budoff's position regarding the population for which the usage of measures of learning potential is crucial resembles Feuerstein's. For both, the underlying beliefs are that (a) there are substantial numbers of individuals who, as a result of their unique educational experiences (e.g., cultural differences or lack of proper education), have their actual capabilities underestimated and so are unfairly viewed and classified by their teachers and the whole educational system, and (b) on average, the performance of mentally retarded individuals, as measured by static tests, is underestimated. These individuals have more learning potential than is usually identified by conventional tests.

Correspondingly, Budoff's work addressed, in essence, two different populations – those low-achieving children unfairly classified as educable but mentally retarded on the basis of IQ tests (primarily minority and low-SES children) and those children correctly diagnosed as educable but mentally retarded, who can demonstrate higher levels of performance when properly tested by other-than conventional tests, and who therefore must be educated in a way that will allow them to maximize their capabilities.

The Paradigm

Budoff (1987a), criticizing Feuerstein's work for lack of standardization, made a concerted effort to standardize the training component of his approach. According to Budoff (1987a), his approach differs from other dynamic testing techniques in which "it is difficult to distinguish the contribution the tester makes to improved student responses from what the student actually understands and can apply" (p.56). There are a number of characteristics of Budoff's approach that make his methodology distinct: (a) The procedure is explicitly designed to serve as an alternative to conventional intelligence tests in selecting and classifying children for purposes of special education; (b) only the use of standardized, reliable, and extensively validated tests is involved and even permitted; (c) the aim of training is to familiarize the students with the demands of the tests, thus attempting to equalize their experiences.

The outcome of the training procedure is conceptualized as the measure of *learning potential*. Budoff views learning potential as a measure of general ability (g) (Budoff 1968) in the disadvantaged population of children. Budoff's g differs from the conventional g in that it does not directly relate to school activities (Budoff 1969) and is explicitly believed to be trainable (Corman & Budoff 1973).

Initially, Budoff and his colleagues (1987a, 1987b) operationalized learning potential in terms of qualitative classification of cases. They distinguished among *high scorers* (those who scored high prior to training), *gainers* (those who performed poorly on the pretest but improved their scores significantly following instruction), and *nongainers* (those who performed poorly at pretest and did not gain from the instruction). However, in response to criticism that this classification could not distinguish among more finely defined groups (e.g., Lidz 1991), the qualitative descriptor of learning potential was replaced with a set of continuous scores, operationalized through *pretraining score, posttraining score,* and *posttraining score adjusted for pretest level* (the residualized score).

Measures of Learning Potential

Budoff and his colleagues have developed dynamic versions of about a dozen well-known standardized tests, including, for example, the Kohs Learning Potential Task, Raven Learning Potential Test, and Picture Word Game. These instruments (referred to by the authors as tests, procedures, or games) can be administered individually or in any combination and are referred to as Budoff's Measures of Learning Potential (Budoff 1987a, 1987b).

Internal consistencies of the tests are satisfactory, averaging around 0.86 (Budoff 1987b). Test–retest reliabilities were evaluated in a number of studies when posttests were administered with different time intervals (from one day to six months). The reliability estimated for the time interval of one month varied from 0.51 (for the Raven test) to 0.95 (for the Kohs test). No evaluation of the reliability of change has been performed.

These tests can be administered in both individual and group formats. For each test there is a specific set of instructions for the examiner. Furthermore, general approaches are suggested to testers at every step of the procedure. Thus, at pretest, the Budoff-based examiner is expected to adopt the style of an examiner in regular standardized static testing. At the training stage, the examiner's role is to direct the student's attention, explain the crucial attributes of the task and the testing procedure, and guide the student in mastering all actions (both cognitive and motor) that are necessary for finding the right solution. For example, training for the Kohs Block Designs involves five coaching strategies, which are printed in the same format and dimensions as the test designs. The coaching emphasizes four principles (Budoff 1987a): (a) maximizing success by pointing out the simplest elements in the design, (b) frequent praise and encouragement, (c) underscoring the importance of checking the block construction against the design card, and (d) emphasizing the two-color design of the blocks. The coaching sequence for an item is designed so that the test-taker initially has to solve the problem from a stimulus card on which the blocks are undifferentiated. In case of failure, the individual is presented one row of the design at a time. If he/she fails again, the blocks are progressively examined and their structure explained on succeeding presentations. The standardization of the training is approximate, not absolute. At the last stage the examiner once again uses the style of traditional static testing. The materials that were presented at pretest are presented twice more – usually, one day and again one month following coaching.

In terms of construct validity, Budoff and his colleagues have presented ample evidence that coaching leads to improvement on posttest (Budoff 1967, 1987a, 1987b; Budoff & Friedman 1964). In terms of concurrent validity, Budoff's findings showed that learning-potential status is related to performance, but not to verbal IQ (Budoff 1967; Budoff & Corman 1974). This finding appears not to be surprising, because most of Budoff's tests measure nonverbal abilities. This result, however, has been challenged by a group of Spanish psychologists (Fernandez-Ballesteros 1996; Fernandez-Ballesteros & Calero 1993, 2000; Fernandez-Ballesteros et al. 1997). Based on Budoff's materials, this group developed a Spanish version of a learning potential assessment device (EPA). The EPA gain scores were predictive of improvement in verbal, but not performance, abilities. The group also found that those who gained on the dynamic test showed superior cognitive performance later on as well. These results are especially unexpected because both the Budoff group and a group of scientists then at Vanderbilt University (and led by Carl Haywood) did not find any evidence of between-domain transfer, either for a pretest predicting intervention performance or for an intervention predicting posttest performance (for a review, see Lidz 1987). For example, it has been found consistently that full-scale intelligence measures do not predict dynamic performance with any great precision. Neither do cross-domain measures. The predictive power of certain subscales, corresponding to the type of cognitive functioning utilized in the dynamic tests, is argued to be higher than the predictive power of the composite total score (e.g., .48 versus .18, Vye et al. 1987). Explaining their results, the authors (Fernández-Ballesteros et al. 1997) argued that although the EPA materials include progressive matrices, the embedded training is verbal; Fernández-Ballesteros et al. appealed to a statement made by Campione and Brown (1979), who claimed that the operation trained during dynamic testing is that of executive verbal control. This result poses a yet unanswered question of what gets trained or coached – a targeted cognitive function or a more general strategy of problem solving.

Despite his early claim that measured learning potential does not directly relate to school achievement, Budoff has conducted a number of school-based predictive-validity studies. In one study utilizing teacher-rated achievement, correlations between the learning-potential posttest and achievement were different for three groups of students (above-average [high scorers], average [gainers], and below-average [nongainers] learners, as identified by the Budoff Learning Potential Measures). Whereas the correlations between posttest and achievement were twice as high as the correlations between IQ scores and achievement ($r = .35$ and $.16$, respectively) for the average and below-average learners, the correlations were comparable ($r = .35$ and $.31$, respectively) for above-average learners (as presented in Laughon, 1990).

The predictive power of Budoff's measure of learning potential was also estimated by correlating it with classroom measures of educational achievement (Budoff, Meskin, & Harrison 1971). Similarly to the teacher-ratings' study, students were classified into groups of below-average, average, and high-average learners based on their scores on Budoff's measures. Students were taught about electricity, and their subsequent performance on the relevant achievement test was correlated with measures of their learning potential. The results showed that the measures of learning potential were more predictive of achievement differences in learning about electricity than was IQ.

Empirical Findings

Within this paradigm, training improves scores for both special- and regular-education children (Budoff 1987a). Moreover, for both nonchallenged and challenged learners, Budoff has reported a high level of correspondence between results of learning-potential testing and teacher indications of students' learning rates (Budoff & Hamilton 1976). The best predictor of the school-achievement criterion for children enrolled in special curriculum programs was found to be the posttraining scores on the learning-potential testing instruments (Budoff, Corman, & Gimon 1976; Budoff et al. 1971).

Most of the empirical work of Budoff and his colleagues has been devoted to exploring correlations between learning potential and other cognitive – as well as demographic, motivational, and emotional – indicators. The designs of these studies are quite similar to one another. Initially, Budoff's battery (or parts of it) are used to evaluate students' learning potential; then the learning potential indicator(s) is (are) correlated with scores from a set of other measures. For example, Budoff and his colleagues conducted a number of large-scale studies ($N > 400$) investigating social, demographic, and psychometric correlates of learning potential (e.g., Budoff 1987a). The participants in these studies were low-IQ pupils who were either students in special-education classes or residents of institutions for the retarded. The results showed that (1) static measures of ability (such as the Stanford-Binet intelligence test) were related more to such variables as noninstitutionalization, family demographic characteristics, and Wechsler (WISC) Verbal IQ than to measures of learning potential (pretraining Kohs scores); (2) immediate effects of training were predicted by gender, family demographics, and static measures of performance IQ; and (3) delayed effects of training were predicted by static measures of performance IQ. Moreover, whereas such variables as race and SES were significantly associated with static measures of IQ, these demographic characteristics did not elicit systematic differences on the scores following training.

Another series of studies conducted by Budoff and his colleagues examined the personality profiles of low-IQ students whose learning potential was evaluated as higher than average for the group of low-IQ students. Children with higher learning potential tended to be friendlier, showed higher motivation for achievement, and were less rigid and less impulsive than were children of similar IQ level but lower learning potential (Budoff 1987a). Budoff also studied socioeconomic class (SES) as a variable that might correlate with learning-potential measures and found that low-SES students needed more training and benefited more from individual than group training in comparison with advantaged students (Budoff 1987a).

In their longitudinal studies (Budoff 1967, 1987a; Budoff & Friedman 1964), Budoff and his colleagues followed various groups of low-IQ children over time. They found that gainers as compared with nongainers were more likely to (a) perform better in special-education programs, (b) attain economic and social independence as adults to a greater degree, (c) be qualified for military service more often, (d) report having friends and dating experience, (e) live away from home and obtain a driver's license, and (f) be released from institutions, if ever institutionalized. However, these findings were obtained from a fairly small group of children and without proper controls for possible covariates (e.g., type and amount of obtained education and family environment).

Four aspects of Budoff's experimental work are important to mention. First are the consistency of methodologies used and the research questions formulated. It appears that Budoff has chosen as his main goal the study of levels of learning potential as a function of various characteristics of students, ranging from their SES to their self-concept. Such consistency has both positive and negative aspects. On the positive side, Budoff has explored correlations between his measure of learning potential and a large number of measures of individual differences, placing learning potential in the context of other individual characteristics. On the negative side, all of these studies are observational and of limited explanatory power. Neither experimental designs nor statistical analyses allowing for fitting causal models have been implemented. In other words, only limited causal or predictive information can be extracted from the obtained data. We do not yet know if the characteristics of learning potential are predictive of positive life outcomes and better life adjustment, or if a higher learning potential is itself a characteristic of a more adaptive person.

Second, correlations have been obtained in samples that have differed in terms of (a) size, ranging from $N = 20$ (Budoff & Pagell 1968) to $N = 627$ (Budoff & Corman 1974); (b) nature, ranging from mainstreamed to institutionalized mentally retarded children; and (c) age, ranging from 12 to 17 years in one study (Budoff & Pagell 1968). The question of comparability of the obtained results in terms both of the meaning of the findings and of the magnitude of the effects has yet to be addressed.

Third, the authors have not been fully concerned with issues such as lack of statistical power to determine the presence of an effect and correcting for multiple comparisons.

Finally, at least in published material, comparatively little attention has been given to the coaching procedures themselves. The initial agenda of Budoff's approach was to standardize the training component of dynamic testing (Budoff 1987a). Based on the published material, it is unclear (a) whether and how the coaching is standardized and (b) how much of the obtained effects can be accounted for by the way in which the coaching is performed.

Evaluation Based on the Proposed Four-Point Profile

How can Budoff's work be evaluated within the 4-dimensional space described above? First, what kinds of information are attainable by Budoff's device? In contrast to Feuerstein's approach, this approach (a) seeks only to improve performance on conventional tests and thus defines learning potential by a simple measure of improvement in performance on conventional tests, and (b) works with a specific population of low-IQ children. Correspondingly, the obtained results are both population- and task-restricted. Budoff's device for assessing learning potential, like Feuerstein's, has been shown to help in differentiating the low-IQ population into distinct groups. In addition, Budoff, like the Soviet defectologists (for details, see Vlasova 1972), suggested that low-IQ students with higher learning potential (high gainers) are educationally disadvantaged rather than mentally retarded. In a similar vein, Feuerstein et al. (1979) have spoken only of retarded performers, not of retarded individuals. These are students whose school progress, for any number of reasons, is not satisfactory, but who, given proper teaching, can progress successfully. Those students whose learning potential is quite low (nongainers) match the profile of mental retardation. This differentiation appears to be helpful and might be utilized by educational practitioners who work with populations of low-IQ students. This theme of Budoff's research is similar to a comparable theme of Feuerstein et al.'s work on modifiability. Those students who gain more (or who are more modifiable) appear to (a) show that their performance is better accounted for by the measure of learning potential than by IQ and (b) have a better overall lifelong prognosis. In sum, in terms of its overall contribution to the theory and methodology of dynamic testing, Budoff's approach has attempted to place learning potential into the broader context of other cognitive, personality, and demographic characteristics.

The differentiation between gainers and nongainers as a way to account for the heterogeneity of the population classified as mentally retarded has been further explored by a number of psychologists interested in dynamic testing. One suggested differentiation is that between "biologically impaired" and "culturally deprived" individuals (Fernández-Ballesteros et al. 1997). In one study, Fernández-Ballesteros and her colleagues (1997) investigated the differences in obtained gains between students with known biological causes of mental retardation (classified as organically impaired) and individuals who did not have any noticeable biological dysfunction (classified as culturally deprived). The researchers found that the gains of students without any known biological dysfunction were about twice as great as, and of a more stable nature than, improvements evidenced by students with a known biological cause of mental retardation.

In terms of the psychometric properties of the device as compared to both static and other dynamic tests, two points should be raised. First, it is not surprising that internal consistencies of the tests are high and match the corresponding static tests, due to the fact that all of the tests composing the battery are slightly modified versions of the static tests themselves. Second, although test–retest reliabilities have been obtained for pretests, what is really needed is an evaluation of the reliabilities of the gain. For example, Carver (1974) suggested utilizing two alternative pretests, followed by highly standardized training and then two alternative posttests. It has been suggested (Embretson 1987b) that the reliability of the gain can be measured by using one pretest but three posttests, a strategy that would allow researchers to evaluate the reliability of change repeatedly. Such (or similar) evaluations have yet to be conducted.

Regarding predictive power, the studies using Budoff's approach, like the studies using the LPAD, have not accumulated enough evidence to suggest a resolution to the dynamic-versus-static testing dilemma. Only two studies have addressed the issue of predictive validity, and their findings, although promising, cannot be interpreted as conclusive. Moreover, similarly to discussions initiated by the followers of Feuerstein's approach, Budoff and his colleagues have questioned the appropriateness of using academic performance as the criterion measure (Budoff 1987a).

The tests constituting the set of *Budoff Learning Potential Measures* are relatively easy to administer and do not require lengthy professional training (Budoff 1987a,b). The results of Budoff's studies are consistent with each other, and it has been claimed that some of the outcomes of these studies (notably, those of high societal significance) have been replicated by independent groups (for a review, see Luther, Cole, & Gamlin 1996). However, after a closer examination of some of the findings, we doubt the conclusiveness of these "replications." For example, Sewell and colleagues (Sewell 1979, 1987; Wurtz, Sewell, & Manni 1985) explored the differential predictive effectiveness of the results of dynamic and static testing. Working with 70 white and 21 black first-graders, Sewell (1979) concluded that the conventional IQ tests provided a more valid estimate of learning potential under varied learning conditions for middle-class children than for lower-class children, whereas posttest performance was the best predictor for lower-class black children. The conclusions were based on two analyses – the comparison of correlation patterns within the two groups and the results of stepwise regression. In the correlational analyses, although the correlations between the IQ score and the achievement tests were significant for whites but not for blacks, Fisher's Z transformation showed that the correlations themselves did not differ from each other, most likely, as a result of the lack of statistical power in the sample of black children. Thus, the conclusion of a difference in the correlation patterns was not warranted statistically. The author chose not to present the details of the stepwise regression analysis (e.g., the variables utilized and the incremental values of R^2). If, however, the regression analyses included all of the variables presented in the correlation table, the results might have been problematic due to the presence of multicollinearity in the equation.

Similarly, when researchers (Wurtz, Sewell, & Manni 1985) attempted to predict learning potential itself (estimated within Budoff's test–teach–test paradigm) utilizing a conventional measure of intelligence (WISC-R IQ, Wechsler 1974) and a so-called measure of Estimated Learning Potential (Mercer 1979), virtually no differences in predictive patterns were found on the basis of statistical analyses. The authors, however, went outside the boundaries of the data by utilizing an "eyeballing" approach to comparing for black versus white children the frequencies of cases classified as mentally retarded, based on the tests of Wechsler and Mercer and the frequencies of Budoff's gainers. Similarly, the authors concluded (without any statistics at all) that the differential impact of using Estimated Learning Potential "is clearly evident" (Wurtz, Sewell, & Manni 1985, p. 301).

CONCLUSION

In sum, the four-point profile of Budoff's measures suggests that the measures are fairly robust instruments for the restricted specific purpose of differentiating the population of low-IQ children in order to conduct proper educational placement and to predict future performance. However, Budoff's search for the best outcome measure has raised an issue that is of concern to everyone working in the field of dynamic testing. This issue has to do with operationalization and interpretation of "responsiveness to training" and "learning." It has been pointed out that it is quite common to find children who show good cognitive test results but have a slow rate of learning and vice versa (see Lidz 1991). Moreover, this discrepancy is present in populations of both challenged (i.e., low-IQ) and nonchallenged (i.e., normal-IQ) learners. We agree with Lidz (1991) that Budoff's decision to change the "gainers" versus "nongainers" paradigm into a paradigm using a set of quantitatively distributed scores solved some analytic issues but also introduced the task of developing population-specific norms that would allow for comparison between obtained and normative scores. This task has yet to be accomplished.

Another concern involves the dearth of incremental-validity studies. Although the relative properties (i.e., its associations with gender, static ability measures, personality traits, and SES) of the measures of learning potential have been investigated in large samples of students, what is missing is "evidence that *Budoff's Learning Potential Assessment* procedures contribute more to prediction of school success than do measures of nonverbal IQ" (Lidz 1991, p. 27). There is, however, evidence of incremental prediction over verbal IQ. Recent Spanish results (Fernández-Ballesteros et al. 1997) suggest that training based on Budoff's approach can lead to an increase in verbal IQ. As a methodology with restricted and well-defined goals, Budoff's methodology appears to be adequate. Moreover, Budoff's is a pioneering, innovative, and important attempt to incorporate carefully developed static tests into a dynamic-testing procedure.

Ultimately, followers of this approach remain committed to the specific goal of obtaining results from standardized tests that are administered dynamically and thus challenge primarily the procedure but not the content of traditional tests. Budoff has not developed any global theoretical paradigm or specific intervention programs based on his approach. Perhaps he or his colleagues will develop such a program in the future.

CHAPTER SIX

Diverse Approaches to Dynamic Testing

In this chapter, we explore a number of diverse approaches to dynamic testing. Specifically, we will present the Graduated Prompts Approach, two European approaches to dynamic testing (Lerntests and Testing-the-Limits approaches), and the Swanson approach.

TESTING VIA LEARNING AND TRANSFER (THE GRADUATED PROMPT APPROACH)

The Framework

The Paradigm

The graduated prompts approach was developed primarily by Campione and Brown (Campione 1989; Campione & Brown 1987) to establish a supportive framework that gradually would assist individuals until they could solve a test problem. Kozulin and Falik (1995) referred to this approach as one that uses the idea of the ZPD as an explicit working concept. The theoretical foundation of this approach is an information-processing theory of intelligence (Campione & Brown 1987).

The key concept of this approach is transfer, or an individual's ability to use learned information flexibly and in a variety of contexts (Campione, Brown, & Bryant 1985). Transfer is considered to be especially important in academic learning situations, where instruction is often incomplete and ambiguous. The ratio of learning (how much instruction is needed for learning to occur) to transfer (how far from the original example an individual can apply the mastered knowledge) is viewed as a measure of individual differences. A special concern here is that the indicators of learning and transfer do not appear to be on the same scale, therefore challenging the meaning of the ratio.

Thus, the operationalization of the theory is in the quantification of indicators of learning and transfer. This quantification is conducted on the basis of a guided-learning paradigm. The typical sequence of testing consists of several sessions that include (a) collection of static, level-of-performance information (pretest); (b) initial learning (hinted stage); (c) static, unmediated maintenance and transfer testing (posttest); and (d) mediated maintenance and transfer testing (hint-assisted posttest). The training procedure is considered successful if (a) performance on the task improves as a consequence of the instruction, (b) the benefit of the training is durable, and (c) the outcome of the training is generalizable – that is, if transfer occurs to tasks other than those on which training took place (Brown & Campione 1981; Brown et al. 1983). Mediation in this approach is delivered by predetermined hints that range from general to specific.

Every new hint is given in response to the child's struggle, failure, or error. Provision of hints stops when the child reaches the level of independent task solution predetermined for this task (e.g., two consecutive items solved correctly). The outcome variables are viewed as measures of the child's efficiency of learning. They are operationalized by the number of prompts and by breadth of transfer in terms of the degree of success with near-transfer (a child's ability to solve problems that are similar both contextually and formally to the training problems) and far-transfer (a child's ability to solve problems that are similar to the training problems contextually, but not necessarily formally).

Consider the following example of a graduated-prompts task, developed by Ferrara (as presented in Campione 1989). At the first, pretest stage of the procedure, the student's ability to solve simple two-digit addition problems ($3 + 2 = ?$) is tested. During the learning session, the student and tester work collaboratively, and the math problems are presented as word problems, such as:

> Cookie Monster starts out with three cookies in his cookie jar, and I'm putting two more in the jar. Now how many cookies are there in the cookie jar?

If the student runs into difficulties, the tester provides a sequence of hints and suggestions about how he or she should proceed. The amount of help needed to master the specific procedure is an outcome of the learning component of the test. Following the learning stage, the student is presented with a variety of transfer problems in the same interactive, assisted format. The new problems are designed so that they require students to apply the procedures originally learned to (a) similar problems of near transfer (e.g., $3 + 1 = ?$), (b) somewhat dissimilar problems of far transfer (e.g., $4 + 3 + 2 = ?$), and (c) very different problems of very far transfer (e.g., $4 + ? = 6$). As in the learning stage, the outcome measure of the transfer session is the amount of help students needed to solve these transfer problems on their own. The final stage of the testing procedure is a posttest, in which the student is given a set of tasks that require utilization of the mastered procedures.

It should be mentioned that, in contrast to previous approaches, this mode of dynamic testing relies on new content rather than on complex tasks (which are typical of standardized tests). The content tends to be at the beginner level, which makes the standardization of hints easier and allows for more differentiation among children at the lower end of the ability distribution.

Formally, the outcome measure (viewed by these researchers as the measure of learning potential) is constructed as the inverse of the minimal number of hints that is necessary for each individual to reach a specified amount of learning (Resing 1993). In other words, rather than concentrating on the amount of improvement in a student's performance, testers determine how much help students need in order to reach a specified criterion and, consequently, how much additional help they need to transfer the learned rules and principles to novel tasks and situations. This position is different from the position of the majority of other dynamic testers (e.g., Budoff, Guthke, Hamer, and Ruijssenaars), who stress the maximal degree of improvement in performance, that is, how much better the individual does on the posttest than on the pretest. Values on the outcome variables within the graduated-prompt approach are calculated as sums of the total number of hints given at each stage of the task (i.e., initial learning, maintenance, and transfer) as well as of the total sum for the whole session. The profile of the outcome measures is viewed as an indicator of the student's zone of proximal development. It is assumed that children with broad ZPDs profit more from the intervention and need less assistance than children with narrow ZPDs.

Target Population

The primary *target population* for this approach is academically weak students, who often are labeled as having learning disabilities or mild mental retardation (Campione & Brown 1987). Researchers working in this paradigm have chosen to standardize the testing procedure, with the goal of producing psychometrically defensible quantitative data (Campione 1989). Types of tasks that are used within this framework include inductive-reasoning problems, such as variants of progressive-matrices problems and series-completion problems, mathematics problems, and reading- and listening-comprehension tasks. Inductive-reasoning measures are especially popular because they have been linked to intelligent performance since the times of Spearman (1927) and because they lend themselves very well to dynamic presentation. Performance can be decomposed into information-processing components that can be taught either separately or as an integrated set of mental events (Resing 1997, 1998, 2000).

Empirical Findings

Researchers using this approach have been concerned with a number of issues. First, they have investigated the role of learning and transfer processes in students at different levels of scholastic performance. To accomplish this goal, the researchers developed measures of learning and transfer and evaluated their concurrent and predictive validity (for a review, see Campione 1989). These measures were implemented in studies conducted to determine whether learning and transfer are related to general ability differences and whether these scores provide information beyond that obtainable from the static tests. The learning and transfer studies indicated that students of lower ability, as compared with higher-ability students, require more instruction to reach the criterion and need more help to show transfer (Campione et al. 1985; Ferrara, Brown, & Campione 1986). For example, a study of this type was conducted among groups of third- and fifth-graders (Ferrara et al. 1986). A test of letter-series completions was presented to each child. Each consecutive step included a specific set of standard and increasingly explicit prompts. The first prompt was a subtle hint, whereas the final one was direct teaching of the problem's solution. The ZPD was operationalized as the inverse of the number of prompts needed for each sequential task: A wide ZPD corresponded to a reduced number of prompts needed from one trial to another, that is, for the effective transfer of a new solution across similar problems. It was found that fifth-graders learned more quickly than did third-graders, and that higher-IQ children needed significantly fewer hints to reach a learning criterion than did average-IQ children. Furthermore, as the number of characteristics distinguishing the learning and transfer tasks increased, the performance differences became progressively more pronounced when younger children were compared with older ones, and when lower-ability students were compared with higher-ability students.

With regard to the superiority of dynamic versus static procedures, Bryant, Brown, and Campione (as cited in Campione 1989) asserted that the learning and transfer scores would provide information beyond that obtainable from static tests. In this study, the individuals' gains from the pretest to the posttest were treated as criterion measures; the intent was to investigate the set of scores that would best predict these gains. It was found that guided learning and transfer scores were the best individual predictors of gain ($r(s) \geq .60$), whereas static ability scores, although predictive, were of secondary importance ($r(s) \geq .45$).

Similarly, the goal of two other studies, one involving a simplified version of the matrices test and the other a simplified version of the series-completion task (Campione & Brown 1987), was to evaluate the magnitude of the contributions of IQ and of measures of training and transfer to the residual gain, calculated on the basis of pretest and posttest scores. It has been found that both learning and transfer measures are associated with the gain measure, over and above measures of abilities (with increments in R^2 of 22% and 17% for the matrices task, and 2% and 22% for the series-completion task, respectively). The ability measures accounted for approximately 37% of the variance, with the estimated IQ explaining 24% and the Raven scores accounting for 14% of the variance.

In addition, Resing (1993) showed that metacognitive training procedures have significant short-term and long-term effects. The test scores of experimental groups that had undergone the training were higher compared with the scores of the control group several months after training. In addition, Resing found that both posttest scores and learning-potential scores, when compared with pretest scores, make a significant contribution to the prediction of school achievement (4% to 40% increase in explained variance, depending on the test). These findings were replicated in a sample of preschool children (Day et al. 1997) who were given pretests, training, and posttests on block design and similarities tasks. Using structural-equation modeling, the researchers demonstrated that the best-fit model was the one that included paths from both pretest and testing of learning to posttest performances within each domain.

Yet another independent replication of these results was obtained in a study of 193 first-grade children (Speece, Cooper, & Kibler 1990).

Based on static ability measures, 104 students were considered at risk for school failure, and 83 were identified as controls of average ability. The researchers designed their own test for 6-year-olds, using the instrument developed by Bryant (as presented in Speece et al. 1990) as a proximal model. Again, the dynamic measure proved superior. Verbal intelligence, pretest knowledge, language variables, and the inverse of the number of prompts needed during training accounted for 48% of the posttest variance, with the prompt measure accounting for a significant amount of variance beyond all other variables in the model. Moreover, although the two groups of children were indistinguishable by standard achievement measures and the inverse of the number of prompts, the groups could be discriminated by the posttest measure.

Second, researchers investigated the role of dynamic testing in clinical assessment. A number of group-comparison studies have been conducted, investigating possible differences between children having and not having mental retardation. Hall and Day (1984, cited in Day & Hall 1987) tested the claim that children with learning disabilities and children of average achievement require less assistance than do children with mental retardation to learn how to find a solution for a novel problem and a way to transfer their learning. There were no group differences during training or close transfer. Performance on the far-transfer task, however, did reflect group differences: The average children did the best, but the differences between their performance and that of the students with learning disabilities were not significant. Children with mental retardation, however, did significantly worse than did children in either of the other two groups and required more hints to learn to solve the problems.

Campione, Brown, Ferrara, Jones, and Steinberg (1985) utilized the Raven matrices test in a comparative study involving mental-age-matched children with and without mental retardation. They found no difference between the groups' means at the learning stage. It was hypothesized that this lack of difference was due to matching procedures that equated the groups for both mental age and entering competence. However, there were significant group differences during both the maintenance and transfer phases, with the children with mental retardation scoring lower. It was found that the greater was the children's need for flexibility in applying the learned rules, the larger were the differences between the children with and without mental retardation. Moreover, in a second study (Campione & Brown 1987), which used letter-series completions, group differences between children with and without mental retardation emerged at the learning stage. More differences appeared at maintenance, as well as during far transfer and very far transfer, once again with the retarded group scoring lower.

Day and Zajakowski (1991) compared assisted and unassisted performance of average readers and readers with learning disabilities and found that children with learning disabilities required significantly more instruction than did average readers to reach a mastery criterion in reading. Resing (1993) studied children from mainstream primary classes, students with learning disabilities, and students with mild mental retardation of the same chronological age. Children in these three groups differed considerably in the mean number of hints needed to reach the established criterion. The three groups also needed a different number of hints per training item. Whereas children from primary school mostly needed metacognitive hints, about 12% of children with learning disabilities and about 25% of children with mild mental retardation needed task-specific instruction in addition to metacognitive hints.

Evaluation Based on the Proposed Four-Point Profile

The evaluation of this work on the four dimensions involves a number of issues. Similar to the findings obtained within other dynamic-testing paradigms, it was observed that children with versus without mental retardation differ in terms of their test performance. In particular, differences were shown in the abilities of children with versus without mental retardation to learn and transfer. The quantification of these differences became possible because performance at both the learning and transfer stages was measured through the number of hints needed to reach the criterion. In other words, the remarkable achievement of this approach is in its creative quantification and standardization of the intervention and transfer stages – an achievement that has not been equally accomplished by either Feuerstein or Budoff.

Another novel piece of information came from studies of normal children, in which the researchers noticed a developmental difference between third- and fifth-graders in terms of the number of requested and processed hints: The older the child, the fewer the number of hints he or she needs in order to find the correct answer. The broader psychological meaning of this finding is that learning potential, as defined by followers of the graduated-prompts approach, changes its properties at different developmental stages, that is, it is itself developmentally dynamic. Based on this finding, a hypothesis might be formed that learning potential has a psychological structure that is developmentally similar to that of any other cognitive function. Thus, it may be possible to intervene in its development, as in the development of other cognitive functions.

As with any research methodology, the graduated prompts approach raises a number of concerns. A first concern has to do with the nature and meaning of the metric of the hints (Lidz 1991). Due to the fact that the nature of hints is very heterogeneous – the hints, for example, vary in terms of their difficulty – hints given at different points of problem solution may not be comparable (nor even additive in their effects). Moreover, hints might have different meanings and significances for individuals of different cognitive profiles. In order to understand the psychological meanings of the outcome measures obtained using this approach, these outcomes need to be studied with more traditional cognitive-developmental indicators (e.g., memory and attention). For example, because a more attentive and reflective child might require fewer hints than might a more impulsive child, the more attentive and reflective child might therefore score higher on measures of learning potential. In this case, the learning-potential measures might merely be proxy measures of the child's attention rather than of his or her learning.

Another concern that needs to be investigated is whether the way learning potential is defined in this paradigm is really qualitatively different from the traditional way abilities are defined in the static-testing paradigm, or whether it merely provides another measure that complements (but is nonidentical to) existing measures. The number of prompted hints reflects the number of subtasks a child cannot solve independently. In other words, a graduated-prompts task might be viewed as a sequence of smaller tasks, each of which can be either solved (no hint is given, the child gets a score) or not solved (a hint is given, the child does not get a score). Thus, test performance could be rescored in terms of counting right and wrong answers rather than hints. When reconceived in this way, the outcome measure of the graduated-prompts approach seems to be more of a static nature than of a dynamic nature.

Moreover, in the graduated-prompts paradigm, the child is not directly taught anything – he or she is led to the discovery of a rule through a system of predetermined hints. What one really wants to know, then, is how the hint-based measures correlate with indicators of other cognitive functions (e.g., memory, cognitive styles, attention, specific abilities). It appears that these outcome measures might correlate higher with other ability measures than with other learning-potential measures.

In contrast to the two traditions discussed above, followers of this approach, as far as can be judged from the published material, have paid significantly less attention to such psychometric properties of their instruments as test–retest reliability and internal consistency. We are aware of only one study (Ferrara et al. 1986) that has addressed reliability issues. This study, however, appears to have been addressing the issue of reliability of change, rather than the issue of the reliability of the tasks themselves. The researchers reported that the amount of instruction needed by participants was similar across two inductive-reasoning tasks, suggesting that learning potential can be measured reliably in the context of different although related tasks.

With regard to predictive validity, this approach is similar to other dynamic-testing approaches, in that it has not yet shown the substantial predictive power of its learning and transfer measures for either school-achievement criteria or other adaptive measures. At present, the empirical research is limited, but we believe it is very promising.

The graduated-prompt approach operates with standardized measures that do not assume any special training and are easy to administer. Moreover, this approach has been used by researchers from laboratories other than those of the initiators of the paradigm (e.g., Day & Cordon 1993; Day & Zajakowski 1991; Speece et al. 1990), suggesting its transportability and applicability in different research contexts.

In sum, the graduated-prompts approach introduced a new feature to dynamic testing – standardization of intervention and transfer. This development has been realized by switching the center of the testing situation from the child to the task. The task and the developed hints anticipate virtually every move a child can make in the search for a solution. The question is not so much *what* the trainer should say to the child in order to lead him or her to the solution. The main issue is *how much* should be said to the child in order for him or her to reach the criterion.

A similar approach, shifting the emphasis from the child to the task, has been implemented within the European tradition, especially in the work of Carlson and Wiedl. The next section discusses this work.

THE EUROPEAN CONTRIBUTION

The Lerntest(s)

The Paradigm

This approach represents an amalgamation of testing procedures, united under the rubric of the Learning Test (*Lerntest* in German).

A German psychologist, Guthke (1992, 1993; Guthke & Stein 1996), has developed a series of tests framed in the pretest–training–posttest paradigm. In this paradigm, training (learning) is based on Gal'perin's theory (1966; see above), the core of which states that every cognitive function can be initially formed (developed) within the child's zone of proximal development under the teacher's assistance and then internalized and assimilated. Guthke and his colleagues have developed several types of learning-potential tests, adjusted to the length of the training phase (Guthke & Beckman 2000; Guthke & Wiedl 1996). They use repetitions, prompts, and systematic feedback during the test in extended training programs interposed between a pretest and a posttest (Beckman & Guthke 1995, 1999). It has been noted (Haywood 1997) that Guthke's procedures are closer to the psychometric tradition than are most of the techniques used in other approaches to dynamic testing.

An example of a learning-potential battery with a long-term (seven-day) training phase is a reasoning battery, the *Reasoning Learning Test*, which consists of two parallel tests (forms A and B) that can be alternated as pre- and posttests. The test is designed to assess reasoning in the basic domains – verbal (through analogies), numerical (through numerical sequences), and figural (through figural sequences). Training is standardized and can be conducted either in groups or individually. During the training phase, the students are provided with instruction manuals. Students are explicitly taught metacognitive strategies for solving the test items. The outcome variable is the posttest score, which is considered to be the result of the learning-potential test.

The short-term battery is designed in such a way that the training phase is embedded in the procedure. These tests do not involve intervention per se, but are based on manipulations within the test situation itself. This approach is similar to the "testing-the-limits" procedures developed by Schmidt (1971). There are two types of short-term batteries: (a) tests providing systematic but fairly limited feedback and (b) tests providing extensive assistance in a standardized form in addition to simple feedback. There are several published German learning-potential tests (for a review, see Guthke 1993). These include the Sequence of Sets Test (for preschool and first-grade children; this test of series completion is designed to assess the learning skills prerequisite for math), the Preschool Learning Potential Test (for 5–7-year-old children); the Situation Learning Potential Test (for 7–9-year-old children), the Speed and Recall Test (for adults with functional brain disorders), and the Reasoning Test. Some of these tests are based on conventional intelligence tests, while others utilize new types of items. An example of a short-term learning test based on a conventional measure is the Raven Short-Term Learning Test (Guthke 1992), which is designed for early identification of developmentally challenged children. At the first stage, the child is tested with the original colored form of the Raven test for children. If problems are not solved, a set of graded hints is given. The hints (presented as a dosaged teaching intervention) are developed according to Gal'perin's theory of learning. All children are led to the correct solution and, if needed, are shown it. The outcome measure is the number of hints needed.

The principles of the Guthke program are summarized by Guthke and Beckman (2000):

1. Ensuring content validity by doing a careful cognitive-psychological analysis of the item pool
2. Sequential construction of test requirements based on analyses of tasks
3. Giving examinees systematic feedback or thinking prompts as an integral part of the test procedure
4. Proceeding to more complex tasks only after examinees achieve independent solution of easier tasks
5. Using adaptive testing, meaning that examinees receive only items that are appropriate for them, and not ones that are too easy or too hard
6. Qualitative analysis of errors
7. Diagnosis of learning processes, not just products

One recent implementation of these principles is in the Adaptive Computer Assisted Intelligence Learning Test Battery (*ACIL*, Guthke et al. 1995). This procedure (as presented in Guthke et al. 1997) is designed for children ages 12 to 16 and is aimed at determining the "core factor of intelligence" in three domains (verbal, numeric, and figural). The procedure is driven by the complexity of items so that a set of target items is determined for each child depending on his or her age, and, if the child fails to solve the target items correctly, the child is rerouted to easier items. If the child makes two consecutive errors, the child is given prompts based on a qualitative analysis of the errors made, and, after the prompts, is presented with an item of equal complexity. If this item is solved correctly, the participant is confronted with items at the level of complexity of the initial error. Thus, the testing is conducted in a circular fashion, so that the child is rerouted between easier and more difficult items, until the criterion is reached and the targeted items are solved, or until the child has repeatedly failed without any progress, or until the time limits are exhausted. This type of testing guarantees a highly individualized approach and provides interesting diagnostic information (e.g., the starting and the ending levels of the items' complexity, the number of errors, and the number of prompts).

Empirical Findings

Researchers investigating the *Lerntest* have addressed various dynamic versus static testing issues, such as the influence of training on performance, group differences on static and dynamic measures, and the predictive validity of their measures. However, due to the fact that European followers of dynamic testing are of different nationalities, and that the majority of them have published their results in their own countries in their own languages, it was difficult to obtain the data from many of these studies. Therefore, the following section is not a comprehensive review, but rather a representative collection of the published studies that were available to the authors.

With regard to training, a number of studies compared a trained experimental group with a control group to which a test was simply administered twice. The experimental group consistently has demonstrated significantly higher gain. Even short-term training has resulted in significant gain in learning (Guthke & Wingenfeld 1992). It appears that pretest scores do not reliably predict either posttest scores or learning gain (e.g., simple repetition of the Raven's test resulted in $r = .70$ between scores obtained on the first administration and the repetition, whereas the correlation between pre- and posttests was only .27, when an interview occurred between testings). At the same time, the predictive validity of posttraining scores, when correlated with school grades and teacher ratings, appears to be fairly high; posttest scores tend to show significantly higher correlations with school performance than do pretest scores (Guthke & Wingenfeld 1992). For example, the posttest scores on the Raven Learning Test obtained for 28 kindergarten children were found to be predictive of school performance evaluated in the first, second, sixth, and seventh school grades, whereas the results of the conventional Colored Progressive Matrices were not found to correlate with school success (Guthke 1992).

In interpreting these results, one should be extremely cautious. First, the sample size appears to be quite small for obtaining the statistical power necessary to detect both the change itself and its magnitude. Second, the presented correlations are all statistically significant only at $p < .05$, suggesting, possibly, that the magnitude of the effects may have been quite low.

Thus, these studies replicate the finding that posttest scores are more informative than scores on both pretest and training measures. Guthke and his colleagues (1992, 1993) summarized the results of a number of learning-potential studies that investigated the associations between the measures of learning potential and other psychological variables. According to these authors (who, unfortunately, did not include the statistical data in their report), learning potential (a) appears to be relatively insensitive to environmental manipulations (e.g., parental support); (b) tends to correlate with creativity – the higher the learning potential, the more creative a student is; and (c) tends to reduce the influence of nonintellectual components (e.g., personality traits) on test performance – the higher the learning potential, the smaller the role played by such factors as irritability and neuroticism.

In a study, utilizing the newly developed ACIL, Guthke and colleagues (Guthke et al. 1997) showed that the learning tests' indicators are, when compared to static tests, (a) better predictors of both knowledge acquisition and knowledge application in the context of a complex problem-solving task, (b) better predictors of the performance on a curriculum-related learning program, and (c) comparable predictors of achievement in math and language arts grades. It is interesting to note that, in these studies, as well as in a study by Guthke and Gitter (1991), these correlations were significantly higher for low-achieving students than for students of higher abilities.

In a study of group differences in learning potential, Groot-Zwaaftink, Ruijssenaars, and Schelbergen (1987) worked with groups of children with versus without cerebral palsy. They used a computerized version of the Tower of Hanoi problem based on the pretest – training – post-test paradigm. They also administered two other learning-potential tests that dynamically approached the question of measuring fluid abilities. The results showed significant group differences in learning potential between affected and normal children. This finding might have turned out to be important had the researchers conducted a comparison of group differences on conventional tests. Had there been such data, especially if the patterns of group differences had been different for affected versus normal children, these data would have offered yet further confirmation of the effectiveness of dynamic testing. Unfortunately, a finding just of group differences between affected and unaffected individuals does not tell us what is added to the usage of a conventional test in similar situations.

Similarly, Heesels and Hamers (1993) conducted a large comparative study (N = 500) of group differences between immigrant children from Turkey and Morocco and native Dutch school-age children. In this study the researchers developed the language-free Dutch Learning Potential Test (DLPT), based on the methodology originated by Guthke and his colleagues. Using factor analyses, the researchers established that the factor structure of the learning-potential measures was virtually the same for all groups. Although the mean difference among the groups was significant on conventional IQ tests, the difference between mean DLPT scores was not significant. In other words, though scoring significantly lower on static tests, immigrant children scored as well as the native Dutch children who participated in the study on the dynamic tests. However, the predictive power of the DLPT was not significantly different from the predictive power of static tests. This finding contradicts findings from the seven-year-long longitudinal study (Guthke 1992) described above. Due to the fact that the sample size of the Dutch study was significantly larger, and that the magnitudes of the effects in the German study were quite small, the inconsistency of the results might be explained by a range of factors; for example, the DLPT and Lerntests – though based on the same methodology – are different tests, the German results were limited, and there were some moderating factors of unknown effect in the Dutch study.

Testing-the-Limits Approach

The Paradigm
A somewhat different methodology has been developed within what has been called a "testing-the-limits approach" (Carlson & Weidl 1978, 1979; Embretson 1987a). Carlson and Wiedl (1980, 1992a, 1992b) have attempted to construct a theoretical framework for their approach by integrating their empirical findings with information-processing theory.

They attributed poor performance on ability tests, at least to some degree, to participants' inability to understand clearly what they were supposed to do and to a set of personality variables (e.g., test anxiety, personality traits, self-esteem). Their conceptual schemata included three components: task characteristics, personal factors, and diagnostic approaches (Carlson & Wiedl 1992b). Their main tasks were Raven matrices and the Cattell Culture-Fair Test of g. Personal factors include cognitive and metacognitive variables. Epistemic (structural) and heuristic (procedural) structures are reflective of previous states of knowledge. Diagnostic approaches represent differentiations of testing strategies that are designed to boost the performance of disadvantaged children. In their work, Carlson and Wiedl have addressed all three of these issues in their model.

This approach, like other dynamic-testing approaches, states that test performance is conceptualized as the result of the dynamic interaction among the individual, the test materials, and the test situation (Carlson & Wiedl 1992b). The special feature of this approach is that it is centered on the testing situation. The initial idea of the testing-the-limits approach was originally formulated by Schmidt (1971), was subsequently developed by Guthke, and later was refined by Carlson and Wiedl. The main assumption of this approach is that, for particular individuals, certain manipulations of the testing situation, designed to compensate for present intellectual or educational deficits, can lead to significant improvements in performance (Carlson & Wiedl 1979). Thus, the task is to find a match between a certain type of disadvantaged student and a certain type of manipulation of the test situation, so that the match evokes the best performance possible.

Researchers working within the testing-the-limits paradigm concentrate their attention on conventional tests (e.g., the Cattell Culture-Fair Tests of g or the Raven Colored Progressive Matrices [RCPM]) in order to develop a system of test administration that can determine which characteristics of the test situation, the test itself, or an individual are related to changes in test performance, and, consequently, can enhance performance. Hence, the researchers are primarily concerned with standardized interventions designed to facilitate performance and to serve as more sensitive measures of abilities.

Empirical Findings

Most fieldwork exploring the effectiveness of the testing-the-limits approach has been conducted with German children (e.g., Bethge, Carlson, & Wiedl 1982; Carlson & Wiedl 1976, 1978, 1979, 1980; Wiedl & Carlson 1976). Initially the work was done with normally developing children, but later it included children with learning difficulties and children of different ethnic groups. In the early studies, researchers compared the six conditions over the course of task administration. These conditions were (a) standard instruction, (b) verbalization during and after solution, (c) verbalization after solution, (d) simple feedback, (e) elaborate feedback, and (f) elaborate feedback plus verbalization during and after solution. For example, Carlson and Wiedl (1976, 1978, 1979) conducted a series of studies employing the RCPM. The test was given to second- and fourth-graders in two forms, the regular booklet and puzzle form. The RCPM was administered under the six conditions described above. The first two studies (Carlson & Wiedl 1976, 1978) demonstrated that test performance improved significantly due to testing condition and the form of the test. The most salient conditions resulting in improved performance were those involving verbalization and feedback. Most effective conditions were conditions (e) and (f), involving verbal descriptions during and after problem solution and elaborated feedback ($p < .05$). However, only the second-grade children showed further increases in performance through feedback (age by testing condition interaction, $F_{p<.01} = 2.22$). Closer analysis of the published results of the analysis of variance, used in the 1978 and 1979 studies, allowed us to compare the magnitude of the main effects specified in these analyses. In the 1978 study, the following main effects (F) and their magnitudes (f) were revealed: for testing condition, $F_{p<.05} = 2.71, f = 0.35$; for version of the test, $F_{p<.001} = 15.55$, $f = 0.38$; and for repeated testing, $F_{p<.001} = 28.68, f = 0.52$. In the 1979 study, when the sample size was increased from 108 to 433 students, the following results were obtained: for testing condition, $F_{p<.01} = 12.63$, $f = 0.38$; for age, $F_{p<.01} = 92.29$, $f = 0.46$; for version of the test, $F_{p<.01} = 61.77, f = 0.38$. Clearly, the magnitude of the effect of testing condition appears to be similar to or smaller than the magnitude of the effect of simple repetition of the test and the effect of the test version.

Once the researchers found that the most effective conditions were verbalization and feedback, they used these conditions and the condition of standard administration for comparison. They restructured the testing situation to incorporate verbalization and elaborate verbal feedback on the participants' performance. While solving the task, the participants are asked to describe both the task and their own cognitive activity (e.g., *Tell me what you see and what you are thinking about as you solve this problem. Tell me why you think the solution you chose is correct. Why do you think it is correct and other possible answers are wrong?*).

In general, the restructuring of testing situations led to higher levels of performance in participants with mental retardation, learning disabilities, or neurological impairments, and in participants of a minority ethnic background. Moreover, it was shown that, when related to general ability test scores and school achievement, the scores obtained in the situations of restructured testing had higher predictive validity than did the scores recorded under conventional testing.

Like the results of the earlier work by Budoff and Corman (1976), the results of these studies showed that the training had the greatest effect on items requiring reasoning by analogy, that is, on those items for which higher level cognitive processes could be modified. Expanding on this finding, researchers (Cormier, Carlson, & Das 1990; Kar et al. 1993) used planning (operationalized by visual search) as an individual-differences dimension in the design and examined the effect of verbalization on task performance. No main effect of verbalization was shown, but there was a significant interaction effect – only poor planners improved. In other words, overt verbalization compensated for intraindividual variability in planning, yielding an interaction between individual differences and test condition. Thus, based on the results from these studies, the testing-the-limits approach appears to be most appropriate for assessing higher level cognitive functions in individuals whose level of performance on corresponding tasks is initially low. Other researchers have also used analogical-reasoning tests in a dynamic mode because they seem particularly sensitive to detecting differences in learning potential, especially for individuals with mental retardation who lack adequate executive functioning (Büchel, Schlatter, & Scharnhorst 1997; Schlatter & Büchel 2000).

Carson and Wiedl (1979) were the first to introduce personality as a variable in dynamic testing. Using the sample from their previous studies, the researchers modified the design and collected data on the introversion, neuroticism, and impulsivity-reflectivity of 203 second- and 230 fourth-grade students. The results showed differential correlational profiles for different testing conditions, with the number of significant correlations between dynamic test performance and various personality measures varying from condition to condition. For example, for the impulsivity-reflectivity indicator, the number of significant correlations varied from 0 out of 6 (condition e) to 5 out of 6 (condition f). However, the patterns of correlations between test performance and personality measures within condition (a) (conventional administration) and condition (f) (elaborate feedback plus verbalization during and after solution) were very similar. This finding suggests that personality variables operate in similar ways in situations of both static testing and testing with elaborate feedback and verbalization. In addition, the researchers tried to predict RCPM scores from personality traits. Whereas same percentage of variation in performance on the Raven can be attributed to personality variables under all testing conditions, no main effects for specific personality traits were found. However, there were some interesting interaction effects. Neuroticism correlated positively with test results under condition (b), but impulsivity correlated with test results under condition (f). This finding was replicated in the 1980 study (cited in Lidz 1987), in which the performance of impulsive children improved when verbalization before and after problem solving took place. Similar results were obtained in a population of children with learning disabilities (cited in Lidz 1987). This general result (performance improving under nonstandard administration) has also been replicated in a study of racially mixed American children (Dillon & Carlson 1978). In this study, Dillon and Carlson administered the RCPM to children of three different ages (5–6, 7–8, and 9–10) and different ethnic backgrounds (White, Mexican-American, and African-American). Three test conditions were used – no help (conventional testing), verbalization, and verbalization plus elaborated feedback. Although there were marked differences in the performance of the three groups in the testing condition of no help, these discrepancies were significantly reduced under the verbalization-plus-feedback condition; the researchers found that racial differences declined markedly under the dynamic conditions, suggesting that the racial differences traditionally registered by static tests could be reduced or perhaps even be eliminated in dynamic-testing settings.

Similarly, Bethge, Carlson, and Wiedl (1982) studied 72 third-grade children and showed that dynamic testing reduces test anxiety and negative orientation to the testing situation. They found that both situation and achievement anxiety indicators are significantly lower in dynamic than in static testing settings ($F_{p<.01} = 5.73$ and $F_{p<.01} = 5.55$ for evaluation and achievement anxiety, respectively).

In sum, the work of Carlson, Wiedl, and their colleagues convincingly demonstrated that specific nontarget variables (e.g., anxiety, impulsivity, poor planning) affect performance on g-loaded factors, but these detrimental impacts could be compensated for by overt verbalization.

One advantage of the Carlson-Wiedl approach (for a review, see Carlson 1989) is that it does not require a pretest, specific training, and a posttest. The studies are designed in such a way that children are randomly assigned to different testing conditions. Thus, the typical dynamic testing paradigm, test–teach–test, is not necessary. Moreover, we are not aware of any published material where the psychometric properties of the Raven Test, as it is administered under systematically different testing conditions, has been evaluated. If testing conditions change the structure of external correlations between test performance and other (e.g., personality) variables, they might change the psychological structure revealed by the test itself, in part by changing the internal consistency of the test. In addition, this approach mitigates methodological problems related to the measurement of change.

The main disadvantage of the approach is in the group nature of the results. In other words, tests are presented in different modes of administration (e.g., standard procedure, verbalization during and after solution, elaborate feedback) to different groups of participants, with the goal of determining which mode is better for which group (e.g., individuals with learning disabilities versus individuals with mental retardation). No individual comparison is possible. However, although the research findings are based on group comparisons, the intervening procedures are highly individualized and targeted to a specific profile of the performance of every child.

Most of the findings obtained within this framework are interactive in nature. Specifically, verbalization and elaborated feedback improve performance in individuals (a) of below-average ability levels, (b) at certain developmental stages, (d) with high levels of anxiety, and (e) on tasks with a certain degree of difficulty that require higher level cognitive processing. This list of requirements limits the target population for whom this approach to testing is most beneficial. However, when the population is defined appropriately, the approach should be adequate. For example, students of below-average ability with a high level of anxiety are expected to demonstrate their best performance on the Raven's test under the testing condition of feedback and verbalization. Thus, the testing-the-limits approach has provided some evidence that when testing approaches are applied differentially and optimal conditions are defined for specific groups of individuals, these individuals are expected to demonstrate their best performance, a performance of higher quality than they would have shown in a situation of conventional testing.

The issue of predictive validity was addressed by Carlson and Wiedl

(1979), who compared correlations of Raven scores under different test-ing conditions with measures of mathematical and language perform-ance. Even though the numbers of participants tested under different conditions are small (ranging from 13 to 21), there is a trend toward im-proving the magnitude of correlations by increasing the degree to which the instruction is dynamic. Later examination of this issue in a sample of German children showed that under effective testing-the-limits pro-cedures (verbalization), both Raven and Cattell scores correlate highly with mathematics performance when the teaching procedures match the testing procedures (Carlson personal communication, September 1997).

In summary, the Carlson-Wiedl approach explores one dimension that is important for dynamic testing – the impact of instruction and feedback. The paradigm is based on group comparison; it serves peda-gogical goals and does not address the issue of individual differences. The results obtained with this methodology can be utilized within re-medial programs for specific disadvantaged populations.

SWANSON'S COGNITIVE PROCESSING TEST

Swanson's work in the field of dynamic testing resulted in creation of the *Swanson Cognitive Processing Test* (*S-CPT*), a dynamic test currently distributed by a major test publisher (Pro-Ed). The development of the S-CPT was triggered by an intention to create an instrument allowing the evaluation of "components of processing ability under standardized dynamic testing conditions" (Swanson 1995b, p. 674). The theoretical roots of the S-CPT are in the information-processing approach to learn-ing disabilities (Swanson 1984a, 1984b, 1988). Swanson's approach to dynamic testing is both methodologically and terminologically linked to the work of his predecessors, especially that of Feuerstein and of Brown and Campione.

Theoretical Model

The main assumption of the model is the central role of working mem-ory (WM), a critical component of many information-processing mod-els, in skill acquisition and learning. Correspondingly, children's learn-ing difficulties are attributed to deficits in WM, whereas children's academic excellence is considered to be linked to high levels of WM (Swanson 1995b). Swanson (1995b) has defined WM as a system that simultaneously holds old and new information that is being manipulated and transformed. Long-term memory is defined as a system of highly interconnected units representing semantic and episodic information. The procedural basis of the model is in the assumption that working-memory encoding occurs when long-term memory representations are engaged in the process of testing as a result of previous learning.

Test Description

The S-CPT consists of 11 subtests (Swanson 1992, 1993) that can be administered as a battery or separately. Administration of the complete S-CPT battery requires approximately three hours. The subtests are *Rhyming, Visual Matrix, Auditory Digit Sequence, Mapping and Directions, Story Retelling, Picture Sequence, Phrase Sequence, Spatial-Organization, Semantic Association, Semantic Categorization,* and *Nonverbal Sequencing.* The test is viewed as an instrument for quantifying *processing potential* (Swanson 1995a). The concept of processing potential is defined by Swanson as being close to Feuerstein's concept of cognitive modifiability. The administration of the S-CPT results in seven composite scores (Swanson 1995b): (1) the *initial* score, indicating the highest level of unassisted performance, that is, the level corresponding to the traditional static score; (2) the *gain* score, indicating the highest score obtained under probing conditions; (3) the *probe* score (also referred to as the *instructional efficiency score*), indicating the number of prompts or hints necessary to achieve the higher score under probing conditions; (4) the *maintenance* score, indicating the stability of the newly achieved highest level of performance without the support of probes or hints; (5) the *processing difference* score, measuring the difference between potential performance as determined under guided assistance and the actual performance level; (6) the *processing stability* score, demonstrating the difference between the maintenance score and the initial score; and (7) the *strategy efficiency* score, demonstrating the strategy used to remember information (obtainable only from subtests 3, 4, 6, 8, 10, and 11).

Although Swanson's terminology is novel, most of his dynamic-testing scores map onto the indices used in other approaches. The initial score corresponds to the pretest score; the gain score corresponds to the intervention score; the maintenance score corresponds to the posttest score, the processing-difference score corresponds to the "intervention score minus pretest score" value, and the processing-stability score corresponds to the "posttest score minus pretest score" value.

In addition to obtaining the dynamic scores, the battery provides the tester with indices of semantic and episodic WM (so-called factorial composites), as well as scores on auditory/verbal, visuo-spatial, prospective, and retrospective memory aspects (the so-called S-CPT components). According to Swanson (1995b), both the factorial composites and the S-CPT components were characterized by high Cronbach alphas (ranging from .86 to .95) in all three conditions (initial, gain, and maintenance).

Practical Context

The S-CPT was initially developed in the context of special education to address two major issues. The first issue is (a) whether children with specific learning disabilities (in particular, reading and math disabilities) demonstrate generalized or specific working-memory deficits when compared with average-achieving children and (b) whether children with these working-memory deficits are distinct from other groups of children experiencing learning problems (e.g., slow learners). The second issue concerns the degree of modifiability of working-memory performance in children with learning disabilities.

Empirical Findings

Most of the studies that have utilized the S-CPT were carried out within a large-scale standardization study of this newly developed test. The majority of the questions raised within this study had to do with evaluating the psychometric properties of Swanson's test. Internal-consistency reliability of the test appears to be satisfactory (generally in the range of .82 to .95, see Swanson, in press).

For example, in order to address the issue of construct validity, 98 children were evaluated through the S-CPT, a sentence-span measure (a working-memory test), a set of achievement tests (PIAT-R, or Peabody Individual Achievement Test, and PPVT-R, or Peabody Picture Vocabulary Test-Revised, L. Dunn & L. Dunn 1981), and short-memory tests (word sequence and object sequence). To evaluate convergent validity, various S-CPT components (i.e., verbal, visuo-spatial, prospective, and retrospective) were correlated with the working-memory test; all correlations were significant. To evaluate divergent validity, both the S-CPT components and the short-memory tests were correlated with achievement scores; the mean partial correlation (holding age and PPVT-R scores constant) of academic performance indicators with S-CPT components was slightly higher than with short-term memory scores, but not statistically different (.37 versus .25, $t = .93$, ns, for mean correlations for S-CPT and the short-term memory measures). Although this difference in correlations is an interesting observation, these data do not warrant any strong conclusions, such as the one made by the author that correlations of higher magnitude were more associated with S-CPT scores than with short-term memory scores (Swanson 1995b, p.678). In reality, the difference in magnitude did not cross the threshold.

Three composite scores (initial, gain, and maintenance) from the data collected in the total sample (1600+ individuals) were subjected to factor analyses (Swanson 1995b). The author chose not to present the total amount of variance explained by the two-factor solutions; for the three scores, the first-factor eigenvalues for the unrotated solutions were 4.43, 5.06, and 4.45, whereas for the second factor, they ranged from 1.01 to 1.17. The best solution was found for the principal factor analysis with a varimax rotation: A two-factor model emerged, reflecting semantic (higher loadings of the rhyming word, phrase sequence, semantic association, and semantic categorization subtests) and episodic (higher loadings of the visual matrix, map/directions, story retelling, and the nonverbal sequencing subtests) memory processes. As a follow-up to the exploratory analysis, a confirmatory factor analysis was conducted. Based on the presented chi-square values (but no other goodness-of-fit indices and no parameter estimates), the author concluded that the confirmatory analysis also supported a two-factor model. Although the presented evidence supports this conclusion, this finding might have been clearer had the author presented his results more fully.

The most interesting outcome of the factor analysis is that, somewhat surprisingly, the factor structures were practically identical for all three composite scores. This finding suggests the viability of either of two possibilities. First, the intervention may have had almost a linear effect, as if a constant were added to every test score. Indeed, the correlational structure of gains was very similar to the structure of the initial scores. Similarly, the maintenance scores appear to be almost in linear dependency from both the initial and the gain scores. Second, the initial, gain, and maintenance scores were highly correlated with each other, so that intraindividual variability introduced by the intervention procedure may have been overshadowed by the magnitude of these correlations. Whereas the former possibility is very unlikely (although possible), the latter is much more likely, and, unfortunately, much less appealing. Perhaps this is why the author did not present the correlations between the composite scores of the test for the total (N = 1600+) sample (Swanson 1995b).

Another piece of evidence suggesting a possibility of high correlations among the three composite scores comes from stepwise regression analysis. Here the intention was to predict how much variance in academic performance might be accounted for by dynamic-testing composites. It is interesting to note that, unlike other investigators in the field (e.g., Campione & Brown 1987), Swanson decided not to include ability measures in his regression equations. In the relevant article (Swanson 1995b), Swanson provided the reader with a single illustration of a stepwise regression predicting a reading-achievement score (Wide Range Achievement Test – WRAT reading subtest, J. F. Jastak & S. Jastak 1978;, S. Jastak & Wilkinson 1984). With the initial score always entered first into the equation, of the four composites entered (initial, gain, probe, and maintenance scores), only the initial score (R^2 = .26, $p < .001$) and the gain score (incremental R^2 = .05, $p < .05$) remained in the equation. Leaving aside a variety of technical and theoretical problems associated with stepwise analyses (Altman & Anderson 1989), we would like to remind the reader that Resing (1993), working in the framework of the graduated-prompt approach, found that both posttest scores and learning-potential scores, when compared with pretest scores, made a significant contribution to the prediction of school achievement (4% to 40% increase in explained variance, depending on the test). Thus, it appears that Swanson's conclusion that his dynamic-testing procedures enhance prediction of school achievement is not yet supported enough by the data in terms of the absolute magnitude of the effect or in terms of its relative magnitude when compared with the results from other approaches.

The matrix of intercorrelations between composite scores (calculated on a much smaller sample of 61 children) published elsewhere (Swanson 1995a) supports our impression. The intercorrelations between the initial, gain, and maintenance scores ranged between 0.85 and 0.88. In this study, the researcher once again used the stepwise-regression paradigm, but now the predictors encompassed both static indices (Full Scale IQ) and dynamic indices (the initial score in one set of equations and the gain score in another set of equations). The results showed that both static and dynamic scores contributed significant amounts of variance: Independently of the order of entry, the initial score explained more variance in achievement scores (14% if entered first, 15% if entered second for reading, and 18% for both orders for math) than did Full Scale IQ (8% for both orders for reading, and 1% if entered first and 2% if entered second for math). In contrast to the results from the total data set (see discussion above), the gain score appeared to be a more powerful predictor than was the initial achievements score. When three composite scores (gain, maintenance, and initial scores), along with Full Scale IQ, were forced into the analysis predicting the reading achievement score, 14% of the variance was attributed to the gain score, 11% to Full Scale IQ, and 4% to the maintenance score; the initial score was dropped from the equation. In predicting the math achievement score, the gain score was the only variable that remained in the equation ($R^2 = .26, p < .001$).

Two studies (Swanson 1994, 1995b) were concerned with the usefulness of dynamic testing in the classification of children with learning disabilities. The children with learning disabilities were classified as such and then subtyped on the basis of their results on static IQ tests (the Wechsler Intelligence Scale for Children – WISC-R; Slosson Intelligence Test-Revised, Slosson 1971; or the PPVT) and on math and reading subtests from a traditional achievement test (WRAT-R). Classification of learning disabilities utilized the "cut-off scores" procedures (e.g., Siegel 1989), rather than the IQ-achievement discrepancy. Dynamic-testing results were utilized in this research in order to distinguish two groups of children with learning disabilities – so-called instructionally or teaching-deficient children (those who improve in information-processing performance relative to their initial test performance) and so-called slow learners (those whose potential score is not discrepant from their achievement score).

The methodology implemented in both studies was quite similar. First, the author investigated the patterns of scores in the group with learning disabilities and in the control group. In both studies, scores on both static and dynamic tests were significantly higher in the control group than in the group with learning disabilities. Then, using stepwise regression analysis, reading and mathematical performance scores were predicted for the total sample. Then the author tried to differentiate two groups (normal and disabled) by the means of discriminant analyses. In both studies, this procedure failed to provide clear-cut information and, therefore, was followed by other types of classification analyses. These analyses resulted in the differentiation of multiple subgroups. Finally, the derived groups were compared with each other.

In the first study (Swanson 1994), one of the research questions was whether ability-group classification, based on traditional IQ and achievement measures, corresponds to the dynamic-testing classification. The sample included 47 average achievers, 26 children with specific reading disability, 24 children with specific math disability, 17 slow learners, and 29 underachievers. This study utilized all composite scores of the S-CPT.

In the initial group comparison, the groups differed from each other on both composite and component dynamic test scores. Although the profiles of the five groups differed significantly, overall, able students did better on both composite and component dynamic measures. However, there were significant differences among groups with disabilities, with the slow learners consistently the lowest group on the dynamic measures. The differences between students with reading and with mathematical disabilities were more subtle.

The stepwise regression analyses were carried out for the whole sample. When the initial score was entered first, the variance in the reading performance score was attributed to the initial ($R^2 = .11, p < .001$), probe (incremental $R^2 = .15, p < .001$), maintenance (incremental $R^2 = .03, p < .01$), and processing-difference (incremental $R^2 = .04, p < .01$) scores. For mathematics, the analysis included the initial ($R^2 = .20, p < .001$) and stability (incremental $R^2 = .12, p < .001$) scores as significant predictors. When there was no fixed order of entry, for reading, the order of the predictors was the gain score ($R^2 = .14, p < .001$), probe (incremental $R^2 = .12, p < .001$), and maintenance (incremental $R^2 = .06, p < .001$) scores; for math, only the gain score ($R^2 = .32, p < .001$) predicted the criterion variance significantly. This pattern of results was similar to the one observed before. Specifically, if the initial score was entered first, the gain and maintenance scores tended not to be significant (probably due to high correlations between the scores). When the order of the entry was random, the gain score appeared to be the most powerful predictor. Some rather small amounts of variance were attributable to other dynamic-testing indicators. As for the results of discriminant analysis, only 42% of the cases were classified correctly among the five groups. The single best discriminatory variable was the initial score. Only two dynamic measures (the probe and processing difference scores) added significant variance to ability group classification. This result was followed up with a stepwise discriminant analysis, the purpose of which was to identify which groups were best predicted by which variables of the three that were significant in the previous analysis. The overall characteristics of the analyses were rather weak, but the author proceeded with an interpretation of the data for specific groups based on the number of cases classified correctly. According to this analysis, the initial score was the best classification variable for slow learners (59% classified correctly) and normal achievers (76%), the probe score was the best classifier for learners with mathematical disabilities (58%), and the processing difference score was helpful in classifying slow learners (52%). None of the variables were informative in classifying students with reading disabilities (the maximum classified correctly was 15%) or underachieving learners (the maximum classified correctly was 38%).

In the second study (Swanson 1995a), 155 poor readers were compared to 351 skilled readers. This study utilized all but the strategy-efficiency composite scores of the S-CPT. As in the 1994 study, a MANOVA revealed group differences on all S-CPT composites, with skilled readers consistently outperforming poor readers. As a follow-up to this result, the author conducted a stepwise discriminant analysis. Unfortunately, the results of this analysis are presented in such a fragmentary fashion that it is difficult to estimate its overall outcome (e.g., the percentage of the cases classified correctly). The author claimed that the best predictor of group classification was the gain score ($R^2 = .05$, $p < .001$). Notice that this result is quite different from the results of the 1994 study (Swanson 1994) discussed above.

Having accomplished less than he perhaps had hoped for with discriminant analysis, the author conducted a type of cluster analysis that supposedly allowed him to identify distinct nonoverlapping clusters in such a way that children would be assigned to only one cluster. (Somehow, however, the number of children in each group increased – there were 155 poor readers before clustering and 156 after; similarly, the group of 351 skilled readers grew in size so that there were 355 of them after clustering.) The clustering was performed based on math achievement scores and two composite S-CPT scores (gain and probe). Unfortunately, the justification of the variables selected for the cluster analysis is somewhat difficult to ascertain – the article does not comprehensibly address why those particular variables and no others were selected. Moreover, no overall statistical characteristics of the procedure were presented. The author stated that eight groups (four nonoverlapping clusters in two reading-skill groups) emerged from this analysis. Based on the analysis of patterns of discrepancies in the values of the criterion variables, these groups were compared with each other. Relying heavily on intuition, the author classified poor readers into slow learners (minimal discrepancy between dynamic and static scores), learners with dyslexia (average math performance and no significant discrepancies between math performance and dynamic variables, but significant discrepancies between reading performance and dynamic variables), instructionally deficient learners (highest gain and probe scores and larger discrepancies between gain and maintenance than between achievement and initial scores), and students with learning disabilities in reading and mathematics (large discrepancies between both reading and mathematics achievement scores and dynamic indices, but low gain and probe scores). The skilled-readers group was classified into subgroups of gifted students (high gain score), low mathematics achievers (low scores in mathematics), skilled mathematics achievers (high mathematics scores), and instructionally responsive children (high probe scores).

As mentioned above, the main purpose of these studies was to investigate whether the dynamic measures contribute more information to the subgrouping of children with learning disabilities (see Swanson, 2000). In other words, on the basis of the first point of comparison from the four-point profile, with what kind of new information does this approach to dynamic testing provide us, or what is the *comparative informativeness* of this approach?

The answer to this question requires an examination of the utilized statistical procedures. There have been a number of warnings issued regarding the usage of stepwise procedures (e.g., Altman & Anderson 1989; Bollen 1989). For example, the F-distribution is unstable, parameter estimates are biased, R^2 tends to be unreliable, and problems of multicollinearity are especially pronounced. Obviously, all these concerns are applicable to the analyses conducted by Swanson. Moreover, this author has a tendency to ignore the widely followed strategy of conservatively interpreting univariate analysis when multivariate models do not fit well (as in the case of the utilized discriminant procedures). In other words, heavy reliance on stepwise procedures and a tendency to forego caution in making statistical inferences put most of Swanson's findings in the gray area of results that require proof by replication. However, the finding that we consider particularly relevant to the field of learning disability is the differentiation of students with learning disabilities into those who are more or less responsive to intervention. The sensitivity of the S-CPT to procedural characteristics of students' learning potential seems to be of special interest. By no means, however, is this a new finding. The very same issue has been addressed in most other approaches to dynamic testing. What is new here is an attempt to identify a specific function, working memory, as central to quantifying learning potential and to classifying both students with learning disabilities and average-achieving students into subgroups based on this function.

Regarding the *power of prediction* of the S-CPT, two comments should be made. First, high levels of correlations between the initial (pretest), gain (intervention), and maintenance (posttest) scores warrant serious investigation. The interpretation of the stepwise-regression results as indicative of the higher predictive power assignable to either the initial or gain scores might be unreliable and due to fluctuations in correlations between the two variables. This is probably why the results of different studies provide competing evidence supporting either the initial score or the gain score as especially informative in predicting school achievement. Confirming previous observations obtained by other dynamic-testing researchers, Swanson's data indicate independent contributions of abilities and indices of learning potential (processing potential in Swanson's terms) to measures of school achievement.

Second, we need to assess the uniqueness of the information provided by the S-CPT compared with the information provided by static tests. Swanson's data support the claim initially made by Vygotsky, which was then supported by evidence from other studies (Day et al. 1997) that static and dynamic measures jointly provide valuable information regarding an individual's performance.

As for the *degree of efficiency* of the S-CPT, the evidence presented in the reviewed publications suggests that the S-CPT is a psychometrically sound and robust instrument that does not require special training of examiners and that may be administered in full in three hours. The effort invested in standardization of the instrument in the general U.S. population exceeds that done for any other dynamic test. Despite this ease of use, the answer to the question of the incremental informational content of the obtained data remains open. The underlying motivation in the creation of this instrument was to tap into cognitive processes rather than cognitive products. Although the correlations between the S-CPT scores and various criterion measures are promising, the link between the profile of dynamic scores and adequate teaching is still missing. In this context, the findings reported in the discriminant analyses of discrepancies between the S-CPT gain and maintenance scores, if shown to be reliable and stable in subsequent research, might be utilized in designing intervention strategies. The assumption here would be that those children who exhibit low initial scores and minimal discrepancy between the initial, gain, and maintenance scores should be viewed as better candidates for special education than those who show a significant discrepancy between the initial score and the gain score, but minimal discrepancy between the gain and maintenance scores (Swanson 1995b).

Our final comment will be on the robustness of the results obtained on the S-CPT so far. The instrument was evaluated using a large heterogeneous sample. However, to our knowledge, all of the data were analyzed simultaneously and by one group. The publication of the S-CPT no doubt will result in the use of the instrument by independent groups whose findings will extend those reviewed above.

CONCLUSION

The approaches discussed in this chapter carry dynamic testing a step beyond the earlier approaches of Feuerstein and Budoff. In some respects, these approaches are less ambitious than the earlier ones. Certainly, they derive from nowhere near the elaborate theoretical base that can be found in Feuerstein's work. At the same time, these tests stay closer to their theoretical base. Much of Feuerstein's theory remained untested and not even clearly operationalized by his test. Brown and Campione, the European theorists, as well as Swanson, stay closer to their theoretical base in their operationalizations. Although none of these tests yet has been shown definitively to provide incremental information that consistently goes beyond the information in static tests, these tests show promise for providing such information and for further development. We therefore are optimistic with regard to them.

PART FOUR

EVALUATING DYNAMIC TESTING

In this part of the book, we consider a general three-part framework for evaluating dynamic testing as a whole as well as considering specific approaches that have been used to implement dynamic testing.

CHAPTER SEVEN

A Three-Pronged Approach to Dynamic Testing

In this book, we have reviewed a number of approaches that identify themselves as dynamic-testing methodologies. We have attempted here to point out their many differences with respect to aims, tasks, training strategies, targeted processes, target populations, and predictive power. Differences among these approaches compromise an accurate evaluation of the comparative efficacies of the various approaches, as well as of the overall efficacy of the dynamic approach in general. Nevertheless, despite variability in points of view, ideas, and concrete techniques, what is characteristic of all the methodologies considered here is that they share an underlying basic hypothesis that cognitive performance, with optimal aid, should provide the most valid testing of learning potential (Minick 1987). The research activity of the last decade in the field of dynamic testing might be characterized as a series of attempts to verify this hypothesis empirically.

The empirical results derived from studies of the testing of learning potential are not homogeneous, however. In this part of the book, we consider some of the factors that may have contributed to the lack of convergence of the empirical findings regarding the usefulness and importance of dynamic testing. Our discussion will center on the issue of correspondence among aims, methodologies, and analytic strategies of dynamic testing. In addition, we will discuss briefly issues of measurement of change and ecological validity of dynamic testing.

GENERAL AIMS: TO EVALUATE, MODIFY, OR BOTH?

It appears that some of the inconsistencies in research findings are due to the multifaceted nature of the goals of dynamic testing. Thus, Embretson (1987b) has delineated three main goals of dynamic testing:

(1) to provide a better estimate of a specified ability construct, (2) to measure new abilities, and (3) to improve mental efficiency. Each of these goals assumes a different approach to testing procedures, testing materials, and data analyses.

For example, the first goal of dynamic testing is applicable to situations in which the test does not measure the same trait for all examinees. In this aspect, dynamic testing can be viewed as a means to increase comparability of individual differences by (a) equating for background, either by training examinees in the content and/or relevant processes or by supplying the outcomes from prerequisite processes for solving items (Sternberg 1977); (b) eliminating test-related artifacts (e.g., anxiety); and (c) taking into account cultural and other group differences between examinees. The a priori assumption that estimates of ability can be changed by varying any of the above aspects, that is, by modifying the conditions under which the test is administered, implies the necessity of having dynamic tests with (a) a fairly high goodness of fit to a latent-trait model, implying a detailed understanding of the effects resulting from modification of the above aspects; (b) high predictive validity; and (c) a clear idea of the impact of various related factors, such as processes, strategies, and executive functions (as mediated by personality and cultural factors) on performance. Another important issue is the particular score that should be utilized. Current research on learning-potential tests consistently shows that a posttest can be considered to be a sound predictor in comparison with a pretest, thus suggesting that perhaps only the former score is interesting in the analyses. However, the predictive validity even of posttests does not appear to be reliably higher than that of conventional intelligence tests. The predictive validity of the tests is dependent, of course, on a number of factors, such as the time period between measurements of the predictor and the criterion, and the types of tasks used as criterion variables. Thus, researchers need to take a very careful approach in designing posttraining studies.

The second goal of dynamic testing, implemented in a number of existing approaches, is not just to improve the estimation of ability, but also to measure a newly formed or newly developed psychological function. Some researchers (e.g., Feuerstein and Budoff) have viewed cognitive modifiability as an independent ability and have instantiated this belief in their testing devices. Other researchers (e.g., Gal'perin) have attempted to develop new specific cognitive functions (e.g., subtraction and addition operations) and then have assessed these newly developed functions.

Finally, the third goal of dynamic testing is to improve people's mental efficiency. The major assumption here is that the level of ability itself should be changed, and that fairly extensive training is required to change it. Examples of this application of dynamic testing procedures are the Feuerstein Instrumental Enrichment program (Feuerstein et al. 1980) and the work of Soviet/Russian defectologists. In pursuing this goal, dynamic testing is closely linked to intervention. The dominant purpose is modifying, changing, and improving cognitive performance. Testing here serves to determine the starting point, direction, and amount of intervention necessary.

Each application of dynamic testing comes with its own corresponding methodological and data-analytic assumptions and limitations. Moreover, each application of dynamic testing reveals unique information beyond that derivable from conventional testing. The varied approaches to dynamic testing arose from different theoretical paradigms are based on different assumptions, and are targeted at different purposes. But the general claim made by dynamic testing promoters and developers seems to have been justified, at least to some extent – dynamic testing does provide data unique to this type of testing.

The multiplicity of the aims of dynamic testing requires a researcher to determine which particular aim of dynamic testing is relevant for a given situation and whether the given procedure will be applicable to this situation. Most likely, the relationship between testing and instruction is viewed differently by teachers and clinicians (who wish to promote change) versus researchers (who are generally more interested in measuring and analyzing the causes of change). Whereas teachers and clinicians are expected to monitor a child's performance closely and to decide when it is beneficial to intervene, researchers conducting testing are typically not expected (and are often unable) to work in such an interactive mode.

Hence, there are three differences between these two types of testing, specifically between testing conducted for the sake of the evaluation and quantification of learning potential and testing conducted for the sake of teaching (Guthke 1993). First, the priorities of the researcher versus the teacher are different. Whereas the researcher typically subordinates the goal of teaching to the goal of determining the difference between child's unassisted and assisted levels of performance, the teacher typically subordinates testing to instruction and modification. Second, the teacher rarely has a chance to work with a student in an individual setting. Thus, the teacher accumulates the feedback he/she is getting from a group of students and adjusts her behavior as part of her conception of the task at hand. Finally, much of what is taught at school cannot be broken down into a well-organized invariant sequence with a distinct path to mastery; on the contrary, there is a spectrum of appropriate reactions by the child, and the teacher is expected to interpret them and flexibly respond to them while teaching.

These differences in attitude are especially important because, recently, there has been a shift in how the role and mission of learning-potential research are viewed. The major changes of emphasis were in (a) the shift from prediction-oriented testing to instruction-oriented testing (Delclos et al. 1992; Ruijssenaars, Castelijns, & Hamers 1993), (b) the shift in emphasis from improved testing of general intelligence toward the analysis and description of learning processes, and (c) the extension of dynamic-testing methodology to groups of nonchallenged children. Researchers have observed the usefulness of the learning-potential tests in (a) the analysis of individual differences in cognitive performance and the causes that lead to these differences, (b) the context of studying so-called differential sensitivity to instruction, and (c) the study of learning processes (Ruijssenaars et al. 1993).

Although this road might well be the most productive one for dynamic testing to take, the methodology that now exists is not fully amenable to this shift, and much background methodological and psychometric research needs to be conducted before it will be feasible to view these goals as representing a new mission for dynamic testing.

MEASUREMENT OF CHANGE

One of the most serious criticisms that has been leveled at the dynamic-testing paradigm is that it lacks a sound psychometric foundation (Snow 1990), particularly in regard to the measurement of change occurring between pretest and posttest. One of the major assumptions of the dynamic-testing paradigm is that training results in better performance. However, it has been shown that approximately 30% of children improve to a statistically significant extent simply due to retesting (Klauer 1993; LeGagnoux et al. 1990). Thus, relatively large changes can be observed simply as an outcome of retesting. For example, in 20–30% of the cases, the absolute value of the retest effect is at least one standard deviation (Klauer 1993). In other words, it appears that the most important components of the change or posttest scores can be traced back to retesting (practice) effects. This issue is especially worrisome for methodologies utilizing standardized tests in their dynamically corrected administration. There are a number of precautions that could be taken in order to minimize the effects of posttesting: (a) to avoid or reduce retest effects through test construction, (b) to control for the effect of retesting by using a control population, and (c) to model possible effects of retesting via mathematical models of dynamic testing.

Even assuming that all potential methodological disturbances have been controlled for and that the dynamic tester has registered the occurrence of true change, another important question arises: How does one measure change? Traditionally, the measurement of change was based on the regression model developed in the framework of Classical Test Theory (CTT, see Cronbach & Furby 1970). Recently, dynamically oriented psychometricians have objected to this approach, stating that its various premises are typically not met (Schöttke, Bartram & Wiedl 1993; Sijtsma 1993). A useful review of harm/benefit ratios that result from applications of different statistical treatments of change has been written by Embretson (1987b). In addition, Chapter 10 of this book discusses some of the aspects of this problem and stresses the methodological link between the measurement of change within a dynamic testing paradigm and the view of abilities as developing expertise.

THE ECOLOGICAL VALIDITY OF DYNAMIC TESTING INSTRUMENTS

Last but not least is the issue of the validity of dynamic-testing instruments. The main criticism of conventional tests of cognitive abilities concerns construct validity – that these tests focus primarily on products rather than on processes, and thus are valid only in terms of product–based criteria, such as tests of school achievement (Lidz 1991).

Much of the early research on dynamic testing (Budoff 1970; Guthke 1977) was devoted to comparing the predictive validities of dynamic versus static tests. Even an advocate of dynamic testing would find it quite difficult to argue that the empirical data, as of now, have consistently showed the higher predictive power of dynamic tests compared with static tests. But there are multiple interpretations of this result.

One is that school achievement, in itself, is a product rather than a process. Thus, naturally, there is a better internal match between conventional tests and school achievement than there is between dynamic tests and school achievement. In support of this statement, it has been shown that the degree of correspondence between learning-potential tests and everyday learning tasks in school (e.g., how well the test represents the material studies at school) is a very important parameter: The higher the correspondence, the greater the test's predictive power. Moreover, researchers have shown that the predictive validity of domain-specific learning-potential tests is higher when criterion tests are also similarly domain-specific (Ruijssenaars et al. 1993). For example, researchers found high correlations ($p < .01$) between a reading-simulation test, administered in kindergarten, and first-grade reading and spelling tests. Consequently, different kinds of dynamic tasks may correspond to different styles of teaching. For example, whereas more traditional test items tend to correspond to more conservative styles of teaching, more dynamic, student-oriented tasks are expected to correspond to more open and progressive styles of teaching to small groups of students.

Thus, the idea of including prototypical learning tasks that match school activities in learning-potential testing devices is very important. For example, European researchers (Hamers, Pennings, & Guthke 1994) have developed a set of domain-specific tasks (e.g., an auditory-analysis test), all of which were assumed to be very important precursors to initial reading, spelling, and arithmetic processes. The results showed that the predictive power of this test was higher for many school achievement tests than was obtained for either domain-general tests of learning potential or a static test of intelligence.

Another idea that could explain the lack of predictive validity of domain-general dynamic tests lies in the mismatch between the active nature of the tested process (e.g., learning) and the passive behavior of the test-takers in many of the dynamic-testing situations. Even in child-centered methodologies such as Feuerstein's, the degree of cognitive activity of the child is minimized and is framed within the understanding of the examiner of what it is that he or she should do in order for a child to reach the criterion of performance. In other words, the examiner frames the child's cognitive activity. An important question is to what extent learning-potential tests are better equipped and better suited than conventional intelligence tests to provide diagnostic and prescriptive information about an active process of learning (for a discussion of this issue, see Lidz & Elliott 2000).

Finally, stressing the need for the ecological validity of *any* tests administered at school, a German educator, Schlee (1985), suggested a merger of static and dynamic approaches to testing by the implementation of treatment-oriented assessment, aimed at the development of interventions suited to the school setting. In this interpretation, the issue of the ecological validity of any type of testing, whether static or dynamic, is eliminated – if the orientation of testing is exclusively pedagogical, then testing itself becomes a part of didactics.

CONCLUSION

Researchers have questioned why dynamic testing has not immediately yielded clear and superior predictive power vis à vis static testing with respect to the prediction of school performance and other criteria. A number of intervening variables may affect the correlation between dynamic tests and other criteria, such as the scoring of dynamic tests, the match between the way the dynamic tests are administered and the way school activities are presented, and so forth. Ultimately, it is important to ensure that the criterion against which the dynamic test is assessed is appropriate for the skills that the test measures. At the same time, to the extent that one's goal is simply to predict performance within an already existing system, such as the system of schooling, it may be the dynamic tests rather than the criteria that need to change to be responsive to the purposes for which the dynamic tests will be used.

PART FIVE

TWO CASE STUDIES OF DYNAMIC TESTING

In this part of the book, we examine two case studies of the use of dynamic testing in our own research program. We do not hold these efforts up as ideals of how work on dynamic testing should be done but merely as exemplars of ways in which such work can be done.

CHAPTER EIGHT

Using Dynamic Testing to Reveal Hidden Potential

In this study, we sought to use dynamic testing to reveal hidden potential in rural Tanzanian school children. The study was done in collaboration with Damaris Ngorosho of MAKWAMI and the University of Dar es Salaam, Erasto Tantufuye of MAKWAMI – Partnership for Child Development, Akundaeli Mbise of the University of Dar es Salaam, Catherine Nokes of the University of Oxford, Matthew Jukes of the University of Oxford, and Donald A. Bundy of the University of Oxford and the World Bank (Sternberg et al. in press).

A researcher from the developed world who has spent much of her life studying school children in developing countries commented to one of the authors of this book that in order to reach children in the developing world, one should treat the children as EMR (educable mentally retarded). This comment seems to reflect the beliefs of at least some psychologists about many children in the developing world (e.g., Herrnstein & Murray 1994).

Individuals who have spent some or all of their careers investigating the intelligence of Black Africans might question this assertion (e.g., Berry et al. 1991; Cole 1996; Mundy-Castle 1967; Serpell 1993; Wober 1974). But much may depend on what is meant by intelligence (Berry 1974; Sternberg 1985; Sternberg & Kaufman 1998; Sternberg, et al. 2000; Wober 1974). To the extent that one values IQ-based measures, one legitimately might wonder why some groups of Black Africans seemingly perform at low mean levels on such measures relative to White American populations as well as other populations.

In this chapter, we propose that one cannot interpret conventional static test scores among certain groups of Black Africans in the same way one might interpret these test scores among members of White majority groups in the United States. In particular, we suggest that conventional static tests systematically may fail fully to elicit the abilities of these African children, in part because the children are not accustomed to the vagaries of taking these tests (see also Cole et al. 1971; Greenfield 1997; Serpell 1993). There is nothing new about this claim (see, e.g., Berry 1974; Greenfield 1997; Laboratory of Comparative Human Cognition 1982; Serpell 2000). But we go beyond this claim to suggest, as have others (e.g., Feuerstein et al. 1979), the use of dynamic testing as an alternative to conventional static testing for use with populations with disadvantages. It may be possible to administer conventional types of tests of intelligence, but through a different mode of administration, in order to allow a more nearly complete display of these children abilities.

As we have seen, interest in dynamic testing has been attributed to the development of certain societal needs and to the formation of more mixed and even critical professional opinion on the usefulness of static testing (Tzuriel & Haywood 1992). As we mentioned above, with regard to societal needs, researchers recognized the desirability of (a) more nearly culture-fair tests that could be used in work with immigrants for the purpose of integrating them into society; (b) tests that would be useful for comparing results obtained in culturally diverse populations; (c) developmental tests appropriate for individuals with deprived educational experiences; and (d) the measurement of learning potential as distinct from what has been learned, regardless of the culture, population, or social group of a tested individual. Such measurement is especially attractive when one considers the relatively modest to moderate forecasting power of most static ability tests for many predictive purposes (e.g., Sternberg 1996). With dynamic testing, we might have a way to reduce the effects of obstruction from all the environmental variables that can affect performance (see Sternberg, Grigorenko, & Nokes 1997) and quantify a person's true potential for growth from wherever he or she may happen to be cognitively at any one moment.

This study was driven by our belief that dynamic testing, based on the theoretical notion of the ZPD, may help one elucidate mental abilities of school children in the developing world that otherwise might remain hidden. To this end, we devised a set of three tasks to be administered to rural school children in villages near Bagamoyo, Tanzania. The tasks were similar or identical to those found on conventional tests of intellectual abilities. Our mode of administration enabled us to obtain both static and dynamic test scores so that we could compare the efficacy of the two methods of testing for illuminating the abilities of the rural Tanzanian school children we tested.

METHODOLOGY OF THE STUDY

A total of 358 experimental-group children, 161 boys and 197 girls, participated in the study. The children were spread throughout four grades (2–5) in 10 schools, even though their age was limited to 11–13 years of age. In terms of grade levels, 4.5% were in second grade, 37.7% were in third grade, 31.8% were in fourth grade, and 26.0% were in fifth grade. The reason for this spread in grades relative to ages was primarily that children first enrolled in formal schooling at different ages. An additional 100 children of the same ages (40 boys and 60 girls) served as controls.

Three tasks were administered dynamically to experimental-group children: Syllogisms, Sorting, and Twenty Questions. Control-group participants received the same pretest and posttest as the experimental-group children without the intervening instruction. Each task measured analytical skills of various kinds. Examiners were always instructed to ensure that the children understood what they were being asked to do. At the very start, if a child did not understand a task, the task was further clarified until he or she did understand it. After each pretest, the examiner would indicate to the child that he or she did very well, but that he or she had made some mistakes. The examiner explained that he/she would now show the child how to solve the problems.

Syllogisms

Thirty-four linear Syllogisms were used – 17 three-term series problems and 17 four-term series problems. Six of each appeared in the pretest, five of each in the intervention, and five of each in the posttest. An example of a three-term series problem would be, "Alan is taller than Ken. Dan is taller than Alan. Who is the tallest, Alan, Ken, or Dan?" An example of a four-term series problem would be, "Bill is smaller than Joe. Joe is smaller than Peter. Peter is smaller than Tom. Who is the smallest, Joe, Peter, or Tom?" Items could be about names of people or about other things, such as lengths of roads, sizes of balls, sounds of school bells, and so forth. The posttest was similar to the pretest. The statements were read aloud to the children. In the intervention, the tester worked with drawings prepared in advance. The child was shown how visual representations of items in a vertical or horizontal line (spatial mental representations) could facilitate problem solution. Children were shown how the same representations that were drawn on a sheet of paper could be visualized mentally.

Scoring of items was for number correct at pretest, intervention, and posttest.

Sorting

The pretest for the Sorting task used the Wisconsin Card Sorting Test (Heaton et al. 1993). Each card contained from one to four identical figures of a single color printed on white cardstock. There were four kinds of figures: stars, crosses, triangles, and circles. There were also four colors in which the figures could appear: red, yellow, blue, and green. Each card, then, could be categorized in terms of number of figures, form, and color.

Children were shown four target stimulus cards. The target cards contained one red triangle, two green stars, three yellow crosses, or four blue circles. The four stimulus cards were placed in front of the child in a row. The children also were given a single pack of 64 cards varying in the attributes described above. The task was to sort the cards in the pack into the four piles. Children were not told any rules for sorting nor were they informed in advance that the rule for sorting would change over the course of sorting the 64 cards.

Whether a given card was sorted correctly depended on a rule that was not disclosed to the child. The rule could be that correct sorting was by form, number, or color. If a child placed a card from the pack under a target stimulus card that matched in the "correct" attribute, the child was told that he or she was correct. Otherwise, the child was told that he or she was incorrect. The child then sorted the next card. After a child did six correct sortings, the rule was changed.

The intervention for the sorting task involved foam figures of four colors (yellow, green, black, and blue), four sizes (large, medium, small, and very small), four shapes (octagon, square, triangle, and rectangle), and four possible numbers of figures (1, 2, 3, and 4). Children were explicitly asked questions about attributes and finding attributes in common between sets of figures. They were shown how to compare relative attributes and sort on the basis of the various attributes.

The posttest for the sorting task involved sorting of threaded beads rather than cards. The beads were of four shapes, four colors, and four combinations (number of beads per thread). The procedure with the beads was comparable to that with the cards.

Scoring of the pretest and posttest was for number of perseverative errors and the number of categories produced. Scoring of the intervention was for number of hints required for the child to reach criterion performance.

Twenty Questions

In the pretest for the Twenty Questions task, the participant was told that the examiner was thinking of an object. The child was then given up to 20 questions to figure out what the object might be. All questions asked by the child had to be answerable either by "yes" or "no." Objects were geometric designs from six rows of figures that varied in shape, size, and color. The shape could be a rectangle, square, or circle. The size could be large, medium, small, or very small. The color could be black or white. There were a total of 24 ($3 \times 4 \times 2$) different objects to choose from.

The intervention consisted of showing the children how to ask those questions that maximally narrowed the search space. For example, they learned that asking whether the figure is "black" would enable them to eliminate all black or white objects, depending upon the examiner's response. Or they learned that asking whether the figure was a rectangle could create an included and an excluded set of 8 and 16 objects, with the identities of the included or excluded objects depending on the examiner's answers.

The posttest for the Twenty Questions task was comparable to the pretest except that it used different attributes. There were crosses, circles, triangles, and rectangles that could be black or white and that could be large or small, for a total of 24 items in all.

Scoring for the pretest, intervention, and posttest was for ratio of constraint-seeking questions to the total number of questions asked.

Reference Ability and Achievement Tests

Results were also available for experimental-group children from a number of other tests of abilities and achievement that serve as reference measures for our own new tests. The reference-abilities tests were digit span forward and backward (averaged), Corsi block, Stroop task, word fluency, and Spanish vocabulary, all of which are used to measure working memory and related cognitive skills. The digit-span forward test involved children's repeating back digits they had heard orally in forward serial order. The Corsi block test involves having children view an examiner tap a number of blocks; the children then have to repeat in forward serial order the pattern of block taps they have seen. The Stroop task was modified for the children so that they either had to say "tick" when they saw a tick and say "cross" when they saw a cross, or else say "cross" when they saw a tick and "tick" when they saw a cross. Word fluency required children to recall, separately, as many foods and animals as quickly as they could. Spanish vocabulary involved the children's learning Spanish vocabulary words (all of which are unfamiliar to them) paired with pictures of objects and then their having to show their recall of the meanings of the words via paired-associates recall. The reference achievement tests were of school achievement in three subject-matter areas: reading, spelling, and arithmetic adapted from the Wide Range Achievement Test (WRAT; Jastak & Jasktak 1978).

The main dependent variables were pretest scores, intervention scores, and posttest scores for our new measures, and reference abilities (digit span, Corsi Block, Spanish, fluency, Stroop errors, Stroop time) and achievement (reading and mathematics). The main independent variables were gender, socioeconomic status, and grade in school.

Dynamic tests were administered in a fixed order: Syllogisms, then Sorting, and then Twenty Questions. All testing was done individually in Kiswahili in an empty classroom that served as a special testing room. Testing occurred in the morning for all participants. It consisted of the three pretests, instruction, and posttests occurring in a single session. Total testing time (actual time spent on tasks), including intervention and instructions for testing, ranged from 42 to 101 minutes. The mean testing time was 71 minutes. Total pure testing time without the intervention or instructions ranged from 14 to 46 minutes with a mean of 25 minutes. Intervention time ranged from 11 to 28 minutes with a mean of 17 minutes. None of these times include time spent in establishing rapport, distributing and collecting materials, changing materials, and so forth.

Static ability tests and educational tests were administered at another earlier time as part of another study.

WHAT WE FOUND

Reliabilities of Measures

Test–retest reliabilities at a two-week interval (for the pretest) were calculated on two distinct weighted (by N) samples of 50 and 19 individuals obtained by two testers. The weighted averages were .54 for Syllogisms, .58 for perseverative errors on the Sorting task and .64 for the number of categories on the Sorting task, and .66 for the Twenty Questions task.

Dynamic testing makes a difference in terms of test performance on posttest versus pretest. To register this difference, we employed general linear modeling analysis (the mixed procedure). Given that pre- and posttest indicators were not independent, we introduced individuals (participants) as a random effect. There was a significant pre- to posttest performance difference for all three tasks.

This set of analyses was followed by profile analyses, whereby the pattern of performance on the three tasks was compared at pretest and posttest. The analysis revealed a significant effect of task, suggesting the importance of task-specific variation; a significant task × time interaction effect, suggesting that the pre- to posttest changes varied across tasks; and a significant task × individual interaction, suggesting that individuals responded differently to different tasks. As for between-subject effects, there was an effect of individual. All within–subject effects were significant.

Scores on all measures showed significant gains from pretest to posttest. Specifically, performance on the Syllogisms task improved by 117%, performance on the Sorting task improved by 111%, and performance on the Twenty Questions task improved by 220%. Moreover, improvement for experimental-group children was significantly greater than for control-group children. For details, see Sternberg et al. (in press).

Associations with Demographic Variables

The results of multivariate analysis of variance showed the presence of a multivariate main effect of grade. The effect of children's grade was significant for all indicators of performance on the Syllogisms task. The effects of SES and attendance were borderline. The effect of SES was significant for both pre- and posttest indicators of numbers of categories in the Sorting task and for performance on the pretest of the Twenty Questions task. The effect of school attendance was significant for all three indicators of intervention performance. There were no multivariate effects of gender or gender × grade interaction. Of the 11 univariate models tested, follow-up analyses revealed four significant for all posttests.

Pretest–Intervention–Posttest Correlations for Dynamic Tests

Of much interest was the analysis of the correlations among scores for pretest, posttest, and intervention both within and between dynamic tests (corrected for attenuation). Two conclusions were drawn from these data.

First, pretest–posttest correlations for experimental-group children ranged from trivial to moderate. They were .05 (NS) for the Syllogisms task, .14 ($p < .01$) for perseverative errors, .42 ($p < .001$) for number of categories on the Sorting Task, and –.02 (NS) for the Twenty Questions task. These generally low correlations suggest that even a very brief and minimal intervention can have substantial effects on ability-test scores. Comparable correlations for the control group were significantly higher: .54, .50, .71, and 1.00, respectively. Clearly, the interaction affected risk order. Conclusions drawn on the basis of the pretest would have to be considered suspect, given the instability of the scores for experimental-group children after the brief intervention. It appears as though it would be unwise to draw strong conclusions about a person's abilities based only on pretest scores. Second, the various dynamic tests were not very highly correlated with each other either. The correlations (corrected for attenuation) ranged from trivial (around 0) to moderate (.43).

Correlations of Dynamic Tests with Reference Ability and Achievement Tests

CORRELATIONS WITH REFERENCE ABILITY TESTS. The correlations with both pretest and posttest scores were in the expected directions and many of them are statistically significant although small in magnitude. On the whole, the tests appeared to be measuring related constructs although probably not the same ones. Note that correlations of the posttests with the reference ability measures tended to be higher than the correlations of the pretests with the reference-ability measures. Comparing pretest and posttest correlations with reference ability tests where at least one correlation in each pair was statistically significant, the pretest correlation with the reference ability measures was higher in absolute value in two instances and the posttest correlation was higher in absolute value in 20 instances, with only two instances where correlations with both pre- and posttest indicators were nonsignificant. (Absolute values were used because for some measures, higher scores indicated higher levels of abilities; whereas for other measures, lower scores indicated higher levels of abilities.) Looked at in another way, the median of the absolute values of the correlations of the pretests with the reference ability measures was .10 and for the posttests was .21. Looked at in still another way, in every case where the disattenuated correlation of the pretest with the reference-ability measures differed significantly from the correlation of the posttest (11 pairs out of 24), the difference in correlation was significant in favor of the posttest. These results suggest that the posttests are better predictors of the reference ability measures than are the pretests.

CORRELATIONS WITH ACHIEVEMENT TESTS. The correlations with the school achievement tests ranged from trivial to moderate. The correlations were variable. In all cases, the correlation of the posttest was higher than the correlation of the pretest. The median correlation of the pretest with the school achievement measures was .08; the median correlation of the posttest with the school achievement measures was .34. Where there were significant differences of the disattenuated correlations between the pre- versus the posttests and the school achievement measures, all seven favored the posttest. Thus, once again, the posttests tended to correlate more highly with the reference measures in this case of school achievement than did the pretests.

CONCLUSION: WHAT DOES IT ALL MEAN?

Our goal in this chapter was to illustrate the value of dynamic testing to explore reasons why Black Africans living in non-Westernized settings might score relatively poorly (relative to other groups) on conventional tests of intelligence. There have been various explanations of this phenomenon, ranging from possible genetic differences (Herrnstein & Murray 1994) to cultural differences in interpretations of test questions (Cole et al. 1971). Our own theoretical conceptualization (Sternberg 1985, 1997a) as well as the theoretical conceptions of others (e.g., Vygotsky 1978) suggested that children growing up in difficult circumstances might have substantial levels of underlying capacities that are reflecting in developing, but not in developed, abilities. Dynamic testing is one means of trying to get past conventional static measures of developed abilities and assess developing abilities generated by these underlying capacities.

In fact, we found that the children in our study seem to have had important intellectual abilities not measured by static intellectual tests. First, we found that performance improved from pretest to posttest following an intervention. Of course, part of the improvement might have been due to a practice effect resulting from their having taken the pretest. But whatever the cause, the gains from pretest to posttest call into question how seriously one can take static test results originating from these children. Second, we found that the correlations between pretests and posttests (following interventions) were relatively weak.

Thus, not only do score levels change after the intervention, but so do rank orders. This finding particularly calls into question the interpretability of the pretest (static) scores. If less than an hour of intervention can result in substantial changes in rank orders, then how seriously can we take pretest (static) scores? Third, we found that the posttest scores generally were better predictors of reference measures of cognitive abilities and achievements than were the pretest scores. Thus, the dynamic-testing procedure truly seems to have been tapping into important abilities that would not have been measured were one only to have considered the pretest (static) scores.

In a related study, conducted in Jamaica (Sternberg, Powell et al. 1997), we found that children who were parasitically infected performed more poorly on complex intellectual tasks than did children who were not infected. This difference did not extend to simpler tasks. Medicating the children with an antiparasitic medication (albendazole) improved their health but not their complex cognitive performance. We suspected that the reason was straightforward: When children grow up with various kinds of environmental press, their ability to profit from the environment, in general, and from school, in particular, is reduced. For example, a child who feels ill every day in school, whether due to parasitic infection or otherwise, will not be in a good position to profit from the lessons taught in the school.

Environmental press goes far beyond parasitic diseases. Any number of illnesses as well as poor nutrition or major responsibilities outside the school may compromise children's ability to profit from school. But we know that amount of schooling affects cognitive-test scores (Ceci & Williams 1997). Therefore, we need to consider the possibility that at least part of the difference in scores between Black African children and children elsewhere may be due to the lesser ability of the former to profit from their school environment. It therefore may be particularly important to measure their developing as well as developed abilities. In this respect, our results are similar to those of many others (e.g., Budoff 1975; Feuerstein et al. 1979) in suggesting that, particularly with children from culturally different backgrounds, dynamic testing may provide complementary information to what can be obtained from static testing. Because the pretest–intervention–posttest design incorporates static testing through the pretest, dynamic testing is not a substitute for static testing, but rather a supplement to it.

CHAPTER NINE

Combining Instruction and Assessment: Measuring Foreign-Language Learning Ability

This chapter describes work done in collaboration with Madeline Ehrman of the U.S. Foreign Service Institute (Grigorenko, Sternberg, & Ehrman, 2000). The ability to learn language has been central to human existence for thousands of years, and the ability to acquire a foreign language (FL) or languages beyond one's native tongue is particularly important for adaptation in today's world. But not everyone learns foreign languages equally easily, whether in classroom settings or everyday life contexts. Even casual observation suggests that some people learn additional languages faster, easier, or better than others do. Because psychologists have observed that people vary in their ability to learn FL, they have tried to formulate theories and design tests of FL learning abilities. Tests can help psychologists and educators (a) know to whom to devote what levels and what kinds of resources, (b) be able to predict success in language learning instruction, and (c) be able to compare actual achievement with the achievement one might expect on the basis of FL learning ability.

Several theories and resulting tests already exist to measure FL learning ability, most notably the Modern Language Aptitude Test (MLAT, Carroll & Sapon 1958). Other well-known language aptitude tests are the Pimsleur Language Aptitude Battery (PLAB, Pimsleur 1966), the Army Language Aptitude Test (ALAT, Horne 1971), the Defense Language Aptitude Battery (DLAB, Petersen & Al-Haik 1976), and the VORD[1] (Parry & Child 1990). In general, these tests emerged from the tradition of psychometric test development and are empirically based, English-rooted, and used for prediction purposes.

The MLAT was constructed on the basis of a model derived from the

---

[1] VORD is the word for "word" in the artificial language used in the text.

results of factor analyses of a large number of individual characteristics thought to contribute to FL learning. The analyses depicted four main factors, namely, phonetic coding ability (auditory capacity and sound-symbol relations), grammatical sensitivity, memory, and inductive language learning. All of these factors are reflected in the scales of the MLAT. Three of these abilities – auditory capacity, the ability to translate sounds into symbols, and grammatical sensitivity – are common to both MLAT and PLAB.

The PLAB (Pimsleur 1966) differs from the MLAT in including a portion addressing the ability to infer language structure from artificial language stimuli. The idea is that a person's abilities as used and integrated in context differs from his or her abilities as used in isolation. Thus, a subtest is included in the PLAB that measured ability to use and integrate FL learning skills.

The ALAT was developed to predict learner success, particularly in learning to speak and read Western Indo-European languages (Horne 1971). It is a 57-item test based on an artificial language of the Western Indo-European type. The artificial language syntax used in the ALAT closely resembles English syntax. The test is highly speeded and relatively short. The examinees are allowed only seven minutes to study grammar and vocabulary, and 20 minutes to solve the problems.

Similarly, the ability to make inferences regarding the structure of an artificial language is the central ability measured by DLAB (Petersen & Al-Haik 1976). The DLAB consists primarily of inductive reasoning items that use a modified version of English. The test includes items that quantify examinees' ability to form language concepts from pictures, learn foreign language sounds (via utterance identification, recognition of vowel patterns, and recognition of stress patterns), and master foreign language sound-symbol association and grammar.

Finally, unlike the previously mentioned tests reflecting the syntactic organization of Western European languages, the VORD was designed to test the ability to cope with grammar systems similar to that of Turkic languages (Parry & Child 1990). This test focuses largely on grammatical analysis (specifically, the analysis of nominal morphology, and verbal morphology, phrase- and sentence-level syntax).

These tests, based on related, but slightly different, theoretical conceptions of FL learning abilities generally have been effective in predicting FL learning success. Thus, the correlations between various tests' subscales (or composite measures or both) and performance measured by tests of actual language proficiency range roughly between .27 and .73 (Ehrman 1996; Parry & Child 1990).

The nature of these correlations, however, is not clear. Notwithstanding the predictive power of foreign language aptitude indicators, the latent abilities captured by the tests and their relationships to measures of intelligence are not well understood. When foreign language aptitude and intelligence tests are used together as predictors of FL learning success, results always reveal significant correlation between the two kinds of tests (Gardner & Lambert 1965; Wesche, Edwards, & Wells 1982).

Yet the tests are not fully redundant. There is empirical evidence showing differential linkages of aptitude and intelligence with foreign language proficiencies. Moreover, Carroll (1981) summarized a number of studies showing that measures of foreign language aptitude and intelligence indicators do not exhibit the same pattern of correlations with FL proficiency. In addition, correlations between intelligence and foreign-language aptitude vary from low/moderate (Gardner & Lambert 1972; Skehan 1989) to moderate/strong (Sasaki 1996; Wesche et al. 1982).

At a theoretical level, the differentiation between measures of intelligence and measures of foreign language aptitude may derive in part from differences in the way the material on them is learned most often. It has been suggested, for example, that conventional tests of crystallized intelligence tend to focus more on material that is explicitly learned than do foreign language aptitude tests, which tend to focus on material that is implicitly learned. Given this view, there well might be two separate systems for learning (Krashen 1981; Reber 1989, 1993; Robinson 1996, 1997). Thus, foreign-language aptitude tests should contribute incrementally over conventional ability tests to the prediction of foreign-language learning success (e.g., Silva & White 1993). At the same time, it seems unlikely that all crystallized skills are explicitly learned, given that much of a person's vocabulary is learned implicitly in context (Sternberg 1985, 1987).

The hypothesis that intelligence and aptitude might play differential roles in FL learning has been investigated within a longitudinal framework (Lett & O'Mara 1990; Skehan 1989). For example, the Defense Language Institute Foreign Language Center (DLIFLC) and the U.S. Army Research Institute conducted a longitudinal project entitled *The Language Skill Change Project* (LSCP, Lett & O'Mara 1990). Each of the 881 LSCP participants on whom all data waves were collected was tracked from entry into one of the DLIFLC language programs through the completion of the program and for the subsequent two years. Each participant's data were gathered on at least 12 different occasions. The administered battery of tests included an extensive array of questionnaires and inventories, designed to measure variables thought to be relevant to the prediction of FL learning outcomes (e.g., DLAB, general ability, memory, verbal ability, attitude, motivation), as well as appropriate language proficiency tests. The results of regression analyses predicting foreign language proficiency achievement demonstrated, on average, an adjusted R^2 of about .14. Where achieved, foreign language proficiency was most strongly predicted (reading and listening versus speaking), general and verbal abilities (R^2 ranging from 0+ to .14) as well as DLAB indicators (with R^2 values ranging from 0+ to .08) contributed prominently to this prediction. Among these predictors, the DLAB appeared to be more valuable than ability indicators in predicting success in the more difficult languages (specifically, Russian and Korean), whereas the ability indicators were more fruitful than the DLAB in predicting proficiencies in the less difficult languages (specifically, German and Spanish).

We have devised a new test of second language learning aptitude; the Cognitive Ability for Novelty in Acquisition of Language as applied to Foreign Language Test (CANAL-FT) that represents one possible instantiation of a cognitive theory of FL acquisition. The test builds on past theories and tests and perhaps goes beyond many of them in being based on a particular cognitive theory of FL acquisition that stresses the role of coping with novelty in such acquisition. The newly developed test is (a) based on a cognitive theory of knowledge acquisition rather than being empirically derived; (b) naturalistic in that it creates a situation in which FL learning occurs naturally, by gradually introducing a simulated language embedded in a multifaceted language context; (c) dynamic rather than static, in that it tests the ability to learn at the time of test; (d) multifunctional in that it both assesses students' levels of ability and provides information on students' strengths and weaknesses, so that appropriate teaching and learning strategies can be devised; and (e) based on item-response theory, thereby permitting adaptive testing and new item development. The test appears to be of some use in its own right, but our primary purpose in presenting it is as a test of the CANAL-F theory.

RATIONALE FOR THE CANAL-F THEORY

The major assumption of the CANAL-F theory is that acquisition of foreign language is a form of developing expertise. The CANAL-F theory holds that one of the central abilities required for FL acquisition is the ability to cope with novelty and ambiguity (Ehrman 1993, 1994, 1996;

Ehrman & Oxford 1995). This ability is a part of the experiential aspect of intelligence as described by the triarchic theory of human intelligence (Sternberg 1985, 1988, 1997a).

Knowledge Acquisition Processes

In its application to FL learning, an expanded list of knowledge acquisition processes specifying the theory includes five knowledge acquisition processes: (a) selective encoding, (b) accidental encoding, (c) selective comparison, (d) selective transfer, and (e) selective combination. Because the FL learner is constantly being exposed to new linguistic material, he or she needs to decide where to focus his or her attention and use these processes accordingly.

1. *Selective encoding* is used to distinguish between more and less relevant information for one's purposes as this information arrives in the stream of incoming data.
2. *Accidental encoding*, in contrast, is used to encode background or secondary information and to grasp the background context of the information stream. This process is very important in FL learning because information accumulated outside the focus of the learner's attention enhances comprehension and increases the knowledge base available for production.
3. *Selective comparison* is used to determine the relevance of old information for current tasks. When using this knowledge-acquisition process, the learner considers how he or she can draw on a knowledge base that already exists to enhance learning (Sternberg 1985). This process is related to the learner's ability to hold contradictory, incomplete, or uninterpretable information in working memory without either rejecting it or coming to premature closure about it (Ehrman 1993, 1996).
4. *Selective transfer* is used to apply decoded or inferred rules to new contexts and tasks. It is particularly helpful to learners in understanding how, based on their previous knowledge, they can carry over to a different context the rules they have learned in a previous situation.
5. *Selective combination* is used to synthesize the disparate pieces of information that have been collected via selective and accidental encoding. These pieces of information are then compared to old information structures and incorporated into a newly created or updated, integrated, and plausible unit of knowledge. Selective

combination also is used to modify the learner's existing cognitive schemata (Ehrman 1993; Sternberg 1985).

Levels of Processing

In FL learning, the five knowledge acquisition processes operate at four levels: lexical, morphological, semantic, and syntactic.

1. The lexical level deals with one's learning, understanding, and use of words.
2. The morphological level deals with the words' structures and derivations.
3. The semantic level deals with one's understanding and use of the meaning of the words, based on information from the higher-order units into which the words combine, such as sentences and paragraphs.
4. The syntactic level deals with one's learning, understanding, and use of the grammatical principles of organization that connect the words to the higher-order units.

Modes of Input

The knowledge acquisition processes of selective and accidental encoding, comparison, transfer, and combination apply at the four levels of lexical, morphological, semantic, and syntactic information processing in two modes of input and output: visual and oral.

1. The visual mode predominates in reading and writing.
2. The oral mode is involved in listening and speaking.

Encoding, Storage, and Retrieval of Information

Finally, for language learning to take place, the linguistic material must be understood and encoded into working memory, and then transferred so that it can be stored in long-term memory for later retrieval. These aspects of encoding, storage, and retrieval can be assessed through two types of recall tasks.

1. Immediate recall occurs right after learning takes place.
2. Delayed recall occurs at some substantial time interval after learning takes place.

In sum, the theory specifies process-based sources of individual differences in FL learning. The test was designed to assess these sources of individual differences.

THE SIMULATION TEST

In order to create a test with a relatively high degree of ecological validity that also capitalizes on modern developments in the psychology of assessment, we designed a dynamic test (see Grigorenko & Sternberg 1998), whereby test-takers are tested at the time they learn. Our particular test is based on a simulation in which the participant was expected to learn elements of a new artificial language (Henmon 1929; Spolsky 1995). This new language (Ursulu) reflects aspects of different existing languages but does not resemble any one language (or linguistic group) in particular. The Ursulu language has a consistent internal structure and stable properties, which were reviewed by linguists at the U.S. Foreign Service Institute, a federal language training institution, and Yale University. If, during the evaluation, the linguists found internal inconsistencies in the Ursulu language or a violation of general linguistic principles, this feedback was taken into account and the new language was reevaluated. Necessary changes to the test then were implemented.

Throughout the simulation, Ursulu is presented gradually, so that, initially, participants have no knowledge of the language; by the end of the test, however, they have mastered enough lexical, morphological, semantic, and syntactic knowledge to cope with a small story in Ursulu. Consider the following example.

In Ursulu, words referring to colors are signified by the ending -oi. Initially, some of these words are introduced by means of implicit learning – the words are embedded in paragraphs, and the meaning of a specific word becomes apparent from contextual clues. This knowledge, then, is supported by means of explicit learning in the section where Ursulu words are learned by their direct comparison with English words: A number of pairs in this section are pairs of Ursulu-English words signifying colors. Finally, in the later sections of the test, words signifying colors are used as key words, the knowledge of which is crucial to understanding the meaning of Ursulu sentences.

Thus, the newly designed test (a) is theory-based, (b) is designed to be of relatively high ecological validity because it simulates a continuous learning situation, (c) utilizes the dynamic paradigm of testing by tapping the processes of knowledge acquisition at the time of test, and

(d) provides diagnostic information that might be suitable for devising optimal teaching and learning strategies. These strategies, based on the CANAL-F theory, can be inferred from patterns of scores on different sections of the test, which address different elements involved in foreign language learning. Specifically, the pattern of CANAL-FT scores permits identification of the preferred modes of learning (auditory vs. visual) and provides indices of students' ability, for example, to extend their vocabulary by means of implicit or explicit learning or both. The test thus potentially enables the tester to expose students' strengths and weaknesses. Obviously, the test represents one instantiation of the CANAL-F theory but by no means the only possible one.

We conducted two studies. The first study examined the relationship of the CANAL-FT to a widely regarded test of FL learning ability as well as to a test of general intelligence in order to assess whether the new test measured FL learning abilities better than general cognitive abilities. In addition, this study was designed to explore associations between CANAL-FT performance and life-long experience with foreign languages. The second study went beyond the first in looking at the quality of prediction provided by CANAL-FT as shown by concurrent validities with performance in foreign-language learning courses.

STUDY 1: EXPLORING CONSTRUCT AND CONTENT VALIDITY OF THE CANAL-FT

Who Participated and What Did They Do?

One hundred fifty-eight (158) individuals participated in Study 1. All participants were recruited through Yale University campus and local newspaper advertisements. Participants were financially compensated for their time.

Ninety-two participants (58.2%) were female and 57 (36.1%) were male. By accident, gender was not recorded for 9 individuals (5.7%). The mean age of participants was 23.9 years, with a range from 18 to 59 years. All participants had attended at least one year of college.

Four aptitude assessment instruments[2] and a background questionnaire were administered to the participants. Each instrument is described in more detail below.

---

[2] The two tests of intelligence were selected because they (a) capture two types of abilities (crystallized and fluid); (b) are considered to be rather difficult and, therefore, suitable for the high-ability population enrolled in this study; and (c) could be group-administered.

CANAL-FT

The CANAL-FT is a dynamic test that comprises nine sections, five of which involve immediate recall, and four of which are identical to these five sections except that they are presented later and involve delayed recall.

The five different sections of the test measure various aspects of the theory in integrated format because, in real FL learning, mental processes are integrated rather than isolated. The sections are:

1. Learning meanings of neologisms from context (immediate and delayed recall).
2. Understanding the meaning of passages (immediate and delayed-recall).
3. Continuous paired-associate learning (immediate and delayed recall).
4. Sentential inference (immediate and delayed recall)
5. Learning language rules. This section is presented last, and so it includes only immediate-recall questions.

In our study, the order of presentation was such that the immediate-recall sections were followed later by delayed-recall sections. For example, a sequence would be learning meanings of neologisms from context (immediate recall), then understanding the meaning of passages (immediate recall), then learning meanings of neologisms from context (delayed recall), then continuous paired-associate learning (immediate recall), and then understanding the meaning of passages (delayed recall), and so on. In Sections 1 through 4, half of the items were presented orally and half of the items were presented visually. All items in Section 5 were presented visually. Examples of types of items are given at the end of the chapter.

SECTION 1 (LEARNING MEANINGS OF NEOLOGISMS FROM CONTEXT). The items in this section were designed to assess all five of the cognitive processes (selective encoding, accidental encoding, selective comparison, selective transfer, and selective combination), primarily at the lexical, morphological, and semantic levels of operation within a language. In some items, however, we also introduced some elements of syntax.

Participants were presented with 24 brief paragraphs within a 2 (type of presentation: oral or visual) × 3 (density of unknown words: low, medium, or high) factorial design. Specifically, half of the passages were presented in written form and half were presented in a standardized (prerecorded) oral form. The paragraphs presented orally were generally shorter than the ones presented in written format, so participants could hold more of the passages in their working memory. In addition, these passages were presented twice: once, when the learner had not yet seen the questions and a second time after the learner had seen the questions.

In one-third of the passages, the density of unknown words was relatively low (approximately 5% unknown), simulating the situation confronted in advanced language learning (or in working with foreign language material in an unfamiliar subject). In another third, the density of unknown words was medium (approximately 10% unknown), simulating the situation in intermediate language learning. In the other third, the density of unknown words was relatively high (approximately 20% unknown), simulating the situation in beginning language learning.

The dependent measure was the demonstrated understanding of the meanings of the neologisms. Understanding was tested via a multiple-choice format, where students were asked to guess which of five alternatives was most likely to correspond to the meaning of the neologism. Two multiple-choice items were presented immediately after receipt of every passage, thereby measuring encoding of information into working memory. One item relevant to every passage was presented at least 30 minutes after receipt of the passages in order to measure storage in long-term memory.

SECTION 2 (UNDERSTANDING THE MEANING OF PASSAGES). Items in this section were designed to measure (a) use of selective and accidental encoding, comparison, and combination (b) for both visually and orally presented material (c) as encoded into working memory and stored in long-term memory (d) for the semantic mode of information. In addition, some elements of semantic processing also were introduced. The six test items in this part were identical in form to those in Section 1, but the dependent measure, which assessed comprehension of whole passages rather than merely of lexical items, was different. As in Section 1, items were presented visually and orally, with varying densities of unknown words: low (10%), medium (15%), and high (20%). However, four questions were posed immediately, and one question was posed after at least 30 minutes. In this section, furthermore, participants were presented with the passage and then were asked questions assessing comprehension of the passage. Thus, the participants needed to comprehend at the sentence and paragraph level, not just at the lexical (word) level. The test differed from standard reading and oral comprehension tests in the inclusion of unknown words in the passages. Such words render these passages more like those that would be encountered in the process of learning an FL.

Four levels of understanding were tested in the measurement of verbal comprehension (see Wagner & Sternberg 1987): comprehension of gist (question 1), comprehension of main ideas (question 2), comprehension of details (question 3), and inference and application (question 4). Delayed questions could address any of the above levels.

SECTION 3 (CONTINUOUS PAIRED-ASSOCIATE LEARNING). This section measured the selective comparison and combination of lexical and morphological material encoded into working memory and stored in long-term memory, in both visual and oral forms. In this test, participants were presented with 60 paired associates (word pairs). The paired associates were equally divided between items that consisted of the pairing of an English word with a neologism and items that consisted of the pairing of a neologism with an English word. Participants were required to learn the successive pairings. As they learned the pairs, they were tested at irregular intervals on words learned more recently as well as less recently. The test differed from a straightforward paired-associates memory test in that there were rules that could facilitate learning. These rules related some of the terms to others. For example, adjectives signifying colors were linked by the -oi ending. Thus, the able language learner would be able to use the cues in the word forms to facilitate his or her learning of the paired associates. In addition, because of the overall design of the test as a learning simulation, some inferences were possible from the tasks in the previous parts. However, it was the participants' responsibility to infer the underlying structure in the lexicon.

Mode of presentation varied in three ways. First, half of the words were presented visually, and half, orally. Second, half of the words were isolates (i.e., they had no cues linking them to other words), whereas the other half of the words were structurally related to each other in some way (i.e., could be derived from each other). Third, the order of English–Ursulu and Ursulu–English pairs was randomized. To assess learning, the participant was required to provide learned paired-associate words. In half of the cases, the participant was asked to provide the English paired associate, and in the other half, the paired associate in the Ursulu language. Some items were presented for immediate recall during the paired-associate stream, whereas other items were presented after a delay of at least 30 minutes.

SECTION 4 (SENTENTIAL INFERENCE). The goal of this section was to measure selective and accidental encoding, selective comparison, selective transfer, and selective combination, primarily at the syntactic and morphological levels and only secondarily at the lexical and semantic levels. The participants received sets of three to five sentences in the Ursulu language with their translations presented either visually or orally. After receiving these sentences and their translations, each participant was presented with a sentence, in either English or Ursulu, and was asked to indicate which of five multiple-choice answers best represented the translation.

Half of the sentence sets were presented visually ($N = 10$) and half orally ($N = 10$). Further, half of the item sets involved only simple sentence structure ($N = 10$) whereas the other item sets involved compound or complex sentence structure ($N = 10$).

The dependent measure had two facets. First, for some of the items, the test-taker needed to respond by guessing the correct sentence in English, whereas for others, the test taker had to guess the correct sentence in Ursulu. The second facet addressed immediate versus delayed recall. To test immediate recall, a question followed every test item. To test delayed recall, four questions (two oral and two written) were presented at least 30 minutes after the completion of this section.

SECTION 5 (LEARNING LANGUAGE RULES). The goal of this section was to measure selective and accidental encoding, selective comparison, and selective combination at the lexical, semantic, morphological, and syntactic levels, for material presented visually and for encoding into working memory and storage in long-term memory. Participants were given some vocabulary, some grammar, and some examples of how the Ursulu language works. From this type of information provided throughout the course of the test, participants were expected to have learned some of the most evident rules of the Ursulu language. To measure this learning, participants were presented with 12 items (lexical, semantic, morphological, and syntactic) testing their understanding of the Ursulu language.

The scoring of the CANAL-FT data was carried out by the means of item response theory (IRT) scaling (Hambleton 1983). Scaling was carried out on a sample of 245 individuals.[3] IRT scaling provides a means

---

[3] Details of test development, participants' information, IRT model fitting, and item characteristics are available from the authors upon request.

to obtain information on both the participants' ability and the administered tasks together. An IRT scale requires a pool of tasks of varying difficulty that assess the same dimension. In this research, such a dimension is the ability to cope with novelty and ambiguity, viewed as a crucial cognitive ability in foreign language acquisition.[4]

The Test of g: Culture-Fair

The Test of g[5]: Culture-Fair, Level III (CFT, Cattell 1940; Cattell & Cattell 1973) is a test of fluid ability designed to reduce as much as possible the influence of verbal comprehension, culture, and educational level. Although the test is called "culture-fair," neither this nor any other test is truly culture-fair (Sternberg 1985). The test consists of four subtests. In the first subtest, Series, individuals are presented with an incomplete, progressive series of figures. The individual's task is to select, from among the choices provided, the answer that best continues the series. In the Classification subtest, individuals are presented with five figures and are expected correctly to identify two figures that are different in some way from the other three. In the Matrices subtest, the task is to complete correctly the matrix presented at the left of each row. The final

---

[4] The CANAL-FT's responses were scaled using the 2-parameter IRT model (Birnbaum 1968), that is, estimating participants' ability to deal with novelty with consideration of the items' difficulty and discriminating power. Four different scaling models were utilized: (a) a single indicator of the ability to deal with novelty (estimated on a complete set of items), (b) indicators of the ability to deal with novelty in oral and visual domains (estimated on two nonoverlapping sets of items – items presented orally and items presented visually), (c) indicators of the ability to deal with novelty and retrieve novel information in immediate or delayed modes (estimated on two nonoverlapping sets of items – items presented while learning and items presented with a delay), (d) indicators of the ability to deal with novelty estimated in different sections of the test. The following α coefficients were obtained for different scalings: (a) $\alpha = .97$ for the total score; (b) $\alpha = .86$ and $\alpha = .96$, for oral and visual modes of presentation, respectively; (c) $\alpha = .96$ and $\alpha = .88$, for immediate and delayed recall scales, respectively; (d) $\alpha = .89$ (Section 1, *Learning meanings of neologisms from context*); $\alpha = .84$ (Section 2, *Understanding the meaning of passages*); (c) $\alpha = .85$ (Section 3, *Continuous paired-associate learning*); (d) $\alpha = .83$ (Section 4, *Sentential inference*); (e) $\alpha = .92$ (Section 5, *Learning language rules*). All scales were normally distributed. For the scaling models with more than one score (e.g., models 2–4) the following intercorrelations between scales scores were obtained. For the scaling scheme b, $r_{245} = .85$ ($p < .001$) for oral and visual scales. For the scaling scheme c, $r_{245} = .77$ ($p < .001$) for immediate and delayed recall scales. For the scaling scheme d, the mean r was .59 (the $r(s)$ ranged from .46 to .70, with all p-values less than .001).

[5] g (G) is an abbreviation for general ability – an ability that is common to all intellectual tasks and is measured to some degree by all tests of intelligence.

subtest, Conditions (or Topology), requires the individual to select, from among the five choices provided, the one that duplicates a target condition with respect to placement of a dot among geometric forms (e.g., the individual is expected to select the figure in which it is possible to place a dot so that it would lie outside the box but inside the circle, as specified in the target condition).

Concept Mastery Test

The Concept Mastery Test (CMT, Terman 1970) largely addresses crystallized ability, or acquired knowledge base (in the cultural context of the United States). It was designed on the premise that people of higher intelligence, all other things being equal, are more likely than those of lesser intelligence to have a rich store of concepts and ideas. Terman (1970) believed that level of vocabulary, general knowledge, and the ability to make inferences of the sort required by verbal analogy items would represent differential levels of concept mastery. In fact, the CMT does successfully differentiate exceptionally gifted adults, people who reach graduate training, undergraduates of several different sorts, and nonstudents from each other (Terman 1970). The test consists of two parts: (1) Synonyms and Antonyms and (2) Analogies. The first part includes 120 pairs of words, and the participant's task is to specify whether the words in each pair are synonyms or antonyms. The second part includes 70 verbal analogies. Each analogy is followed by the word for which an analogous word should be selected from among three possible answers so that the constructed analogy will resemble the structure of the analogy given in the example. Ability to solve the analogies depends strongly on vocabulary and general information.

Modern Language Aptitude Test (MLAT)

The MLAT (Carroll & Sapon 1958) is perhaps the benchmark FL aptitude test. The test consists of 146 items divided into five parts: (a) number learning, a measure of memory and auditory alertness; (b) phonetic script (actually phonemic transcription), a measure of the test-taker's ability to establish associations between sounds and symbols presented orally; (c) spelling clues, an English-based subtest of the ability to establish associations between sounds and symbols presented in a written format; (d) words in sentences, an English-based measure of sensitivity to grammatical structure; and (e) paired associates, a measure of the test-taker's ability to memorize pairs of words. Despite its age, the MLAT continues to enjoy substantial discriminatory and predictive power (Ehrman 1994; Ehrman & Oxford 1995; Sparks, Ganschow, & Patton 1995).

Prior Language Experience Questionnaire

This brief eight-item questionnaire was designed to obtain information about the prior language experience of the participants. We asked participants (a) about their education and field of study, (b) which foreign language(s) they knew, (c) their degree of mastery of these foreign languages, (d) how they studied these languages, and (e) how difficult they find learning a foreign language.

Results

External Construct Validity

In order to assess the external construct validity of the CANAL-FT, a series of correlational analyses was conducted. The CANAL-FT scores were validated against the MLAT, the benchmark test of foreign language aptitude, and two difficult tests of intelligence, one of crystallized intelligence (the Concept Mastery Test) and one of fluid intelligence (the Cattell Culture-Fair Test of g, Scale 3, Form B). Both discriminant and convergent types of validity (Campbell & Fiske 1959) of the measurements provided by our test were evaluated. Specifically, the convergent validity of the measurement provided by the CANAL-FT was appraised by means of its correlations with the MLAT, whereas the discriminant validity of the measurement provided by the CANAL-FT was assessed through the test's correlations with the intelligence measures.

Two aspects of these results, reflected in correlations between the CANAL-FT, MLAT, and intelligence tests and in correlations between different CANAL-FT scales and the MLAT, were key. First, the correlations between all scores of the CANAL-FT and the MLAT were either significantly higher or not significantly lower than correlations between the CANAL-FT scores and the indicators of crystallized and fluid abilities, demonstrating convergent-discriminant validity of the measurement provided by the CANAL-FT. To illustrate this point, we compared the most discrepant pairs of $r(s)$ between CANAL-FT and MLAT subscores. Specifically, the correlation between the CANAL-FT / Section 3 (Continuous paired-associate learning) and the MLAT / Part 5 (Paired associates) was significantly higher than that between the CANAL-FT / Section 3 and the CMT. On the contrary, the correlation between the CANAL-FT / Section 4 and the MLAT / Part 4 and the correlation between the CANAL-FT and the CFT were not statistically different. The correlation between the CANAL-FT Total and the MLAT Total is significantly higher than either the correlation between the CANAL-ST Total and the CFT or the correlation between the CANAL-FT Total and the CMT.

The correlation matrix between scores of five sections of the CANAL-FT, five parts of the MLAT, and the CMT and CFT scores was subjected to a factor analysis. The method of extraction was principal-components[6] followed by an oblique rotation ($\delta = 0$). The initial extraction revealed two components with eigenvalues higher than 1 (5.18 and 1.29, respectively). When rotated, the two factors together explained 53.9% of the variance (eigenvalues of 4.71 and 2.73, respectively). The first factor included: (1) CANAL-FT Section 1 (Understanding meanings of neologisms from context, factor loading .78), (2) CANAL-FT Section 2 (Understanding the meaning of passages, factor loading .68), (3) CANAL-FT Section 4 (Sentential inference, factor loading .65), (4) CANAL-FT Section 5 (Learning language rules, factor loading .67), (5) MLAT Part 1 (Number learning, factor loading .71), (6) MLAT Part 2 (Phonetic script, factor loading .70), (7) MLAT Part 4 (Words in sentences, factor loading .61), (8) CMT (factor loading .61), and (9) CFT (factor loading .68). The second factor included: (1) CANAL-FT Section 1 (Understanding meanings of neologisms from context, factor loading .51), (2) CANAL-FT Section 3 (Continuous paired-associate learning, factor loading .73), (3) CANAL-FT Section 4 (Sentential inference, factor loading .59), (4) CANAL-FT Section 5 (Learning language rules, factor loading .69), and (5) MLAT Part 5 (Paired associated, factor loading .76). Thus, the first factor probably accounts for the g-factor-related performance on these tests, whereas the second factor accounts for the g-factor-unrelated performance on the CANAL-FT and *MLAT*. Notice that more subtests of the CANAL-FT than of the MLAT contributed to the second factor.

In sum, the results of the construct validity analyses suggest that the CANAL-FT is a valid measure of foreign-language aptitude, which, as expected, is related to but not equivalent to both crystallized and fluid abilities.

---

[6] Principal axis factoring followed by an oblique rotation revealed a very similar pattern of results, but there was a loss of explained variance (the total explained variance was 44.8%, with eigenvalues for rotated factors of 4.3 and 2.4, for the first and second factors, respectively).

Prior Language Experience

Four questions in the Prior Language Experience Questionnaire were of special interest. First, participants were asked to report on languages they spoke, read, and wrote. Only 5 (3.2%) of participants did not speak and 35 (22.2%) did not write any additional language other than English. Thirty-four (21.5%) participants spoke, read, and wrote in one foreign language. Sixty-seven (42.4%) participants spoke and 44 (27.8%) read and wrote in two foreign languages. Finally, 52 (32.9%) participants in the sample could communicate and 45 (28.5%) could read and write in three foreign languages. These proportions are similar to those found at the U.S. Foreign Service Institute (Ehrman & Oxford 1995).

A series of analyses was conducted to investigate whether the number of foreign languages a person speaks/reads/writes is associated with the CANAL-FT Total indicator. Univariate analyses of variance revealed significant F values, with means showing a stable linear trend linking the number of foreign languages in which participants could communicate with higher CANAL-FT performance. The analyses did not reveal any noticeable associations between the MLAT Total score and the number of languages mastered.

Thus, the more languages the person can speak, read, and write, the easier the CANAL-FT is for the person and the better the person's performance on it. Higher performance on the CANAL-FT could come from language learning experience, or, alternatively, those who learn multiple languages might tend to have higher levels of the kinds of abilities that the CANAL-FT measures. The chances are that both influences have a reciprocal effect.

The answers to two other questions from the Prior Language Experience Questionnaire also were investigated. We wanted to test whether contact with foreign languages when participants were growing up ("Were you ever in contact with other languages while growing up?") or attitude toward learning a foreign language ("Do you find learning foreign languages easy?") reflected a difference in terms of CANAL-FT performance. In this sample, 51.2% of participants were not in contact with a foreign language while growing up, whereas 48.8% were in contact. Fifty-five percent of the participants in the sample said that learning a foreign language was an easy task, whereas 45% said that it was not an easy task. The analysis of variance conducted on the CANAL-FT Total and MLAT Total indicators did not reveal main effects of either self-reported early experiences with language or of participants' attitudes toward learning foreign languages.

STUDY 2: EXLORING CRITERION-RELATED VALIDITY OF THE CANAL-FT

Participants and Materials

The participants in Study 2 were 63 Yale University college students. The mean age of the participants was 19.6 years, with a range from 18 to 22 years. Among the participants, there were 34 females and 25 males. By accident, gender was not recorded for four individuals (6.3%). All participants were recruited through Yale University campus advertisements. The conditions for enrollment in the study were that participants took at least one foreign language course at Yale and were willing to grant permission for the investigators to contact their Yale foreign-language instructors. Participants were studying a variety of different languages. The participants were compensated financially for their time. All participants took the CANAL-FT and the MLAT tests (see Study 1). Only three MLAT subtests (Parts 3, 4, and 5) were administered in this study. In addition, the participants' language instructors at Yale were asked to fill out a report on the participants' skills relevant to the study.

On a scale of poor, below average, average, above average, and outstanding, this report, the Language Instructors' Survey, asked the teachers to rate the students' communication, vocabulary, writing skills, their knowledge of the language the instructor taught, and their ability to master the language the instructor taught.

What Did We Find?

To ascertain the criterion validity data on the CANAL-FT scales, we obtained rank-order correlations between CANAL-FT and MLAT indicators and the data from the Language Instructors' Survey.

A principal-components analysis was done on the instructors' survey ratings in order to facilitate interpretation of the results. This analysis revealed a single principal component with an eigenvalue of 3.9, which accounted for 78% of the variance in the data. All other factors were trivial (eigenvalues less than 1).

Correlations of the CANAL-FT with instructors' ratings were statistically significant in all but two cases, and generally the correlations also were substantial. The mean correlation between specific instructors' ratings and the CANAL-FT total score was .40. The correlations of the CANAL-FT subtests were at least comparable to those for the MLAT (the average correlation between specific instructors' ratings and the CANAL-FT was .27, $p < .05$, and the average correlation between specific instructors' ratings and the MLAT was .23, $p < .10$. It is notable that two CANAL-FT subtests (Understanding Meaning of Neologisms from Context and Understanding the Meaning of Passages) did not correlate with instructors' ratings. This result might be reflective of the preferred mode of foreign language instruction at Yale, which is primarily conversation-based and communication-skill-oriented. In other words, Yale language courses are targeted primarily at the development of speaking rather than at reading and writing proficiency. When the average correlation between specific instructors' ratings and the other three subtests of the CANAL-FT is calculated, it reaches .37 ($p < .01$). These results show that the CANAL-FT predicts instructors' ratings of students' foreign-language performance.

CONCLUSION: WHAT DOES IT ALL MEAN?

In this work, we attempted to present the rationale, description, and partial construct validation of a new theory and test of foreign language aptitude: the CANAL-F. The theory served as the basis for construction of the test, and the favorable results for the test indicate the viability of the theory, although of course these results do not "prove" the correctness of the theory.

The test was intended to be (a) theory-based (i.e., representing a current in cognitive theory in psychology), (b) ecologically valid (i.e., representing the activities and processes that are involved in learning a foreign language), (c) dynamic rather than static in its form of assessment (i.e., measuring the ability to learn rather than acquired knowledge), (d) suitable for a population of restricted range in IQ (i.e., differentiating highly educated people at the higher end of the IQ distribution), and (e) flexible (i.e., suiting different needs with different items of portions of the general test). The test was created to meet the specific goals of federal intensive language programs and to serve simultaneously as a theory-based instrument providing information regarding (a) prediction of success in learning a foreign language, (b) individual profiles of learners' stylistic preferences, and (c) the best possible placement of learners within a program. All of these requirements were met.

In addition to the results on the initial validation of the CANAL-F theory of foreign-language learning, the study contributed to the literature on foreign language acquisition in three specific ways. First, the data showed that, when factor-analyzed, the CANAL-FT subtests load on two factors: an intelligence-related factor and a language-specific factor, to which substantial contributions are made by all subtests of the CANAL-FT and only two subtests of the MLAT (Paired Associates and Spelling Clues). This finding contributes to the search for the explanation of the first-order correlations between intelligence and foreign language aptitude: It appears that there is an overlap between these two factors (Sawyer & Ranta 1999; Skehan 1998). The structure of the loadings on the second factor suggests the desirability of the inclusion of various working-memory measures in further research with CANAL-FT (Harrington & Sawyer 1992; Osaka & Osaka 1992; Osaka, Osaka, & Groner 1993; Skehan 1998).

Second, we collected data to address the issue of the links between previous exposure to foreign-language learning and foreign-language aptitude. In concordance with some studies (Eisenstein 1980; Sparks et al. 1995) and in contrast to other studies (Harley & Hart 1997; Sawyer 1992), we found an association between the number of languages the person can speak/read/write and higher levels of language aptitude. The interpretation of this finding, however, should be tentative – a mere association does not reveal underlying causal relations. In particular, there is strong evidence in the literature that foreign-language aptitude is much more than a matter of experience (e.g., Sawyer & Ranta 1999; Skehan 1989, 1990), and more research is needed to sort out the modifiable aspects of the aptitude. Foreign-language aptitude is itself a form of developing expertise, which presumably can be increased to some extent through the focused learning of languages and the rule systems underlying them.

Third, this research demonstrated, in concordance with many studies (for review, see Sawyer & Ranta 1999) that foreign-language aptitude indicators are linked to various indicators of actual language learning.

In sum, our attempt to structure this test as a holistic situation with one dominant factor (ability to deal with novelty), as manifested in different tasks encountered by a language learner (vocabulary acquisition, sentence/paragraph comprehension, mastery of syntax and grammar, and semantic inference), requiring the coaction of different processes involved in foreign-language learning (selective and accidental encoding, selective combination, selective comparison, and selective transfer), appears to be promising. In general, this work should be viewed as a foundation for further development rather than as a completed effort.

Like any new test, the CANAL-FT requires further validation and refinement, in particular, further external validation with larger samples, a broader range of foreign-language learners, and a greater variety of foreign languages to be learned. The results of content, construct, and criterion validation suggest that the psychometric properties of the CANAL-FT are generally satisfactory and that the test may be suitable for a variety of applications, ranging from diagnostic to educational and remedial purposes, including construction of profiles of learners' strengths and weaknesses.

If the theory upon which the CANAL-FT is based is indeed correct, then it leads to a somewhat different view of language aptitude than the traditional one that looks at language aptitude as largely fixed (e.g., Skehan 1990). Language aptitude is based, in part, on expertise in certain kinds of information processing that, like any other kinds of expertise, can be developed (Sternberg 1998). Thus, language aptitude is a form of developing expertise rather than an entity fixed at birth. Whether, indeed, this is the case will need to be explored through studies that determine whether language aptitude training can, in fact, result in increased language performance and perhaps performance on the CANAL-FT.

CANAL-FT ITEM EXAMPLES

Section 1 *Immediate-Recall*
Rising tuition costs and increasingly large loans aren't the only financial issues facing *mukulu nafe-de*; the latest threat to *yuve-yuve ya-pama-de* pocketbooks comes from mandatory *twok-de*. One *laka* will require entering freshmen *fru hujuk* a *mukulu*-specified laptop *twok* at a cost of $3,000. Another *laka* has mandated that *nafe-de* have uninterrupted 24-hour access to a PC but is not dictating which model. *Nafe-de* have protested at both institutions, fearing that financial aid will not keep pace with *twok* costs, and will lower the economic diversity of the *nafe* body. Despite these protests, however, *mukulu-de* are forging ahead with yuve-yuve plans.

Fru hujuk most likely means: (a) to arrange; (b) having; (c) carrying; (d) to purchase; (e) to rent.

Mukulu in line (3) most likely means: (a) schools; (b) student; (c) parent; (d) universities; (e) college

Section 2 *Immediate-Recall*
The wealthy hunting *femo-de* of late glacial Europe might have maintained or even enriched culture, or *unta-u erto* to stagnate *ik* decline: *yuve* could hardly have advanced *erto* to a higher form of civilization, for the environment *neunta-u erto*. But *yuve-yuve* future *cutta-u* not left in *yuve-yuve* own *sima-de*. Inexorably, although no doubt to *twum* imperceptibly, the climate changed: *kojok-de* grew longer *ik* warmer, ice-sheets shrank, *ik* glaciers

retreated. Enslaved to climate, plant *ik* animal *kiz* had to change also. The mammoth, rhinoceros, *ik* reindeer in turn *rika-u* from western Europe, *yuve-yuve* going perhaps accelerated by the inroads of the *hudum* hunters themselves. On what had been open grassland of tundra with a scrub of dwarf *whiten ik* willow, *tudu* spread, stocked with the appropriate *pretudu* animals – *urkoi* deer *ik* wild pig. With the withdrawal or extinction of the great herds on which *yuve* had preyed, the *presufum* basis of the hunting *femo-de cutta-u* cut away *ik yuve-yuve* carefully adjusted culture made obsolete. This *cutta-u* one of the *putta-de* when early *kupu cutta-u* able to prove the full advantage of *Yut-Yut* self-made equipment over the biological *roji* of the beasts: the reindeer found *Yut-Yut* coat intolerably *preledu ik* had to quit; *kupu* merely took *Yut-Yut* off *ik* readjusted *Yut-Yut* habits.

The passage is largely concerned with: (a) man's conflict with his environment; (b) the effect of climate on man's way of life; (c) changes in plant and animal life in South America; (d) primitive hunting tribes and their culture; (e) extinct prehistoric animals

Fru neunta (see line 3 for a reference) most likely means: (a) to prevent; (b) to allow; (c) because of; (d) to permit; (e) factor

The disappearance of certain animals from western Europe was: (a) caused by the growth of cities; (b) disastrous to primitive man; (c) the direct result of man's self-equipment; (d) the immediate result of a more advanced culture; (e) caused by the movements of glaciers

The primitive hunting societies were forced to change their way of life because: (a) they were victims of an alien invasion; (b) they were incapable of enriching their lives; (c) they were stagnating; (d) the animals which they hunted disappeared; (e) their culture was allowed to decline.

Section 1 *Delayed-Recall*
In the passage mentioning an increase in the cost of studying at universities, *twok* most likely meant a: (a) microscope; (b) textbook; (c) computer; (d) equipment; (e) camera

Section 3 *Immediate-Recall*

kiss	=	lutik
maki smelano	=	floweret
to oppose	=	fru prostoto
threerish	=	two
to luxuriate	=	fru shikta
unteriapremu	=	fairytale
to learn	=	fru umbrad
juk-de	=	fingers
yellow	=	hukoi
pjze_min-de	=	workers

In Ursulu,
floweret most likely means: (a) *maki smelano;* (b) *ummake;* (c) *lutik;* (d) *pjze_min;* (e) *maki juk*

fru umbrad most likely means: (a) to eat; (b) to go; (c) to learn; (d) to kiss; (e) to dream

Section 2 Delayed-Recall
The author of the passage about the hunting society apparently believes that levels of civilization are determined by: (a) economic luck; (b) a balance of solar energy; (c) the ambitions of the people; (d) a piece of magic; (e) climatic conditions

Section 4 Immediate-Recall
In Ursulu,

Panlin-u Sumu Twah chuck	means	I handed a stick to him.
Panlin-u Yut Twa dozz	means	He handed an umbrella to me.
Panilcos-u Yut Twa flexta	means	He handed a piece of paper to me.
Panleh-u Sumu Twah chuchu	means	I handed a rope to him.

The sentence: *Panilcos-u Sumu Twah otikum* most likely means: (a) He handed a rod to me; (b) I handed a cord to him; (c) I handed a postcard to him; (d) I handed a waterhose to him; (e) I handed a tree-branch to her.

Section 3 Delayed-Recall
In Ursulu,
opposer most likely means: (a) *pjze_prostoto;* (b) *pjze_juk;* (c) *pjze_mor;* (d) *pjze_tenin;* (e) *pjze_jok*

Section 5 Immediate-Recall
In Ursulu, ya-bum baqlo means "the chief's mule," ya being the possessive and ya-bum the modifier of the noun baqlo "mule."

Match the corresponding pairs

ya-fuama pokka	corresponds to
preumma chicca-de	corresponds to
ya-xori gazza	corresponds to
prebrutama tepla-de	corresponds to
ya-ayama xrosyo	corresponds to
preuntam rutuma	corresponds to

(a) monkey's smile; (b) alligator gloves; (c) sheep wool; (d) cat's tail; (e) gigantic tiger; (f) wife's book

Section 4 Delayed-Recall

"Good afternoon" is most likely translated in the Ursulu language as: (a) *Cutta Sumu demiourgu;* (b) *Cutta Yuo preyakute demiourgu;* (c) *Preuntam eme-toi smelano-de;* (d) *Fimeduk fuddo;* (e) *Ubdara preyakute.*

PART SIX

MEASURING CHANGE

In this part of the book we discuss issues and problems in the measurement of change.

CHAPTER TEN

Measurement Aspects of Dynamic Testing: Quantifying Change[1]

The last chapter of this book brings the discussion back to the point of the first chapter. In fact, if we are to view dynamic testing as the means of testing developing expertise, one of the important questions is how to measure the acquisition of expertise. Specifically, the question brings us back to the issue we have touched upon very briefly, but have not explored – that of quantifying and analyzing change.

The agenda of this chapter is to summarize some of the current developments in the field of measurement that both directly and indirectly address the issue of quantifying change in its aspect that is relevant to dynamic testing.

Different types of change have been recognized and different methods of quantifying change have been developed (e.g., Collins & Horn, 1991; Harris 1963). In presenting the relevant material, we will concentrate on both old and new approaches to measuring change.

TYPES OF CHANGE

Throughout the book we have not concerned ourselves with a clear distinction between the terms *learning, development*, and *acquired expertise*. The theoreticians whose work we discussed earlier (see Chapters 4–6) take differing positions with regard to the definitions and interlinkages between these terms. Moreover, these theoreticians also differ in terms of defining the forms and types of learning that take place within the framework of dynamic assessment. The point we would like to make

[1] This chapter is somewhat more technical than the preceding chapters, but we believe readers will find it worth their trouble to read through the chapter in order to understand some of the developmental models that can help explain psychological and statistical changes that occur in the process of dynamic testing.

here is that, although the three processes (learning, development, and acquisition of expertise) do have distinct dissimilarities, they also have a sufficient number of overlapping properties (e.g., Pascual-Leone 1995; van Geert 1995; Vygotsky 1962/1934). Specifically, all three processes (a) mark the emergence of something new (skill, function, or level), (b) assume both procedural continuity and discontinuity, and (c) presume directionality.

There are many distinct models of learning and development, and their comprehensive discussion is outside of the frame of this book. Here we present only one of the many developmental models, stressing its potential relevance to the issues of measuring change in dynamic testing.

The general growth model (van Geert 1995) indicates that the change in a developing skill (i.e., one that is being learned or acquired), such as linear syllogistic reasoning, depends on (a) a growth parameter (e.g., indicators of a child's ability to reason deductively), (b) the current state of the growth process (e.g., the degree of familiarity with linear-syllogism problems), and (c) a set of scaffolding factors immediately available to the child (with factors ranging from motivational to instrumental scaffolding).

These "contributors" to growth can occur in a number of combinations so they can explain various types of growth. Among these various types of growth are classical learning curves, S-shaped learning curves, saltatory growth, and stepwise growth.

The classical learning curve assumes continuity of skill acquisition – the higher the ability of the child, and the more the child knows, the easier it is for the child to acquire new knowledge and the easier it is to find additional sources of knowledge. Thus, all three parameters contribute to the process of learning in a continuous (either linear or nonlinear–exponential) way. Translating these models into the language of dynamic testing, the gain in a skill observed at the posttest can be explained by the child's ability, the child's familiarity with the skill shown at the pretest, and the amount of help offered to the child at the intervention period of the testing. The assumption of this model is that the higher the ability level, the higher the level of familiarity with the skill, and the more scaffolding, the better the outcome.

S-shaped learning curves are considered to be quite characteristic of a number of learning and developmental processes (Fischer & Rose 1994). The modification of the learning curve into the S-shaped curve originates when there is an explicit maximum level to the skill that is being learned. S-shaped curves describe situations in which the learning in the middle of the process occurs at a much higher speed than at either the beginning or the end of the process. In its application to dynamic assessment, this model will assume a lack of response to the initial stages of training, rapid increase in skill at the middle stages of training, and a slowed-down response to intervention at the end of training. Once again, this model assumes the presence of the criterion in teaching for the skill.

Saltatory learning curves depict situations when, after an extended initial period with practically no increase at all, a sudden acceleration occurs so that the skill improves dramatically and performance achieves its maximum possible level (van der Maas & Molenaar 1992). Similarly, these models assume the presence of the maximum level of performance (the criterion) in the acquisition of the skill. In terms of patterns observed within the dynamic-testing paradigm, these curves can be observed when no improvement is initially shown in response to the intervention, and then suddenly the performance halts at its maximum possible level.

Finally, stepwise curves assume the presence of fluctuation in skill acquisition (e.g., correct solutions are intermixed with failures). However, the "unevenness" of the learning curve (marked by forward and backward movements) is such that correct solutions outweigh wrong ones. These types of curves might be of interest to those researchers in the field of dynamic assessment who work with the acquisition of skills, conditional on the acquisition of other skills (e.g., the skill of solving linear syllogisms depends on the capacity of working memory – if that capacity is low and few mental tools are available to the child, wavering performance on the syllogism tasks might be due, not to inability to solve syllogisms, but to the unstable functioning of working memory).

Obviously, these patterns fall into two general categories – the first and second types of learning curves describe continuous changes, whereas the third and fourth types describe discrete changes. All four types of growth can appear within the framework of dynamic testing, signifying changes from pre- to posttest. What are our means of quantifying these changes?

OLD APPROACHES TO MEASURING CHANGE

Conventional approaches to measuring change utilized primarily simple change scores, quantified as the difference between raw scores on pre- and posttests. Multiple problems arise with the use of simple change scores (e.g., Bereiter 1963). These problems are due to (1) the apparent lack of reliability of gain scores, (2) the presence of ceiling effects in subgroups of a sample, and (3) the disturbance of the equal-interval scale assumption encountered at the higher and lower ends of ability distributions with regard to the quantification of gain (i.e., when raw difference scores [gain scores] obtained at the lower and higher ends of the ability distribution are compared, the equality of raw scores does not translate into the equality in latent ability gains).

The first and most apparent problem of gain scores is their lack of reliability. Specifically, it has been shown that the reliability of a gain score is substantially impacted by the relative standard deviations of the test in a given sample, the placement of the test on the ability distribution, the distribution of item difficulty in the test, and a number of other factors. Interestingly, the reliability of change scores has been found to increase whereas the correlation between the pre- and posttest measures decreases. The paradoxical nature of this link is in that the decreasing correlation between the two measures of the same trait indicates low reliabilities of at least one of the two measures. Moreover, simple measures of change tend to correlate (spuriously!) negatively with the pretest indicators, suggesting the presence of a negative bias.

Second, the ceiling effect often originates when the same test is administered twice, at the pretest (when the test tends to be more difficult because it is more novel) and the posttest (when the test tends to be easier because it is more familiar). The issue here is that high-ability students often perform "well enough" at both pretest and posttest to demonstrate ceiling effects and, correspondingly, zero or near-zero gains. The trouble is that, when those zero (or near-zero) gains are interpreted in group data analyses and researchers consider only arithmetical data, not making an allowance for ceiling effect, the two most frequent interpretations are that (1) the particular intervention failed because a group of highly able children did not show any gain, or (2) the scores of the less able increased faster than those of more able. There are at least two explanations for these "no-gain" (or "slow-gain") findings that deserve serious consideration. The first explanation is that the trained sample contained a group of children who possessed the skill targeted by the training (a high-ability group of children), the training did not benefit these children at all, and therefore the training was useless to them. The second explanation is that the higher-ability children did benefit from the training, not in terms of obtaining better scores, but rather in terms of improving their strategies of problem solving. In sum, due to the frequent presence of a ceiling effect in intervention data, the group of high-ability nongainers should be analyzed with particular caution.

Finally, the nature of the scale on which change is measured is not well understood. It is clear, however, that the meaning of scale units is not constant along the continuum of simple change. In other words, the meaning of a given level of change can be different at different levels of ability). Specifically, a relatively small change obtained when performance improves from a high level to an even higher level may have a different psychological meaning and result from a different psychological mechanism than the same small change from a low or a moderate score. The very presence of a ceiling effect in the data on the administration of the same test twice, at pretest and posttest, calls for ensuring that the tests administered at the pretest and posttest are easy enough and can distinguish students at the lower level of abilities (and show variability at the higher level of ability) and are difficult enough to distinguish students at the higher level of abilities (and show variability at the lower level of ability). The only arrangement that satisfies these two conditions is a careful assembly of the pre- and posttest items. Otherwise, the comparative quantification of gains in high- and low-ability populations is very difficult.

To illustrate, suppose that we used two different tests at pretest (an easier one and a harder one) and two different tests at posttest (an easier one and a harder one). Then, the higher-ability group might well show a very small pre- to posttest gain on the easier test (simply because they did very well on the pretest) and a huge gain on the harder test. An opposite effect might be observed for the lower-ability group. When the easier test was employed, the gain was huge, and when the harder test was employed, the gain was very small (i.e., the lower-ability individuals did badly on the harder test at the pretest, and they did badly again at the posttest). Thus, the interpretation of gains in higher- and lower-ability groups should take into account psychometric characteristics of the pre- and posttest items, specifically, the items' degree of difficulty and their discriminating power.

Much professional attention has been devoted to ways of compensating for these weaknesses in change scores (e.g., Cohen & Cohen 1975), but none of the procedures that has been developed has been universally accepted (see, e.g., Campbell & Kenny 1999; Ragosa, Grant, & Zimowski 1982). In an attempt to circumvent the weaknesses of simple change scores, researchers have tried to avoid using them. They stopped trying to quantify changes at the individual level and started to address the issue of quantifying change at the group level (Cronbach & Furby 1970). Yet, this strategy did not work – it has been shown that simple *t*-tests (Maxwell & Delaney 1985), tests of interaction effects (Embretson 1994, 1996), and complex growth-curve analyses (Embretson 1994) on classical test scores can produce biased results. Needless to say, the large majority of dynamic-testing applications are based on the classical theory approach.

Of the three problems discussed above, the third appears to be the most fundamental one. Apparently, this problem cannot be compensated for by means of the classical test theory approach, but it can be addressed by means of modern psychometric theories (Embretson & Reise 2000).

MODERN APPROACHES TO MEASURING CHANGE

Item response theory (IRT) and related applications (e.g., Embretson & Reise 2000; Hambleton, Swaminathan, & Rogers 1991) constitute a rapidly developing field of research. IRT was introduced to the field of measurement in the early 1950s (Lord 1952), gained popularity in the 1960s, 1970s, and 1980s (e.g., Lord 1980; Wright & Stone 1979), and today is the major tool in test development (e.g., Embretson & Reise 2000; Hambleton, Swaminathan, & Roger 1991). It has been demonstrated that IRT has many theoretical and practical advantages (Hambleton & Slater 1997). The distinguishing features of IRT are (1) the invariance property of item and person parameters – i.e., properties of the items remain stable in the population in which this item has been developed and applied, and the person's ability level can be accurately estimated by a variety of items of various degrees of difficulty; (2) reporting items and examinees on a common reporting scale – i.e., a person is measured in the context of his or her interaction with the item so that ability estimates vary as a function of both the person's responses and the properties of the item; (3) the capability of providing a measure of precision for each ability score – i.e., ability levels can be equally accurately determined by different items; and (4) the presence of item information functions – i.e., the ability to determine the contributions of items to measurement precision along the ability continuum.

There are many IRT models (Hambleton et al. 1991), but they can all be roughly divided into two large classes: unidimensional and multidimensional IRT models. Among the unidimensional models, the Rasch (1960/1980) model is the most well- known and well-studied one. In this model, item success/failure is predicted from the simple difference between the item's difficulty and the person's ability based on the logistic distribution in which the parameters are exponents. In other words, Rasch connected item difficulty and the probability of an item's being solved correctly as it is attempted by an individual of a certain level of ability (or skill). Thus, the general goal of the Rasch model is to provide a probabilistic interpretation of skill acquisition along a scale of expertise. More complex unidimensional models consider additional item properties (e.g., an item's capacity to discriminate different levels of ability or its susceptibility to guessing).

Multidimensional IRT models assume that test items are complex tasks requiring the recruitment of multiple abilities (either simultaneously or sequentially). In other words, the item-solving probability is determined by many abilities rather than one.

Measuring Change under the Assumption of Continuity

The assumption of continuity implies that any subsequent step in developing expertise is an uninterrupted continuation of the previous step. In other words, increases or decreases between pre- and posttest are based on gradual processes. Under the assumption of continuity, the observed gradual changes can be both linear and nonlinear. The concept of "linearity" refers to simple proportionality. In other words, if the change in a trait is proportional to the amount of training, then a change is a linear function of training. Correspondingly, the concept of "nonlinearity" refers to the change occurring in a nonproportional fashion with respect to the amount of training received. IRT models exist for quantifying change for continuous linear and nonlinear growth curves.

Several IRT models have been adopted for the purposes of dynamic testing. One such example is the multidimensional Rasch-family model for learning and change (MRMLS, Embertson 1991). This model includes a number of estimable parameters, among which are initial level of ability and indexes of modifiability (as indicated by changes between successive evaluations of ability), and item difficulty indexes.

Consider the following illustration (Schmidt-McCollam, 1998). A dynamic test of spatial visualization ability was administered at three time points to adults, divided into older and younger groups. The following indicators of ability were available: (1) base-level ability, (2) indicators of ability after physical analogues training, and (3) indicators of ability after verbal–analytical training. The point of the research was to compare the initial levels of ability and indices of modifiability in younger and older adults. It was found that although the younger adults showed higher levels of ability at the baseline (pretest), the indicators of modifiability did not differ across ages.

Dynamic Models of Change

A concept relevant for our further discussion is the neo-Piagetian concept of mental capacity, defined as the maximum number of things or aspects that an individual is able to attend to simultaneously (Case 1992; Pascual-Leone & Ijaz 1989). Mental capacity is intimately related to cognitive stage-based development and is purported to serve as an indicator of the speed and quality of this development (i.e., an indicator of learning potential). The acquisition of mental capacity takes place in the form of mastering different types of schemes (e.g., figurative-declarative, operative-procedural, and executive). To measure mental capacity, Pascual-Leone and colleagues developed a set of tasks (so-called M-capacity tasks). One of these tasks is the Figural Intersections Task (FIT). In the FIT, the child is presented with a set of simple figures and a complex figure that includes intercrossing simple figures. The child is asked to identify all simple figures that are included in the complex figure, and then to place a dot inside the complex figure so that the dot is simultaneously inside all the simple figures. A similar task is found on the Cattell Culture-Fair Test of g.

In the application of the FIT and other mental capacities, the point of interest to our discussion is the administration protocol. Prior to testing, all participants are taught all mental schemes that are thought to be required for successful task performance (e.g., they are taught how to find simple figures in a complex figure and how to identify the placement of the dot). Thus, the assumption is that the participant has obtained all relevant skills prior to testing, so that the indicator of learning potential is his or her ability to manipulate those learned skills. According to Pascual-Leone, M-capacity can be symbolized by the formula $e + k$, where e is the child's "given" potential, which is fully expressed by the age of two, and k is the acquired mental capacity, which grows by increments of one unit every other year from three years of age until adolescence. This definition of M-capacity permits the formulation of an assumption that the rate of k-growth can be approximated by the outcome of practicing within one testing session.

Pascual-Leone and his collaborators have shown that M-capacity can be assessed in multiple domains (e.g., language, memory) and have claimed that this assessed M-capacity can be assumed to be the same available for use in any content domain (Pascual-Leone & Ijaz 1989). The proponents of M-capacity tasks argue that they maximize certain advantages of dynamic testing (e.g., they are relatively insensitive to the participant's previous knowledge base) and minimize its certain disadvantages (e.g., they offer a measurement scale with known properties instead of dealing with change indicators).

It is important to note that Pascual-Leone and his colleagues, using IRT analyses, investigated the linearity and continuity assumption for the acquisition of M-capacity. Specifically, Pennings and Hessels (1996) scored figural M-capacity items for mental demand from the stimulus properties, taking into account the following links: (1) the link between item difficulty and mental capacity, and (2) the link between age and mental capacity. A Rasch-model scaling of these items generally supported the assumption of Pascual-Leone that M-capacity increases linearly with age. However, when the assumption of continuity was analyzed, it was concluded that M-capacity develops in a discrete fashion (Pascual-Leone & Baillargeon 1994). The argument that was put forward in the explanation of this finding is that M-capacity is an indicator of the number of mental schemes the individual has mastered, and this mastery occurs in a discrete fashion. Thus, it has been argued (Pascual-Leone & Johnson in press) that a comprehensive M-capacity theory of acquiring cognitive change (in the process of skill acquisition) can be constructed so that every observed change can be predicted in terms of the type and quantity of the mastered schemes.

The finding of Pascual-Leone and his colleagues stressing that acquisition of a skill might have a discrete nature is not unique in the field. On the contrary, there is a large body of literature that discusses the discontinuous nature of development. Here we briefly review some major assumptions of this literature, with the aim of summarizing those of its aspects that can be relevant to the discussion of the issue of quantifying change.

Measuring Change under the Assumption of Discontinuity

A number of investigators view the developmental process as a dynamic one, applying the knowledge of nonlinear systems that originated in other sciences to the science of developmental psychology (e.g., van Geert 1998). Nonlinear systems are characterized by sudden changes that qualitatively change the trait of interest. The process of skill acquisition in this context is viewed discontinuously, so that, in a time sequence, a fairly slow continuous process of building up skill components is interrupted by abrupt events of skill mastery. Subsequent to such abrupt changes, nonlinear systems tend to stabilize temporarily, converging into a so-called attractor state, where, once again, slow continuous processes can unfold (e.g., Wimmers et al. 1998). Having stabilized, with time, the system becomes autonomous. Then, once again, the period of structural stability gets interrupted by an abrupt change in organization, with the emergence of a qualitatively different mode of stability.

The general assumption of these models is that, under the (mostly) stable pressure of independent variables (such as biological foundation [e.g., genetic makeup] or environmental context [e.g., educational patterns, SES]), dependent (cognitive, behavioral, and social–emotional) variables tend to reach certain stable states (attractors). However, reflecting changes in independent variables, attractors can change suddenly. In other words, if the attractor stability is challenged by perturbation (in the language of this book, if the relevant stability of a cognitive skill is challenged by an appropriate intervention), the skill can be forced to fall apart or to be transformed into a different (higher-order) skill in a discontinuous manner. The claim of methodological approaches based on nonlinear dynamic systems theory is that there are well-defined ways permitting the establishment of linkages between changes in independent variables and changes in attractors.

To illustrate, consider as an example syllogistic reasoning. Supposedly, there is a syllogism construction device that takes some previous outputs of reasoning development (e.g., the child's skill to perform a conjunction with the logical operator *and*) and an external intervention (e.g., instruction on how to solve linear syllogisms) as its input. Thus, the adequate intervention transfers the first stage of reasoning development into a new stage of reasoning development (knowing how to solve linear syllogisms). This transformation, according to the dynamic systems approach, can be of a discontinuous nature. However, after the skill has been mastered in principle, each subsequent intervention will strengthen the reasoning but will keep it within the attractor stage, not changing the principle of finding the solution to a syllogism task. Currently the dynamic systems approach, in spite of its broadening applications, occupies a minor position in developmental psychology. An example of such application is a dynamic model of motor development (Thelen 1992; Thelen & Smith 1994, 1998).

Understandably, these models of development have attracted the attention of researchers interested in dynamic testing. The explanation is simple: The principles of dynamic systems – the iterative nature of operations or mechanisms and the existence of various attractors – can help reformulate problems previously encountered by dynamic testing approaches. This type of developmental model permits more accurate modeling of the temporal course and the time scale of development. Specifically, the very idea of dynamic testing is based on the child's experiencing new cognitive stages in collaboration with the teacher (instructor, coach), and then growing up to these stages as a result of these "learning encounters" (the term of van Geert 1997). The issues here are that neither does a child reach to these new cognitive "masteries" (or levels of expertise) in a linear fashion, nor does the progression of these masteries correspond directly to the amount of instruction the child receives. As a result, an accurate time estimate will be related to the amount of time each learning encounter takes (e.g., how quickly a child can master a certain skill) and to the amount of time between learning encounters (e.g., how these learning encounters should be spaced to maximize developmental outcomes). Notice that both between- and within-learning encounter times might vary from child to child and from task to task, calling for applications of highly specialized statistical approaches.

One of the models used for uncovering discontinuous change in the development of psychological processes is the model of transition in catastrophe theory (Thom 1975). Catastrophe theory is a mathematical theory allowing the detection of phase shifts in dynamic systems (i.e., a system in which time-based change is inherent). The catastrophe (or transformation) stage of a dynamic system is defined by eight necessary, mathematically defined indicators (Gilmore 1981; van der Maas & Molenaar 1992). A number of these indicators, specifically, bimodality of the trait distribution, inaccessibility of the skill, sudden jump, anomalous variance, and critical slowing down, have been studied in the context of developmental research (e.g., the development of analogical reasoning, Hosenfeld, van der Maas, & van den Boom 1997b).

Yet another example of the nonlinear growth model is expressed in the form of the so-called Verhulst model (van Geert 1991, 1993, 1994). Here, the variable whose change in time is observed is referred to as a "grower"; growers take off from some arbitrary level (seed) and then grow (positively, increase, or negatively, decrease) to reach some equilibrium state (which in turn can change as an outcome of some disturbance). This model has been explored in the domain of language development (Ruthland & van Geert 1998).

Although there has been a limited number of specific applications of the models described above in the psychological literature, researchers have found many indicators of bimodality (separating those who have and have not mastered the skills) in developmental data in performance on tasks such as conservation, classification, the understanding of horizontality and verticality, and analogical reasoning (Hosenfeld, van de Maas, & van den Boom 1997a; Thomas 1989; Thomas & Lohaus 1993; Thomas & Turner 1991). Because a major goal of dynamic testing is to offer the child a cognitive tool to master and then to see whether the child can or cannot master this tool, some of the data collected within the dynamic-testing paradigm are bimodal because two distributions are created – one of children who master the tool and one of children who do not. One of the apparent examples of such bimodality comes from the research of Budoff: It is the bimodality of skill mastery that he attempted to reflect in his distinction between gainers and nongainers.

To illustrate the relevance of these ideas to the field of dynamic testing, consider a simple and hypothetical case. Suppose that a theory hypothesizes that there are two kinds of students – those who benefit from instruction and those who do not. (In fact, our own view is that students benefit in varying degrees.) Suppose a given dynamic test consists of four items, each of which is designed to show whether the student has benefited from a specific set of instructions and has improved his or her performance from the pretest to the posttest. Those who benefit from the instruction will show it by improving their performance on each single item. This situation can be represented by the pattern 1111, where 1 stands for "improved." Those who have not benefited from the instruction will get every item wrong. This situation can be represented by the pattern 0000, where 0 stands for "not improved." Unfortunately, items are almost certainly not perfect (e.g., some posttest items may be much harder for the test-takers than are many pretest items). Moreover, students' responses to these items may not reflect their true level of abilities (e.g., some students who have mastered the rule and benefited from the instruction may not show improved performance on a specific item); we may expect a few students to fail to demonstrate better performance due to carelessness, fatigue, misunderstanding, less interest, and so on. In addition, there may be students who, having not mastered the rule discussed in instruction, may show improved performance accidentally, by guessing or just by luck. Thus, as a result of the imperfect nature of the items as well as fluctuations in students' performance, we will see patterns different from the two "perfect" patterns described above. Specifically, assuming error of measurement and fluctuations in individual performance, all 16 patterns (1110, 1100, 1000, and so on) are possible.

If the whole spectrum of profiles is encountered, there are two procedural options. We can assume that the learning trait we are trying to quantify is a continuous trait. We then can place our students on the corresponding scale, interpreting their summary scores as indicators of their position (0, 1, 2, 3, or 4, based on the number of items on which the students show an improvement). Alternatively, we can trust our theoretical model, assuming the presence of two major classes of students – those who benefit from instruction and those who do not – but presume that erroneous factors such as those mentioned above may result in the manifestation of other classes. Thus, due to the manifestation of error, the true class of a student is not directly observed and, therefore, is not easily detectable, but needs to be inferred through an analysis of the pattern of right and wrong answers. This true class is referred to as the latent (unobserved) class. Latent classes can be detected with the help of computer programs.

Thus, the application of dynamic systems models in the field of dynamic testing might help us to formalize and understand nonlinear effects essential to situations of intervention. Most dynamic testing models (and corresponding data-analytic procedures) are based on the assumption of linearity – that is, they suppose that the effect is proportional to the magnitude of the input of some controlling variables (the better the intervention, the better the outcome). However, there are many accounts of observations when an intervention leads to proportional effects only up to a certain point (or starting from a certain point), but then, as (or before) a threshold is reached, the impact of the intervention may change both qualitatively and quantitatively. The point here is that nonlinear effects of intervention and the nonlinear nature of parameters are often ignored in the context of traditional group-difference-based approaches to dynamic testing data. For example, an impact of standardized training might be especially substantial for those children who are close to the acquisition of the skill, but very small for those children who are far away from mastery of the skill (van der Maas & Molenaar 1992). Specifically, if the distance to the "mastery point" is short, training can introduce enough dynamics into the system (instability, expressed as increased variability in performance, in terms of van der Maas & Molenaar 1992) so that transition to the mastery can occur.

Moreover, the impact of the intervention within the dynamic testing paradigm might be modeled as a nonlinear dynamic system where complex dynamic forms can be realized from relatively simple equations (Glass & Mackay 1988; May 1976; Newell & Molenaar 1998). The overarching goal of these analyses might be the identification of the relevant developmental variables that are, or may be, acting as critical variables in the shaping of the dynamics of the developing system over time. Two assumptions underlie these analyses: (1) the mastery of the skill is the product of the coalescing of many constraints to action imposed by critical variables (e.g., Newell 1986), (2) small qualitative changes in critical variables may result in large-scale qualitative changes in the emerging skills, and (3) the stability-transformation dynamics of the emergence and the transformation of skills are linked to the interplay between sets of cooperating and competing critical variables.

So, what are the means available to the professional who is interested in quantifying the discrete changes encountered in dynamic testing?

Latent Class Analysis (LCA)

Some theorists have argued that the ultimate purpose of dynamic testing is to see whether the tested individual benefits from instruction. According to this point of view, the indicators of gains are not so important; what is important is whether an individual gains or not. This point of view is especially popular among some developmentalists interested in studying the development of competencies and the acquisition of skills. In other words, what is important is not how much better the child solves the tasks at the posttest, but rather whether the child solves the task better at posttest than he or she did at pretest.

Latent class analysis (LCA) provides effective statistical tools to test for multimodality that require quite unproblematic assumptions. As a data-analytic technique, LCA can be compared to cluster analysis, in that both search for underlying groups or types. However, LCA has a number of advantages, including maximum-likelihood estimation, well-behaved statistics, and model flexibility.

LCA is a member of a family of multivariate analysis methods (log-linear models, factor analysis, latent trait models, and cluster analysis; Rindskopf 1987) that permits modeling noncontinuous variables measured at either the nominal or the ordinal level of measurement. Moreover, this approach does not make assumptions of linearity and permits modeling nonlinear relationships (e.g., nonlinear developmental transformations of cognitive performance and behavior). There are two types of variables distinguished: latent variables (unobserved ability or unobserved behavioral type) and manifest variables (specific responses to a set of items or specific patterns of development). This distinction provides a method for determining whether relationships within a set of observed measures are due to some unmeasured explanatory variable – specifically, whether the level of the latent variable explains the pattern of responses to the manifest variables (McCutcheon 1987). The latent-class analyses result in the estimation of two types of parameters – the unconditional probabilities of being in a latent class (e.g., gainers versus nongainers) and the conditional probabilities of making a particular response or demonstrating a particular behavior, given membership in a certain latent class (e.g., the acquisition of mastery).

The Guttman's Scalogram Model and the Saltus Model

Guttman's scalogram analysis (1944, 1950) was initially derived from analyses of attitude questionnaires. The techniques assume that there is one item per level of trait. The assignment of a respondent to a trait level is carried out as follows: (1) based on a scalable response – a participant is at level n if he or she has provided correct responses to all items below and at the level n and has failed the items at all other levels starting at the level $n + 1$; (2) based on a nonscalable response – a participant is not at level n if his or her response does not follow (1). Thus, the major assumption (and the major shortcoming) of the Guttman model is the notion that only scalable responses are usable in a scale showing the point of the skill acquisition at which the child is. Although such a linear picture of skill acquisition has been widely applied to developmental data (e.g., Siegel 1971; Wohtwill 1960), a number of researchers (e.g., Kofsky 1966) have argued that often the process of skill acquisition is probabilistic (due to both errors of measurement and the discontinuous nature of development), assuming discontinuities in the mastery of the skill's components.

The Saltus (saltus is Latin for "leap") developmental model can be viewed as both an extension of Guttman's scalogram model (1944) and the Rasch model (1966). Similarly to the Rasch model, the Saltus connects the item difficulty and its probability of being solved correctly through the expertise level of the respondent, but it also conditions this probability on the item level. The presence of the level in this equation indicates the assumption that all members of the group who are at this level of performance will apply the strategies typical at this level consistently across all items. The Saltus model is designed to measure state changes by using multiple tasks at each of various developmental levels, so that it can register so-called first-order changes (i.e., discontinuous leaps in a single ability) and second-order changes (i.e., discontinuous leaps in at least two abilities). The innovation of this model lies in the addition to the scalogram model and the model of multiple tasks a probabilistic framework (as introduced by the IRT model incorporating parameters for subjects, tasks, and levels). Thus, the parameter estimates obtained by Saltus modeling have been viewed as a solution to a Rasch model with a special set of constraints (Wilson 1989). Specifically, this set of constraints links performances in certain groups (i.e., groups at different levels of expertise) on certain item types, in which the person's group classification (i.e., level of expertise) is determined from the data (Fischer 1983a, 1983b, 1987).

The Mixed Population Rasch Model

Rost (1990) developed a mixed population Rasch model (MIRA) that combines IRT with latent class analysis. In this model, a person is characterized by only one trait level (the IRT part), but the meaning of the trait level depends on the class to which the person belongs (the latent-class-analysis part). Consequently, item difficulties are scored differently, depending on latent-class membership.

Consider the following illustration of the relevance of the MIRA model to dynamic testing applications. Supposedly, items are presented in two forms, with listen-to and read-yourself instructions. It appears that items' difficulties vary depending on the format of instruction (e.g., on item latent class). In addition, the relative likelihood of a student's wrong/right response pattern under the two formats of instruction determines the probability of the student's preference of a mode of instruction (some students learn better when instructions are explained to them, whereas others learn better when instructions are delivered to them in written form). Once having applied this model, a dynamic tester may detect the preferred mode of instruction of the testee.

The General Component Latent-Trait Model

The general component latent-trait model allows researchers to apply a process–decomposition approach to the ability task. For example, a cognitive task can be broken down, in equation form, into procedural contributors of its level of difficulty (e.g., a Raven's item's difficulty level can be decomposed into difficulty attributable to working memory and difficulty attributable to sequential processing). Then these decomposed items can be administered to children assessed by dynamic tests on two different occasions (pre- and posttest). The results can demonstrate componential improvements in different abilities in different latent classes of children.

CONCLUSION

In this chapter, we have attempted to bring to the attention of researchers and others interested in applications of dynamic testing a number of methodological issues regarding the quantification of change. The problem of quantifying change has been long discussed among researchers interested in developmental changes, but it has not been central to the work of the methodologists interested in dynamic testing. It appears to us that there is much to learn and utilize from modern psychometrics and developmental psychology in our attempts to push forward the development of the field of dynamic testing. The diverse studies presented above only suggest possible directions, but they point to several paths of interest for methodologists in the field of dynamic assessment. Moreover, the applications briefly described in this chapter are supported by publicly available pieces of software (e.g., Embretson & Reise 2000).

Epilogue

We started this book by stating that the field of dynamic testing, as a result of a number of historical and ideological circumstances, has experienced insufficient critical attention from the scientific community. We have suggested a number of dimensions along which dynamic-testing studies can be reviewed and compared, and we have conducted such a comparison. We have arrived at three conclusions.

First, as of today, it is difficult to argue that this approach has proven its usefulness and has shown distinct advantages over traditional static testing, relative to the resources that need to be expended. Second, certain requirements, once met, will make dynamic-testing studies more compelling and, correspondingly, will make the field of dynamic testing stronger and its data more compelling. These requirements are of two types – macro and micro. The macro-requirements are related to theoretical issues of defining dynamic testing as an important and worthwhile tradition in the psychology of testing, with its own goals, methods, and applied techniques. The micro-requirements are specific to empirical issues and underscore the necessity of conducting studies that involve larger participant populations, validating dynamic-testing results against educational or professional criteria, and replicating results from different laboratories that independently use developed methodologies to arrive at similar findings. Third, the work on dynamic testing might benefit, both theoretically and methodologically, from adopting the perspective of abilities as developing expertise. It might also benefit from taking into account the different styles with which people think and learn (Sternberg 1997b).

The field of dynamic testing has grown up largely out of dissatisfaction with conventional static testing. But it is important to realize that static and dynamic testing are, to some extent, on a continuum rather than representing two total different perspectives. For one thing, many of the dynamic tests are adaptations of tests that originally have been used in static form. For another, static tests themselves involve learning. As one takes a static test, or when one takes a test (or an alternate form of a test) for the second time, learning can occur. Jan-Eric Gustafsson (2000) has even collected data suggesting that such learning takes place. The learning may be self- rather than other-guided. But it is learning nevertheless. Thus, dynamic testing makes explicit what may be, to some extent, implicit in some static tests. Rather than viewing static and dynamic tests as competitive, greater progress may be made by a synthesis of the two traditions that builds on the strengths of each.

In sum, work in the field of dynamic testing has suggested interesting paradigms and ideas as well as promising findings. The question is whether this potential can be realized in a branch of psychological testing characterized by consistently converging results and techniques that provide information over and above the data collected by conventional tests. We believe that dynamic testing will ultimately meet these challenges and will prove to be a valuable resource to the psychological profession and to the world.

References

Altman, D. G., & Andersen, P. K. (1989). Bootstrap investigation of the stability of a Cox regression model. *Statistics in Medicine, 8,* 771–783.

Amabile, T. M. (1996). *Creativity in context.* Boulder, CO: Westview.

Anastasi, A., & Urbina, S. (1997). *Psychological testing* (7ᵗʰ ed.). Upper Saddle River, NJ: Prentice-Hall.

Ashman, A. F. (1985). Process-based interventions for retarded students. *Mental Retardation and Learning Disability Bulletin, 13,* 62–74.

Ashman, A. F. (1992). Process-based instruction: Integrating testing and instruction. In H. C. Haywood & D. Tzuriel (Eds.), *Interactive testing* (pp. 375–396). New York: Springer-Verlag.

Baltes, M. M., Kühl, K. P., & Sowarka, D. (1992). Testing for limits of cognitive reserve capacity: A promising strategy for early diagnosis of dementia? *Journal of Gerontology, 47,* 165–167.

Bandura, A. (1977). Self-efficacy: Toward a unifying theory of behavioral change. *Psychological Review, 84,* 181–215.

Bandura, A. (1996). *Self-efficacy: The exercise of control.* New York: Freeman.

Barr, P. M., & Samuels, M. T. (1988). Dynamic testing of cognitive and affective factors contributing to learning difficulties in adults: A case study approach. *Professional Psychology: Research and Practice, 19,* 6–13.

Beckman, J. F., & Guthke, J. (1995). Complex problem solving, intelligence status and learning ability. In J. Funke & P. Frensch (Eds.), *Complex problem solving: The European perspective* (pp. 177–200). Hillsdale, NJ: Erlbaum.

Beckman, J. R., & Guthke, J. (1999). *Psychodiagnostik des schlussfolgernden Denkens (Assessing reasoning ability).* Göttingen: Hogrefe.

Bereiter, C. (1963). Some persisting dilemmas in the measurement of change. In C. W. Harris (Ed.), *Problems in measuring change* (pp. 3–20). Madison: University of Wisconsin Press.

Berry, J. W. (1974). Radical cultural relativism and the concept of intelligence. In J. W. Berry & P. R. Dasen (Eds.), *Culture and cognition: Readings in cross-cultural psychology* (pp. 225–229). London: Methuen.

Berry, J. W., Poortinga, Y. H., Segall, M. H., & Dasen, P. R. (1992). *Cross-cultural psychology: Research and applications.* New York: Cambridge University Press.

Bethge, H., Carlson, J. S., & Wiedl, K. H. (1982). The effects of dynamic testing procedures on Raven Matrices performance, visual search behavior, test anxiety and test orientation. *Intelligence, 6,* 89–97.

Binet, A. (1909). *Les idées modernes sur les enfants* [*Modern concepts concerning children*]. Paris: Flammarion.

Binet, A., & Simon, T. (1905). Méthodes nouvelles pour le diagnostic du niveau intellectuel des anormaux. *L'Année Psychologique, 11,* 191–336.

Birnbaum, A. (1968). Some latent trait models and their use in inferring an examinee's ability. In F. M. Lord and M. R. Novick, *Statistical theories of mental test scores* (pp. 397–479). Reading, MA: Addison-Wesley.

Blagg, N. (1991). *Can we teach intelligence?* Hillsdale, NJ: Lawrence Erlbaum.

Bodrova, E., & Leong, D. J. (1996). *Tools of the mind. The Vygotskian approach to early childhood education.* Englewood Cliffs, NJ: Prentice Hall.

Bolig, E. E., & Day, J. D. (1993). Dynamic testing and giftedness: The promise of assessing training responsiveness. *Roeper Review, 16,* 110–113.

Bollen, K. A. (1989). *Structural equations with latent variables.* New York: Wiley.

Borland, J. H., & Wright, L. (1994). Identifying young, potentially gifted, economically disadvantaged students. *Gifted Child Quarterly, 38,* 164–171,

Bradley, T. B. (1983). Remediation of cognitive deficits: A critical appraisal of the Feuerstein model. *Journal of Mental Deficiency Research, 27,* 79–92.

Bransford, J. D., Stein, B. S., Arbitman-Smith, R., & Vye, N. J. (1985). Improving thinking and learning skills: An analysis of three approaches. In J. Segal, S. F. Chipman, & R. Glaser (Eds.), *Thinking and learning skills: Relating instruction to research* (Vol. 1, pp. 133–208). Hillsdale, NJ: Erlbaum.

Bronfenbrenner, U. (1977). Toward an experimental ecology of human development. *American Psychologist, 32,* 513–551.

Brown, A. L., Bransford, J. D., Ferrara, R. A., & Campione, J. C. (1983). Learning, remembering, and understanding. In J. H. Flavell & E. M. Markman (Eds.), *Handbook of child psychology (Vol. III).* New York: Wiley.

Brown, A. L., & Campione, J. C. (1981). Inducing flexible thinking: A problem of access. In M. Friedman, J. P. Das, & N. O'Connor (Eds.), *Intelligence and learning.* New York: Plenum Press.

Brown, A. L., Campione, J. C., Webber, L. S., & McGilly, K. (1992). Interactive learning environments: A new look at assessment and instruction. In B. R. Gifford & M. C. O'Connor (Eds.), *Changing assessments.* Boston: Kluwer.

Brown, A. L., & Ferrara, R. A. (1985). Diagnosing zones of proximal development. In J. V. Wertsch (Ed.), *Culture, communication, and cognition: Vygotskian perspectives* (pp. 273–305). New York: Cambridge University Press.

Brown, A. L., & French, L. (1979). The zone of potential development: Implications for intelligence testing in the year 2000. *Intelligence, 3,* 255–273.

Brownell, M. T., Mellard, D. F., & Deshler, D. D. (1993). Differences in the learning and transfer performance between students with learning disabilities and other low-achieving students on problem-solving tasks. *Learning Disability Quarterly, 16,* 138–156.

Büchel, F. P., Scharnhorst, U. (1993). The Learning Potential Testing Device (*LPAD*): Discussion of theoretical and methodological problems. In J. H. M. Hamers, K. Sijtsma, & A. J. J. M. Ruijssenaars (Eds.), *Learning potential testing* (pp. 83–111). Amsterdam: Swets & Zeitlinger.

Büchel, F. P., Schlatter, C., & Scharnhorst, U. (1997). Training and assessment of analogical reasoning in students with severe learning difficulties. *Educational and Child Psychology, 14,* 83–94.

Buckingham, B. R. (1921). Intelligence and its measurement: A symposium. *Journal of Educational Psychology, 12,* 271–275.

Budoff, M. (1967). Learning potential among institutionalized young adult retardates. *American Journal of Mental Deficiency, 72,* 404–411.

Budoff, M. (1968). Learning potential as a supplementary testing procedure. In J. Hellmuth (Ed.), *Learning disorders* (Vol. 3) (pp. 295–343). Seattle, WA: Special Child.

Budoff, M. (1969). Learning potential: A supplementary procedure for assessing the ability to reason. *Seminar in Psychiatry, 1,* 278–290.

Budoff, M. (1970). Learning potential: A supplementary procedure for assessing the ability to reason. *Acta Paedopsychiatrics, 37,* 293–309. (ERIC Document Reproduction Service No. ED 048 703).

Budoff, M. (1975). *Learning potential among educable retarded pupils.* Final report, Research Institute for Educational Problems, 29 Ware Street, Cambridge, MA.

Budoff, M. (1987a). The validity of learning potential assessment. In C. S. Lidz (Ed.) *Dynamic assessment: An interactional approach to evaluating learning potential* (pp. 52–81). New York: The Guilford Press.

Budoff, M. (1987b). Measures for assessing learning potential. In C. S. Lidz (Ed.) *Dynamic assessment: An interactional approach to evaluating learning potential* (pp. 173–195). New York: The Guilford Press.

Budoff, M., & Corman, L. (1974). Demographic and psychometric factors related to improved performance on the Kohs learning-potential procedure. *American Journal of Mental Deficiency, 78,* 578–585.

Budoff, M., & Corman, L. (1976). Effectiveness of a learning potential procedure in improving problem-solving skills to retarded and nonretarded children. *American Journal of Mental Deficiency, 81,* 260–264.

Budoff, M., Corman, L., & Gimon, A. (1976). An educational test of learning potential testing with Spanish-speaking youth. *Interamerican Journal of Psychology, 10,* 13–24.

Budoff, M. & Friedman, M. (1964). "Learning potential" as a testing approach to the adolescent mentally retarded. *Journal of Consulting Psychology, 28,* 434–439.

Budoff, M., & Hamilton, J. (1976). Optimizing test performance of the moderately and severely mentally retarded. *American Journal of Mental Deficiency, 81,* 49–57.

Budoff, M., Meskin, J., & Harrison, R. G. (1971). An educational test of the learning potential hypothesis. *American Journal of Mental Deficiency, 76,* 159–169.

Budoff, M., & Pagell, W. (1968). Learning potential and rigidity in the adolescent mentally retarded. *Journal of Abnormal Psychology, 73,* 479–486.

Burns, M. S. (1991). Comparison of two types of dynamic testing and static testing with young children. *The International Journal of Dynamic Testing and Instruction, 2,* 29–42.

Burns, M. S. (1996). Dynamic assessment: Easier said than done. In M. Luther,

E. Cole, & P. Gamlin. *Dynamic assessment for instruction: from theory to application* (pp. 182–187). North York, Canada: Captus Press, Inc.

Burns, M. S., Delclos, V. R., Vye, N. J., & Sloan, K. (1992). Changes in cognitive strategies in dynamic testing. *International Journal of Dynamic Testing and Instruction, 2*, 45–54.

Burns, M. S., Vye, N., Bransford, J., Delclos, V., & Ogan, T. (1987). Static and dynamic measures of learning in young handicapped children. *Diagnostique, 12(2)*, 59–73.

Campbell, D. T., & Fiske, D. W. (1959). Convergent and discriminant validation by the multitrait-multimethod matrix. *Psychological Bulletin, 56*, 81–105.

Campbell, D. T., & Kenny, D. A. (1999). *A primer on regression artifacts.* New York: Guilford Press.

Campione, J. C. (1989). Assisted testing: A taxonomy of approaches and an outline of strengths and weaknesses. *Journal of Learning Disabilities, 22*, 151–165.

Campione, J. C., & Brown, A. L. (1979). *Human intelligence.* Norwood, NJ: Albex.

Campione, J. C., & Brown, A. L. (1987). Linking dynamic testing with school achievement. In C. S. Lidz (Ed.), *Dynamic assessment: An interactional approach to evaluating learning potential* (pp. 82–115). New York: The Guilford Press.

Campione, J. C., Brown, A., & Bryant, N. (1985). Individual differences in learning and memory. In R. J. Sternberg (Ed.), *Human abilities: An information-processing approach* (pp. 103–126). New York: Freeman.

Campione, J. C., Brown, A. L., Ferrara, R. A., Jones, R. S., & Steinberg, E. (1985). Differences between retarded and non-retarded children in transfer following equivalent learning performance: Breakdowns in flexible use of information. *Intelligence, 9*, 297–315.

Carlson, J. S. (1989). Advances in research on intelligence: The dynamic assessment approach. *Mental Retardation and Learning Disability Bulletin, 17*, 1–20.

Carlson, J.S. (Ed.) (1992). *Cognition and educational practice: An international perspective.* Greenwich, CT: JAI Press, Inc.

Carlson, J. S. (personal communication, Stellenbosch, South Africa, September 10, 1997).

Carlson, J. S., & Wiedl, K. H. (1976). The factorial analysis of perceptual and abstract reasoning abilities in tests of concrete operational thought. *Educational and Psychological Measurement, 36*, 1015–1019.

Carlson, J. S., & Weidl, K. H. (1978). Use of testing-the-limits procedures in the testing of intellectual capabilities in children with learning difficulties. *American Journal of Mental Deficiency, 11*, 559–564.

Carlson, J. S., & Wiedl, K. H. (1979). Toward a differential testing approach: Testing-the-limits employing the Raven matrices. *Intelligence, 3*, 323–344.

Carlson, J. S., & Wiedl, K. H. (1980). Applications of a dynamic testing approach: Empirical results and theoretical formulations. *Zeitschrift für Differentielle und Diagnostische Psychologie, 4*, 303–318.

Carlson, J. S., & Wiedl, K. H. (1992a). Principles of dynamic testing: The application of a specific model. *Learning and Individual Differences, 4*, 153–166.

Carlson, J. S., & Wiedl, K. H. (1992b). The dynamic testing of intelligence. In H. C. Haywood & D. Tzuriel (Eds.) *Interactive testing* (pp. 167–186). New York: Springer-Verlag.

Carlson, J. S., & Wiedl, K. H. (2000). The validity of dynamic assessment. In C. S. Lidz & J. G. Elliott (Eds.), *Dynamic assessment: Prevailing models and applications* (pp. 681–712). Greenwich, CT: Elsevier.

Carroll, J. B. (1981). Twenty-five years of research on foreign language aptitude. In K. C. Diller (Ed.), *Individual differences and universals in language learning aptitude* (pp. 83–118). Rowley, MA: Newbury House.

Carroll, J. B. (1993). *Human cognitive abilities: A survey of factor-analytic studies.* New York: Cambridge University Press.

Carroll, J., & Sapon, S. M. (1958). *Modern Language Aptitude Test.* New York: Psychological Corporation.

Carver, R. (1974). Two dimensions of tests: Psychometric and edumetric. *American Psychologist, 29,* 512–518.

Case, R. (1992). Neo-Piagetian theories of child development. In R. J. Sternberg & C. A. Berg (Eds.), *Intellectual development* (pp. 161–196). New York: Cambridge University Press.

Cattell, R. B. (1940). A culture free intelligence test. I. *Journal of Educational Psychology, 31,* 161–180.

Cattell, R. B. (1971). *Abilities: Their structure, growth, and action.* Boston: Houghton-Mifflin.

Cattell, R. B., & Cattell, (1973). *Measuring intelligence with the Culture Fair Tests.* Champaign, IL: Institute for Personality and Ability Testing.

Cazden, C. B. (1981). Performance before competence: Assistance to child discourse in the zone of proximal development. *Quarterly Newsletter of the Laboratory of Comparative Human Cognition, 3,* 5–8.

Ceci, S. J., & Liker, J. (1986). Academic and nonacademic intelligence: An experimental separation. In R. J. Sternberg & R. K. Wagner (Eds.), *Practical intelligence: Nature and origins of competence in the everyday world* (pp. 119–142). New York: Cambridge University Press.

Ceci, S. J. & Roazzi, A. (1994). The effects of context on cognition: Postcards from Brazil. In R. J. Sternberg & R. K. Wagner (Eds.), *Mind in context: Interactionist perspectives on human intelligence* (pp. 74–101). New York: Cambridge University Press.

Ceci, S. J. & Williams, W.M. (1997). Schooling, intelligence, and income. *American Psychologist, 52*(10), 1051–1058.

Chi, M. T. H., Glaser, R., & Farr, M. J. (Eds.) (1988). *The nature of expertise.* Hillsdale, NJ: Erlbaum.

Cohen, J., & Cohen, P. (1975). Applied multiple regression/correlation analysis for the behavioral sciences. Hillsdale, NJ: Lawrence Erlbaum Press.

Coker, C. C. (1990). Dynamic testing, learning curve analysis and the training quotient. *Vocational Evaluation and Work Adjustment Bulletin, 23,* 139–147.

Cole, M. (1985). The zone of proximal development: where culture and cognition create each other. In J. V. Wertsch (Ed.), *Culture, communication, and cognition: Vygotskian perspectives* (pp. 146–161). New York: Cambridge University Press.

Cole, M. (1996). *Cultural psychology: A once and future discipline.* Cambridge, MA: Harvard University Press.

Cole, M., Gay, J., Glick, J., & Sharp, D.W. (1971). *The cultural context of learning and thinking.* New York: Basic Books.

Collins, L. M., & Horn, J. L. (Eds.) Best methods for the analysis of change: Recent advances, unanswered questions, future directions. Washington, DC: American Psychological Association.

Corman, L., & Budoff, M. (1973). *A comparison of group and individual training procedures on the Raven Learning Potential Measure.* RIEPrint #56. Cambridge, MA: Research Institute for Educational Problems. (ERIC Document Reproduction Service No. ED 086 924).

Cormier, P., Carlson, J. S., & Das, J. P. (1990). Planning ability and cognitive performance: The compensatory effects of a dynamic testing approach. *Learning and Individual Differences, 2,* 437–449.

Coxhead, P., & Gupta, R. M. (1988). Construction of a test battery to measure learning potential. In R. M. Gupta & P. Coxhead (Eds.), *Cultural diversity and learning efficiency. Recent developments in testing.* London: Macmillan Press.

Cronbach, L. J., & Furby, L. (1970). How we should measure "change" – Or should we? *Psychological Bulletin, 74,* 68–80.

Das, J. P. (1984). Simultaneous and successive processing in children with learning disability. *Topics in Language Disorders, 4,* 34–47.

Das, J. P., & Conway, R. N. F. (1992). Reflections on remediation and transfer: A Vygotskian perspective. In H. C. Haywood & D. Tzuriel (Eds.) *Interactive testing* (pp. 94–115). New York: Springer-Verlag.

Das, J. P., Kirby, J. R., & Jarman, R. F. (1979). *Simultaneous and successive cognitive processes.* New York: Academic Press.

Davydov, V. V. (1986). *Problemy razvivaiushchego obuchenia. [Issues in developing learning].* Moskva: Pedagogika.

Davydov, V. V., Pushkin, V. N., & Pushkina, A. G. (1972). Zavisimost' razvitia myshlenia mladshikh shkol'nikov ot kharaktera oluchenia [Relationships between the development of thinking of elementary schools students and instruction]. *Voprosy Psikhologii, 6,* 124–132.

Day, J. D., & Cordon, L. A. (1993). Static and dynamic measures of ability: An experimental comparison. *Journal of Educational Psychology, 85,* 75–82.

Day, J. D., Engelhardt, J. L., Maxwell, S. E., & Bolig, E. E. (1997). Comparison of static and dynamic assessment procedures and their relation to independent performance. *Journal of Educational Psychology, 89*(2), 358–368.

Day, J. D., & Hall, L. K. (1987). Cognitive testing, intelligence, and instruction. In J. D. Day & J. G. Borkowski (Eds.), *Intelligence and exceptionality: New directions for theory, testing, and instructional practice* (pp. 57–80). Norwood, NJ: Ablex Publishing Corporation.

Day, J. D., & Zajakowski, A. (1991). Comparisons of learning ease and transfer propensity in poor and average readers. *Journal of Learning Disabilities, 24,* 421–428.

Dearborn, W. F. (1921). Intelligence and its measurement. *Journal of Educational Psychology, 12,* 210–212.

Delclos, V. R., Burns, M. S., & Kulewitz, S. J. (1987). Effects of dynamic assessment on teachers' expectations of handicapped children. *American Educational Research Journal, 24,* 325–336.

Delclos, V. R., Burns, M. S., & Vye, N. J. (1993). A comparison of teachers' responses to dynamic and traditional assessment reports. *Journal of Psychoeducational Assessment, 11,*46–55.

Delclos, V. R., Vye, N. J., Burns, M. S., Bransford, J. D., & Hasselbring, T. S. (1992). Improving the quality of instruction: Roles for dynamic testing. In H. C. Haywood & D. Tzuriel (Eds.), *Interactive testing* (pp. 317–332). New York: Springer-Verlag.

DeWeerdt, E. H. (1927). A study of the improvability of fifth grade school children in certain mental functions. *Journal of Educational Psychology, 18,* 547–557.

Dillon, R. F., & Carlson, J. S. (1978). Testing for competence in three ethnic groups. *Educational and Psychological Measurement, 38,* 436–443.

Dmitriev, D. (1997). Pedagogical psychology and the development of education in Russia. In E. L. Grigorenko, P. Ruzgis, & R. J. Sternberg (Eds.), *Russian psychology: Past, present, and future* (pp. 225–265). Commack, NY: Nova.

Downs, S. (1985). *Testing trainability.* Oxford: NFER Nelson.

Dunn, L., & Dunn, L. (1981). *Peabody Picture Vocabulary Test-Revised.* Circle Pines, MN: American Guidance Service.

Ehrman, M. E. (1993). Ego boundaries revisited: Toward a model of personality and learning. In J. A. Alaties (Ed.), *Georgetown University roundtable on languages and linguistics* (pp. 331–362). Washington, DC: Georgetown University Press.

Ehrman, M. E. (1994). Weakest and strongest learners in intensive language training: A study of extremes. In C. Klee (Ed.), *Faces in a crowd: Individual learners in multisection programs* (pp. 81–118). Boston, MA: Heinle & Heinle.

Ehrman, M. E. (1996). *Understanding second language learning difficulties.* Thousand Oaks, CA: Sage.

Ehrman, M. E., & Oxford, R. L. (1995). Cognition plus: Correlates of language learning success. *Modern Language Journal, 79,* 67–89.

Eisenstein, M. (1980). Childhood bilingualism and adult language learning aptitude. *International Review of Applied Psychology, 29,* 159–174.

El'konin, D. B. (1960). Opyt psikhologicheskogo issledovaniia v eksperimental'nom klasse [A sample of psychological research in an intervention class]. *Voprosy Psikhologii, 5,* 30–40.

Elliott, J. (1993). Assisted testing: If it is "dynamic" why is it so rarely employed? *Educational and Child Psychology, 10,* 48–58.

Embretson, S. E. (1987a). Improving the measurement of spatial aptitude by dynamic testing. *Intelligence, 11,* 333–358.

Embretson, S. E. (1987b). Toward development of a psychometric approach. In C. S. Lidz (Ed.), *Dynamic assessment: An interactional approach to evaluating learning potential* (pp. 141–172). New York: The Guilford Press.

Embretson, S. E. (1991). A multidimensional latent trait model for measuring learning and change. *Psychometrika, 56,* 495–516.

Embretson, S. E., (1994). Comparing changes between groups: Some perplexities arising from psychometrics. In D. Laveault, B. D. Zumbo, M. E. Gessaroli, & M. W. Boss (Eds.), *Modern theories of measurement: Problems and issues.* Ottawa: Edumetric Research Group, University of Ottawa.

Embretson, S. E. (1996). Item response theory models and inferential bias in multiple group comparisons. *Applied Psychological Measurement, 20,* 201–212.

Embretson, S. E., & Reise, S. R. (2000). *Item response theory for psychologists.* Mahwah, NJ: Erlbaum Publishers.

Ericsson, K. A. (Ed.) (1996). *The road to excellence: The acquisition of expert performance in the arts and sciences, sports and games.* Hillsdale, NJ: Erlbaum.

Ericsson, K. A., & Smith, J. (Eds.) (1991). *Toward a general theory of expertise: Prospects and limits.* New York: Cambridge University Press.

Fernandez-Ballesteros, R. (1996). Cuestiones de fiabilidad y la validez en la evaluación del potencial de aprendizaje. [Questions of reliability and validity in the evaluation of learning potential.] In S. Molina & M. Fandos (Comp.), *Educación cognitive* (Vol. 1). Zaragoza, Spain: Mira.

Fernandez-Ballesteros, R. & Calero, M. D. (1993). Measuring learning potential. *Inernational Journal of Cognitive Education and Mediated Learning, 3,* 9–20.

Fernandez-Ballesteros, R., & Calero, M. D. (2000). The assessment of learning potential: The EPA instrument. In C. S. Lidz & J. G. Elliott (Eds.), *Dynamic assessment: Prevailing models and applications.* (pp. 293–323) Greenwich, CT: Elsevier-JAI.

Fernández-Ballesteros, R., Juan-Espinosa, M., Colom, R., & Calero, M. D. (1997). Contextual and personal sources of individual differences in intelligence: Empirical results. In J. Kingma, & W. Tomic (Eds.), *Advances in Cognition and Educational Practice* (Vol. 4, pp. 221–274). Greenwich, CT: JAI Press Inc.

Ferrara, R. A., Brown, A. L., & Campione, J. C. (1986). Children's learning and transfer of inductive reasoning rules: Studies in proximal development. *Child Development, 57,* 1087–1099.

Feuerstein, R., Feuerstein, R., & Gross, S. (in press). The Learning Potential Assessment Device: History, theory, application, and results. In D. P. Flanagan, J. L. Genshaft, & P. L. Harrison (Eds.), *Beyond traditional intellectual assessment: Contemporary and emerging theories, tests, and issues.* New York: Guilford.

Feuerstein, R., Feuerstein, R., & Schur, Y. (in press). Process as content in regular education and in particular in education of the low functioning retarded performer. In A. L. Costa & R. M. Liebmann (Eds.), *If process were content: Sustaining the spirit of learning.* Thousand Oaks, CA: Corwin Press.

Feuerstein, R., & Krasilowsky, D. (1972). Interventional strategies for the significant modification of cognitive functioning in the disadvantaged adolescent. *Journal of the American Academy of Child Psychiatry, 11,* 572–582.

Feuerstein, R., & Rand, Y. (1974). Mediated learning experiences: An outline of proximal etiology for differential development of cognitive functions. *International Understanding, 9–10,* 7–37.

Feuerstein, R., Rand, Y., Haywood, H. C., Hoffman, M., & Jensen, M. (1985). *The learning potential testing device (LPAD). Examiners' Manual.* Hadassah–Wizo–Canada Research Institute, Jerusalem, Israel.

Feuerstein, R., Rand, Y., & Hoffman, M. B. (1979). *The Dynamic Assessment of Retarded Performers: The Learning Potential Assessment Device Theory, Instruments, and Techniques.* Baltimore, MD: University Park Press.

Feuerstein, R., Rand, Y., Hoffman, M. B., & Miller, R. (1980). *Instrumental enrichment.* Baltimore: University Park Press.

Feuerstein, R., Rand, Y., Jensen, M. R., Kaniel, S., & Tzuriel, D. (1987). Prerequisites for testing of learning potential: The *LPAD* model. In C. S. Lidz (Ed.), *Dy-*

namic assessment: An interactional approach to evaluating learning potential (pp. 35–51). New York: The Guilford Press.

Feuerstein, R., Rand, J., & Rynders, J. E. (1988). *Don't accept me as I am: Helping "retarded" people to excel.* New York: Plenum Press.

Fischer, G. H. (1983a). Some latent trait models for measuring change in qualitative observations. In D. J. Weis (Ed.), *New horizons in testing.* New York: Academic Press.

Fischer, G. H. (1983b). Logistic latent trait models with linear constraints. *Psychometrika, 48,* 3–26.

Fischer, G. H. (1987). Applying the principles of specific objectivity and of generalizability to the measurement of change. *Psychometrika, 52,* 565–587.

Fischer, K. W., & Rose, S. P. (1994). Development of coordination of components in brain and behavior: A framework for theory and research. In G. Dawson & K. W. Fisher (Eds.), *Human behavior and the developing brain* (pp. 3–66). New York: Guilford.

Flynn, J. R. (1987). Massive IQ gains in 14 nations: What IQ tests really measure. *Psychological Bulletin, 101,* 171–191.

Frawley, W., & Lantolf, J. P. (1985). Second language discourse: A Vygotskyan perspective. *Applied Linguistics, 6(1),* 21–43.

Frisby, C. L., & Braden, J. P. (1992). Feuerstein's dynamic testing approach: A semantic, logical, and empirical critique. *Journal of Special Education, 26,* 281–301.

Gal'perin, P. Ya. (1966). Kucheniui ob interiorizatsii [Toward the theory of interiorization]. *Voprosy Psikhologii, 6,* 20–29.

Gardner, H. (1983). *Frames of mind: The theory of multiple intelligences.* New York: Basic Books.

Gardner, H. (1999). *Reframing intelligence.* New York: Basic Books.

Gardner, R. C., & Lambert, W. E. (1965). Language aptitude, intelligence and second-language achievement. *Journal of Educational Psychology, 56,* 191–199.

Gardner, R. C., & Lambert, W. E. (1972). *Attitudes and motivation in second-language learning.* Rowley, MA: Newbury House.

Gerber, M. M. (2000). Dynamic assessment for students with learning disabilities: Lessons in theory and design. In C. A. Lidz & J. G. Elliott (Eds.), *Dynamic assessment: Prevailing models and applications* (pp. 263–292). Greenwich, CT: Elsevier-JAI.

Gerber, M. M., Semmel, D. S., & Semmel, M. I. (1994). Computer-based dynamic assessment of multidigit multiplication. *Exceptional Children, 61,* 114–125.

Gick, M. L., & Holyoak, K. J. (1980). Analogical problem solving. *Cognitive Psychology, 12,* 306–355.

Gilmore, R. (1981). *Catastrophe theory for scientists and engineers.* New York: Wiley.

Ginzburg, M. P. (1981). O vozmozhnoi interpretatsii poniatia zony blizhaishego razvitia [On a possible interpretation of the concept of the zone of proximal development]. In D. B. El'konin & A. L. Venger (Eds.), *Diagnostika uchebnoi diatel'nosti i intellectual'nogo razvitia detei,* pp. 145–155. Moskva: APN

Glass, L., & Mackey, M. (1988). *From clocks to chaos: The rhythms of life.* Princeton, NJ: Princeton University Press.

Goncharova, E. L. (1990). Nekotorye voprosy vyshego obrazovania vzroslykh slepoglukhikh [On higher education for the deaf-blind]. In V. N. Chulkov, V. I. Lubovsky, & E. N. Martsinovskaia, (Eds.). *Differentsirovannyi podkhod pri obuchenii i vospitanii slepoglukhikh detei* (pp. 56–70). Moscow: Academia Pedagogicheskikh Nauk SSSR.

Goncharova, E. L., Akshonina, A. Ia., & Zarechnova, E. A. (1990). Formirovanie motivatsionnoi osnovy chtenia u detei s glubokimi narusheniiami zreniia i slukha [The formation of motivation for reading in children with severe visual and auditorial handicaps]. In V. N. Chulkov, V. I. Lubovsky, & E. N. Martsinovskaia (Eds.), *Differentsirovannyi podkhod pri obuchenii i vospitanii slepoglukhikh detei* (pp. 105–121). Moscow: Academia Pedagogicheskikh Nauk SSSR.

Greenfield, P. M. (1997). You can't take it with you: Why ability assessments don't cross cultures. *American Psychologist, 52,* 1115–1124.

Grigorenko, E. L. (1998). Russian defectology: Anticipating perestroika in the field. *Journal of Learning Disabilities, 31,* 193–207.

Grigorenko, E. L., & Sternberg, R. J. (1998). Dynamic testing. *Psychological Bulletin, 124,* 75–111.

Grigorenko, E. L., Sternberg, R. J., & Ehrman, M. E. (2000). A theory-based approach to the measurement of foreign language learning ability: The CANAL-FT theory and test. *The Modern Language Journal, 84,* 390–405.

Groot-Zwaaftink, T., Ruijssenaars, A. J. J. M., & Schelbergen, I. (1987). Computer controlled learning test. Learning test research with cerebral paresis. In F. J. Maarse, L. J. M. Mulder, W. P. B. Sjouw, & A. E. Akkerman (Eds.), *Computers in psychology: Methods, instrumentation and psychodiagnostics.* Lisse: Swets & Zeitlinger.

Gustafsson, J.-E. (2000). Personal communication, Nicosia, Cyprus, November 26.

Guthke, J. (1977). *Zur Diagnostik der intellekturllen Lernähigkeit.* Berlin: VEB Deutscher Verlag der Wissenschafen.

Guthke, J. (1992). Learning tests: The concept, main research findings, problems and trends. *Learning and Individual Differences, 4,* 137–151.

Guthke, J. (1993). Current trends in theories and testing of intelligence. In J. H. M. Hamers, K. Sijtsma, & A. J. J. M. Ruijssenaars (Eds.) *Learning potential testing* (pp. 13–20). Amsterdam: Swets & Zeitlinger.

Guthke, J., & Beckman, J. (2000). The learning test concept and its application in practice. In C. S. Lidz & J. G. Elliott (Eds.), *Dynamic assessment: Prevailing models and applications* (pp. 17–69). Greenwich, CT: Elsevier-JAI.

Guthke, J., Beckman, J. F., & Dobat, H. (1997). Dynamic testing-problems, uses, trends, and evidence of validity. *Educational and Child Psychology, 14,* 17–32.

Guthke, J., Beckman, J. F., Stein, H., Vahle, H., & Rittner, S. (1995). *Adaptive Computergestützte Intelligenz Lerntestbatterie (ACIL)* [The adaptive, computer-assisted intelligence learning test battery]. Mödlingen: Schuhfried GmbH.

Guthke, J., & Gitter, K. (1991). Prognose der Schulleistungsentwicklung mittels Status- und Lerntests in der Vorschulzeit [Predicting school achievement by means of static and learning tests applied to preschoolers]. In H. Teichmann, B. Meyer-Probst, & D. Roether (Eds.). *Risikobewältigung in der lebenslangen psychischen Entwicklung* (pp. 141–147). Berling: Vergla Gesundheit.

Guthke, J., & Stein, H. (1996). Are learning tests the better version of intelligence tests? *European Journal of Psychological Assessment, 12*, 1–13.

Guthke, J., & Wiedl, K. H. (1996). *Dynamisches Testen [Dynamic assessment]*. Göttingen, Germany: Hogrefe.

Guthke, J., & Wingenfeld, S. (1992). The Learning Test concept: Origins, state of art, and trends. In H. C. Haywood & D. Tzuriel (Eds.), *Interactive testing* (pp. 64–93). New York: Springer-Verlag.

Gutierrez-Clellen, V. F., Pena, E., & Quinn, R. (1995). Accommodating cultural differences in narrative style: multicultural perspective. *Topics in Language Disorders, 15*, 54–67.

Guttman, L. A. (1944). A basis for scaling qualitative data. *American Sociological Review, 9*, 139–150.

Guttman, L. A. (1950). The basis for scalogram analysis. In S. A. Stouffer, F. A. Suchman, P. F. Lazarfeld, S. A. Star, & J. A. Clausen (Eds.), *Studies in social psychology in World War II: Vol 4. Measurement and prediction*. Princeton, NJ: Princeton University Press.

Guttman, L. A. (1965). A faceted definition of intelligence. In R. R. Eiferman (Ed.), *Scripta Hierosolymitana* (Vol. 14). Jerusalem: Magnes Press.

Haenen, J. (1996). *Piotr Gal'perin: psychologist in Vygotsky's footsteps*. Commack, NY: Nova Science Publishers.

Hambleton, R. K. (1983). *Applications of item response theory*. Vancouver, BC: Educational Research Institute of British Columbia.

Hambelton, R. K., & Slater, S. C. (1997). Item response theory models and testing practices: current international status and future directions. *European Journal of Psychological Assessment, 13*, 21–28.

Hambleton, R. K., Swaminathan, H. (1985). *Item response theory*. Boston, MA: Kluwer Nijhoff.

Hambleton, R. K., Swaminathan, H., & Rogers, H. J. (1991). *Fundamentals of item response theory*. Newbury Park, CA: Sage.

Hamers, J. H. M., Hessels, M. G. P., & Pennings, A. H. (1996). Learning potential in ethnic minority children. *European Journal of Psychological Assessment, 12*, 183–192.

Hamers, J. H. M., Hessels, M. G. P., & Van Luit, J. E. H. (1991). *Learning potential test for ethnic minorities (LEM). Manual and test*. Lisse: Swets & Zeitlinger.

Hamers, J. H. M., Pennings, A., & Guthke, J. (1994). Training-based assessment of school achievement. *Learning and Instruction, 4*, 347–360.

Harley, B., & Hart, D. (1997). Language aptitude and second language proficiency in classroom learners of different starting ages. *Studies in Second Language Acquisition, 19*, 379–400.

Harrington, M., & Sawyer, M. (1992). L2 working memory capacity and L2 reading skill. *Studies in Second Language Acquisition, 14*, 25–38.

Harris, C. W. (Ed.) (1963). *Problems in measuring change*. Madison: University of Wisconsin Press.

Haywood, H. C. (1997). Interactive assessment. In R. Taylor (Ed.), *Assessment of individuals with mental retardation* San Diego: Singular Publishing Group.

Haywood, H. C., & Arbitman-Smith, R. (1981). Modification of cognitive functions in slow-learning adolescents. In P. Mittler (Ed.) *Frontiers of knowledge in mental retardation* (Vol. 1). Baltimore. MD: University Park Press.

Haywood, H. C., & Menal, C. (1992). Cognitive developmental psychotherapy: A case study. *International Journal of Cognitive Education and Mediated Learning, 2,* 43–54.

Haywood, H. C., & Tzuriel, D. (Eds.) (1992). *Interactive assessment.* New York: Springer-Verlag.

Haywood, H. C., & Wingenfeld, S. A. (1992). Interactive testing as a research tool. *The Journal of Special Education, 26,* 253–268.

Heaton, R. K., Chelune, G. J., Talley, J. L., Kay, G. G., & Curtiss, G. (1993). *Wisconsin Card Sorting Test Manual* (revised and expanded). Odessa, FL: Psychological Assessment Resources.

Hedegaard, M. (1990). The zone of proximal development as the basis for instruction. In L. Moll (Ed.), *Vygotsky and education: Instructions and applications of sociohistorical psychology* (pp. 349–372). Cambridge: Cambridge University Press.

Hedlund, J., Sternberg, R. J., Horvath, J. A., & Dennis, M. (1998, April). The acquisition of tacit knowledge for military leadership: Implications for training. Paper presented at the Society for Industrial and Organizational Psychology Conference, Dallas, Texas.

Henmon, V. A. C. (Ed.) (1929). *Prognosis tests in the modern foreign languages.* New York: Macmillan.

Herrnstein, R. J., & Murray, C. (1994). *The bell curve.* New York: Free Press.

Hessels, M. G. P. (1996). Ethnic differences in learning potential test scores: Research into item and test bias in the Learning Potential Test for ethnic minorities. *Journal of Cognitive Education, 5,* 133–153.

Hessels, M. G. P. (1997). Low IQ but high learning potential: Why Zeyneb and Moussa do not belong in special education. *Educational and Child Psychology, 14,* 121–136.

Hessels, M. G. P. (2000). The Learning Potential Test for ethnic minorities (LEM): A tool for standardized assessment of children in kindergarten and the first years of primary school. In C. S. Lidz & J. G. Elliott (Eds.), *Dynamic assessment: Prevailing models and applications* (pp. 109–131). Greenwich, CT: Elsevier-JAI.

Hessels, M. G. P., & Hamers, J. H. M. (1993). The learning potential test for ethnic minorities. In J. H. M. Hamers, K. Sijtsma, & A. J. J. M. Ruijssenaars (Eds.) *Learning potential testing* (pp. 285–311). Amsterdam: Swets & Zeitlinger.

Hickson, J., & Skuy, M. (1990). Creativity and cognitive modifiability in gifted disadvantaged pupils: A promising alliance. *School Psychology International, 11,* 295–301.

Hoffman, R. R. (Ed.) (1992). *The psychology of expertise: Cognitive research and empirical AI.* New York: Springer-Verlag.

Horn, J. L. (1994). Fluid and crystallized intelligence, theory of. In R. J. Sternberg (Ed.), *Encyclopedia of human intelligence* (Vol. 1, pp. 443–451). New York: Macmillan.

Horne, K. M. (1971). *Differential prediction of foreign language testing.* Paper presented before the Bureau of International Language Coordination, London.

Hosenfeld, B., van der Maas, H. L. J., & van den Boom, D. C. (1997a). Detecting bimodality in the analogical reasoning performance of elementary school-children. *International Journal of Behavioral Development, 20,* 529–547.

Hosenfeld, B., van der Maas, H. L. J., van den Boom, D. C. (1997b). Indicators of discontinuous change in the development of analogical reasoning. *Journal of Experimental Child Psychology, 64,* 367–395.

Hoy, M. P., & Retish, P. M. (1984). A comparison of two types of assessment reports. *Exceptional Children, 51,* 225–229.

Jastak, J. F., & Jastak, S. R. (1978). *The Wide Range Achievement Test* (rev. ed.). Washington, DC: Jastak Associates.

Jastak, S., & Wilkinson, G. S. (1984). *The Wide Range Achievement Test-Revised: Administration manual.* Washington, DC: Jastak Associates.

Jensen, M. R. (1992). Principles of change models in school psychology and education. In J. Carlson (Ed.), *Cognition and educational practice* (Vol. 1B, pp. 47–72). Greenwich, CT: JAI.

Jensen, M. R. (1998). *MindLadder projects: Student, school, family and community learning in the information age.* Unpublished manuscript, International Center for Mediated Learning, American InterContinental University.

Jensen, M. R. (2000). The mindladder model: Using dynamic assessment to help students learn to assemble and use knowledge. In C. S. Lidz & J. G. Elliott (Eds.), *Dynamic assessment: Prevailing models and applications* (pp. 187–227). Greenwich, CT: Elsevier-JAI.

Jensen, M. R., Robinson-Zañarty, C., & Jensen, M. L. (1992). *Dynamic testing and mediated learning: Testing and intervention for developing cognitive and knowledge structures.* Sacramento, CA: The California Department of Education. The Advisory Committee on the Reform of California's Testing Procedures in Special Education.

Jepsen, R. H. (2000). Dynamic assessment of learners with severe developmental disabilities. In C. S. Lidz & J. G. Elliott (Eds.), *Dynamic assessment: Prevailing models and applications* (pp. 577–605). Greenwich, CT: Elsevier-JAI.

Jitendra, A. K., & Kameenui, E. J. (1993). Dynamic testing as a compensatory testing approach: A description and analysis. *RASE: Remedial and Special Education, 14,* 6–18.

Kahn, R. J. (2000). Dynamic assessment of infants and toddlers. In C. S. Lidz & J. G. Elliott (Eds.), *Dynamic assessment: Prevailing models and applications* (pp. 325–373). Greenwich, CT: Elsevier-JAI.

Kalmykova, S. J. (1975). Problemy diagnostiki psikhicheskogo razvitiia shkol'nikov [*Testing of schoolchildren's mental development*]. Moskva: Pedagogika.

Kaniel, S., & Tzuriel, D. (1992). Mediated learning experience approach in the assessment and treatment of borderline psychotic adolescents. In H. C. Haywood & D. Tzuriel (Eds.), *Interactive assessment* (pp. 399–418). New York: Springer-Verlag.

Kaniel, S., Tzuriel, D., Feuerstein, R., Ben-Shachar, N., & Eitan, T. (1991). Dynamic assessment, learning, and transfer abilities of Jewish Ethiopian immigrants to Israel. In R. Feuerstein, P. S. Klein, & A. Tannenbaum (Eds.), *Mediated learning experience* (pp. 179–209). London: Freund.

Kar, B. C., Dash, U. N., Das, J. P., & Carlson, J. (1993). Two experiments on the dynamic testing of planning. *Learning and Individual Differences, 5,* 13–29.

Karpov, Y. V., & Gindis, B. (2000). Dynamic assessment of the level of internalization of elementary school children's problem-solving activity. In C. S. Lidz & J. G. Elliott (Eds.), *Dynamic assessment: Prevailing models and applications* (pp. 133–154). Greenwich, CT: Elsevier-JAI.

Katz, M., & Bucholz, E. (1984). Use of the LPAD for cognitive enrichment of a deaf child. *School Psychology Review, 13,* 99–106.

Keane, K. J., & Kretschmer, R. (1987). The effect of mediated learning intervention on cognitive task performance with a deaf population. *Journal of Educational Psychology, 79,* 49–53.

Keane, K. J., Tannenbaum, A. J., & Krapf, G. F. (1992). Cognitive competence: Reality and potential in the deaf. In H. C. Haywood & D. Tzuriel (Eds.) *Interactive assessment* (pp. 300–316). New York: Springer-Verlag.

Kern, B. (1930). *Winkungsformen der Überg [Effects in training].* Munster, Germany: Helios.

Kirschenbaum, R. J. (1998). Dynamic assessment and its use with underserved gifted and talented populations. *Gifted Child Quartely, 42,* 140–147.

Klauer, K. J. (1993). Evaluation einer Evaluation. Stellungsnahme zum Beitrag von Hager und Hasselhorn [Evaluation of an evaluation: A critique of the study by Hager and Hasselhorn]. *Zeitschrift fur Entwicklungspsychologie und Padagogische Psychologie, 25,* 322–327.

Klein, S. (1987). *The effects of modern mathematics.* Budapest: Akademia.

Kliegl, R., & Baltes, P. B. (1987). Theory-guided analysis of development and aging mechanisms through testing-the-limits and research on expertise. In C. Schooler & K. W. Schaie (Eds.), *Cognitive functioning and social structures over the life course.* Norwood: Ablex.

Kliegl, R., Smith, J., & Baltes, P. B. (1989). Testing-the-limits and the study of adult age differences in cognitive plasticity of a mnemonic skill. *Developmental Psychology, 25,* 247–256.

Kofsky, E. (1966). A scalogram study of classificatory development. *Child Development, 37,* 191–204.

Kozulin, A. (1984). *Psychology in Utopia.* Cambridge: MIT Press.

Kozulin, A. (1990). *Vygotsky's psychology (A biography of ideas).* New York: Harvester Wheatsheaf.

Kozulin, A. (1998). Profiles of immigrant students' cognitive performance on Raven's Progressive Matrices. *Perceptual and Motor Skills, 87,* 1311–1314.

Kozulin, A., & Falik, L. (1995). Dynamic cognitive assessment of the child. *Current Directions in Psychological Science, 4(6),* 192–196.

Krashen, S. (1981). *Second language acquisition and second language learning.* Oxford: Oxford University Press.

Laboratory of Comparative Human Cognition (1982). Culture and intelligence. In R. J. Sternberg (Ed.), *Handbook of human intelligence* (pp. 642–719). New York: Cambridge University Press.

Laughon, P. (1990). The dynamic testing of intelligence: A review of three approaches. *School Psychology Review, 19,* 459–470.

Lave, J. (1989). *Cognition in practice.* New York: Cambridge University Press.

LeGagnoux, G., Michael, W. B., Hocevar, D., & Maxwell, V. (1990). Retest effects on standardized structure-of-intellect ability measures for a sample of elementary school children. *Educational and Psychological Measurement, 50,* 475–492.

Lett, J. A., & O'Mara, F. E. (1990). Predictors of success in an intensive foreign language learning context: Correlates of language learning at the Defense Language Institute Foreign Language Center. In T. Parry & C. W. Stansfield (Eds.), *Language aptitude reconsidered* (pp. 222–260). Englewood Cliffs, NJ: Prentice Hall Regents.

Levina, R.E. (Ed.) (1968). *Osnovy teorii i praktiki logopedii [Fundamentals of logopaedic theory and practice].* Moskva: Pedagogika.

Lidz, C. S. (Ed.) (1987). *Dynamic assessment: An interactional approach to evaluating learning potential.* New York: Guilford Press.

Lidz, C. S. (1991). *Practitioner's guide to dynamic testing.* New York: Guilford Press.

Lidz, C. S. (1995). Dynamic assessment and the legacy of L. S. Vygotsky. *School Psychology International, 16,* 143–153.

Lidz, C. S. (1997). Dynamic assessment approaches. In D. P. Flanagan, J. L. Genshaft, & P. L. Harrison (Eds.), *Contemporary approaches to assessment of intelligence* (pp. 281–296). New York: Guilford.

Lidz, C. S. (2000). The application of Cognitive Functions Scale (ACFS): An example of curriculum-based dynamic assessment. In C. S. Lidz & J. G. Elliott (Eds.), *Dynamic assessment: Prevailing models and applications* (pp. 407–439). Greenwich, CT: Elsevier-JAI.

Lidz, C. S., & Elliott, J. G. (Eds.) (2000). *Dynamic assessment: Prevailing models and applications.* Greenwich, CT: Elsevier-JAI.

Lidz, C. S., & Thomas, C. (1987). The Preschool Learning Testing Device: Extension of a static approach. In C. S. Lidz (Ed.), *Dynamic assessment: An interactional approach to evaluating learning potential* (pp. 288–326). New York: Guilford.

Lord, F. M. (1952). A theory of mental test scores. *Psychometric Monograph No 7.*

Lord, F. M. (1980). *Applications of item response theory to practical testing problems.* Hillsdale, NJ: Erlbaum.

Luria, A. R. (1973). *The working brain.* New York: Basic Books.

Luther, M., Cole, E., Gamlin, P. (Eds.) (1996). *Dynamic testing for instruction: From theory to application.* North York: Captus University Publications.

Maxwell, S. E., Delaney, H. D., & Manheimer, J. M. (1985). ANOVA of residuals and ANCOVA: Correcting an illusion by using model comparisons and graphs. *Journal of Educational Statistics, 10,* 197–209.

May, R. M. (1976). Simple mathematical models with very complicated dynamics. *Nature, 261,* 459–467.

McClelland, D. C. (1985). *Human motivation.* New York: Scott Foresman.

McClelland, D. C., Atkinson, J. W., Clark, R. A., & Lowell, E. L. (1976). *The achievement motive.* New York: Irvington.

McCutcheon, A. L. (1987). *Latent class analysis.* Beverly Hills: Sage.

McLane, J. B. (1990). Writing as a social process. In L. Moll (Ed.), *Vygotsky and education* (pp. 304–318). Cambridge. MA: Cambridge University Press.

McNamee, G. D. (1990). Learning to read and write in an inner-city setting: a longitudinal study of community change. In L. Moll (Ed.), *Vygotsky and education* (pp. 287–303). Cambridge. MA: Cambridge University Press.

McNamee, G. D., McLane, J. B., Cooper, P. M., & Kerwin, S. M. (1985). Cognition and affect in early literacy development. *Early Childhood Development and Cure, 20,* 229–244.

Mercer, J. R. (1979). *Technical manual: SOMPA.* New York: Psychological Corporation.

Minick, N. (1987). Implications of Vygotsky's theories of dynamic assessment. In C. S. Lidz (Ed.), *Dynamic assessment: An interactional approach to evaluating learning potential* (pp. 116–140). New York: Guilford Press.

Missiuna, C., & Samuels, M. T. (1988). Dynamic testing: Review and critique. *Special Services in the Schools, 5,* 1–22.

Missiuna, C., & Samuels, M. T. (1989). Dynamic testing of preschool children with special needs: Comparison of mediation and instruction. *RASE: Remedial and Special Education, 10,* 53–62.

Molina, S., & Perez, A. A. (1993). Cognitive processes in the child with Down syndrome. *Developmental Disabilities Bulletin, 21,* 21–35.

Moll, L., & Greenberg, J. (1990). Creating zones of possibilities: combining social contexts for instruction. In L. Moll (Ed.), *Vygotsky and education* (pp. 319–348). Cambridge, MA: Cambridge University Press.

Mundy-Castle, A. C. (1967). An experimental study of prediction among Ghanaian children. *Journal of Social Psychology, 73,* 161–168.

Naglieri, J. A., & Das, J. P. (1988). Planning-attention-simultaneous-successive (PASS): A model for testing. *School Psychology Review, 19,* 423–458.

Neisser, U. (Ed.) (1998). *The rising curve.* Washington, DC: American Psychological Association.

Newell, K. M. (1986). Constraints on the development of coordination. In M. G. Wade & H. T. A. Whiting (Eds.) *Motor development in children: Aspects of coordination and control* (pp. 341–360). Dordrecht, Netherlands: Martinus Nijhoff.

Newell, K. M., & Molenaar, P. C. M. (Eds.) (1998). *Applications of nonlinear dynsmics to developmental process modeling.*

Newman, D., Griffin, P., & Cole, M. (Eds.) (1989). *The construction zone: Working for cognitive change in school.* New York: Cambridge University Press.

Newman, F., & Holzman, L. (1993). *Lev Vygotsky: Revolutionary scientist.* London: Routledge.

Nikolaeva, S. M. (1995). Vidy raboty po korrektsii narusheny pis'mennoi rechi u pervoklassnikov [Correcting written language problems in first-graders]. *Defectologiia, 3,* 76–81.

Nuñes, T. (1994). Street intelligence. In R. J. Sternberg (Ed.), *Encyclopedia of human intelligence* (Vol. 2, pp. 1045–1049). New York: Macmillan.

Obukhova, L. F. (1972). Etapy razvitia detskogo myshlenia [Stages of the development of children's thinking]. Moscow: Moscow University Press.

Okagaki, L., & Sternberg, R. J. (1993). Parental beliefs and children's school performance. *Child Development, 64,* 36–56.

Olswang, L. B., & Bain, B. A. (1996). Testing information for predicting upcoming change in language production. *Journal of Speech and Hearing Research, 39,* 414–423.

Ombrédane, A., Robayer, F., & Plumail, H. (1956). Résultats d'une application répétée du matrix-couleur à une population de Noirs Congolais. *Bulletin, Centre d'Etudes et Recherches Psychotechniques, 6,* 129–147.

Osaka, M., & Osaka, N. (1992). Language-independent working memory as measured by Japanese and English reading span tests. *Bulletin of the Psychonomic Society, 30,* 287–289.

Osaka, M., Osaka, N., & Groner, R. (1993). Language-independent working memory: Evidence from German and French span tests. *Bulletin of the Psychonomic Society, 31,* 117–118.

Palincsar, A. S., & Brown, A. L. (1984). Reciprocal teaching of comprehension-fostering and comprehension-monitoring activities. *Cognition and Instruction, 1,* 117–175.

Palincsar, A. S., & Brown, A. L. (1988). Teaching and practical thinking skills to promote comprehension in the context of group problem solving. *RASE, 9,* 53–59.

Palincsar, A. S., Brown, A., & Campione, J. (1991). Dynamic assessment. In H. L. Swanson (Ed.), *Handbook on the assessment of learning disabilities: theory, research, and practice* (pp. 75–95). Austin, TX: PRO-ED.

Paour, J.-L. (1992). Induction of logic structures in the mentally retarded: A testing and intervention instrument. In H. C. Haywood & D. Tzuriel (Eds.), *Interactive testing* (pp. 119–166). New York: Springer-Verlag.

Parry, T. S., & Child, J. R. (1990). Preliminary investigation of the relationship between *VORD, MLAT,* and language proficiency. In T. Parry & C. W. Stansfield (Eds.), *Language aptitude reconsidered* (pp. 30–66). Englewood Cliffs, NJ: Prentice Hall.

Pascual-Leone, J. (1995). Learning and development as dialectical factors in cognitive growth. *Human Development, 38,* 338–348.

Pascual-Leone, J., & Baillargeon, R. (1994). Developmental measurement of mental attention. *International Journal of Behavioral Development, 17,* 161–200.

Pascual-Leone, J., & Johnson, J. (in press). Culture-fair assessment and the processes of mental attention. In A. Kozulin & Y. Rand (Eds.), *Experience of mediated learning: An impact of Feuerstein's theory in education and psychology.* Amsterdam: Elsevier.

Pascual-Leone, J., & Ijaz, H. (1989). Mental capacity testing as a form of intellectual-developmental assessment. In R. J. Samuda, S. L. Kong, J. Cummins, J. Pascual-Leone, & J. Lewis (Eds.), *Assessment and placement of minority students* (pp.143–171). Toronto, Canada: C. J. Hogrefe.

Peña, E., (1996). Dynamic assessment: The model and language applications. In K. Cole, P. Dale, & D. Thal (Eds.), *Assessment of communication and language* (pp. 2810307). Baltimore: P. H. Brookes.

Peña, E. (in press). Measurement of modifiability in children from culturally and linguistically diverse backgrounds: An initial report. *Journal of Childhood Communicative Disorders.*

Peña, E., & Gillam, R. (2000). Dynamic assessment of children referred for speech and language evaluations. In C. S. Lidz & J. G. Elliott (Eds.), *Dynamic assessment: Prevailing models and applications* (pp. 543–575). Greenwich, CT: Elsevier-JAI.

Peña, E., Quinn, R., & Iglesias, A. (1992). The application of dynamic methods to language testing: A nonbiased procedure. *Journal of Special Education, 26,* 269–280.

Pennings, A. H., & Hessels, M. G. P. (1996). The measurement of mental attentional capacity: A neo-Piagetian developmental study. *Intelligence, 23,* 59–78.

Penrose, L. S. (1934). *Mental defect.* New York: Farrar and Rinehart.

Petersen, C. R., & Al-Haik, A. R. (1976). The development of the Defense Language Aptitude Battery *(DLAB). Educational and Psychological Measurement, 6,* 369–380.

Pimsleur, P. (1966). *The Pimsleur Language Aptitude Battery.* New York: Harcourt, Brace, Jovanovich.

Pozhilenko, E. A. (1995). Ispol'zovanie nagliadnukh posoby i igrovykh priemov v korrektsii rechi doshkol'nikov [Usage of visual materials and play in the speech correction of preschoolers]. *Defectologiia, 3,* 61–68.

Ragosa, D., Brandt, D., & Zimowskyk, M. (1982). A growth curve approach to the measurement of change. *Psychological Bulletin, 92,* 726–748.

Rand, Y., & Kaniel, S. (1987). Group administration of the LPAD. In C. S. Lidz (Ed.), *Dynamic assessment: An interactional approach to evaluating learning potential* (pp. 196–214). New York: Guilford.

Rasch, G. (1980). *Probabilistic models for some intelligence and attainment tests.* Chicago: University of Chicago Press. (Original work published in 1960: Rasch, G. *Probabilistic models for some intelligence and attainment tests.* Copenhagen: Danmarks Paedagogiske Institut).

Raven, J. C. (1956). *Guide to using the Coloured Progressive Matrices: Sets A, Ab, and B.* London: H. K. Lewis.

Razvities psikhiki shkol 'nikov v protesse vehebnoi deiatel'nosti [Schoolchildren's psychological development in learning activity]. Moscow: Pedagogika.

Reber, A. S. (1989). Implicit learning and tacit knowledge. *Journal of Experimental Psychology: General, 188,* 219–235.

Reber, A. S. (1993). *Implicit learning and tacit knowledge.* Oxford: Clarendon Press.

Resing, W. C. M. (1993). Measuring inductive reasoning skills: The construction of a learning potential test. In J. H. M. Hamers, K. Sijtsma, & A. J. J. M. Ruijssenaars (Eds.) *Learning potential testing* (pp. 219–242). Amsterdam: Swets & Zeitlinger.

Resing, W. C. M. (1997). Learning potential assessment: The alternative for measuring intelligence? *Educational and Child Psychology, 14,* 68–82.

Resing, W. C. M. (1998). Intelligence and learning potential. Theoretical and research issues. In W. Tomic & J. Kingma (Eds.), *Advances in cognition and educational practice (Vol. 5): Conceptual issues in research on intelligence.* Greenwich, CT: JAI Press.

Resing, W. C. M. (2000). Assessing the learning potential for inductive reasoning (LIR) in young children. In C. S. Lidz & J. G. Elliott (Eds.), *Dynamic assessment: Prevailing models and applications* (pp. 224–262). Greenwich, CT: Elsevier-JAI.

Rey, A. (1934). D'un procédé pour èvaluer l'éducabilité [A method for assessing educability]. *Archives de Psychologie, 24,* 297–337.

Rindskopf, D. (1987). Using latent class analysis to test developmental models. *Developmental Review, 7,* 66–85.

Robertson, I. T., & Mindel, R. M. (1980). A study of trainability testing. *Journal of Occupational Psychology, 53,* 131–138.

Robinson, P. (1996). Learning simple and complex second language rules under implicit, incidental, rule-search and instructed conditions. *Studies in Second Language Acquisition, 18,* 27–67.

Robinson, P. (1997). Individual differences and the fundamental similarity of implicit and explicit adult second language learning. *Language Learning, 47,* 45–99.

Robinson-Zañartu, C. A., & Sloan Aganza, J. (2000). Dynamic assessment and sociocultural context: Assessing the whole child. In C. S. Lidz & J. G. Elliott (Eds.), *Dynamic assessment: Prevailing models and applications* (pp. 443–487). Greenwich, CT: Elsevier-JAI.

Rogoff, B. (1990). *Apprenticeship in thinking. Cognitive development in social context.* New York: Oxford University Press.

Rogoff, B., & J. V. Wertsch (Eds.) (1984). *Children's learning in the "zone of proximal development."* In *New Directions for Child Development, 23.* San Francisco: Jossey-Bass.

Rost, J. (1990). Rasch models in latent classes: An integration of two approaches to item analysis. *Applied Psychological Measurement, 14,* 271–282.

Royer, J. M., Carlo, M. S., Dufresne, R., & Mestre, J. (1996). The assessment of levels of domain expertise while reading. *Cognition and Instruction, 14,* 373–408.

Rubinstein, S. L. (1946). *Osnovy obshchei psikhologii* [Foundation of general psychology]. Moscow: Uchpedgiz.

Rubtsov, V. V. (1981). The role of cooperation in the development of intelligence. *Soviet Psychology, 19(4),* 41–62.

Ruijssenaars, A. J. J. M., Castelijns, J. H. M., & Hamers, J. H. M. (1993). The validity of learning potential tests. In J. H. M. Hamers, K. Sijtsma, & A. J. J. M. Ruijssenaars (Eds.) *Learning potential testing* (pp. 69–82). Amsterdam: Swets & Zeitlinger.

Ruthland, A. F., & Campbell, R. N. (1996). Relevance of Vygotsky's theory of the zone of proximal development to the testing of children with intellectual disabilities. *Journal of Intellectual Disability Research, 40,* 151–158.

Rutland, R., & van Geert, P. (1998). Jumping into syntax: transitions in the development of closed class words. *British Journal of Developmental Psychology, 16,* 65–95.

Salmina, N., & Kolmogorova, L. S. (1980). Usvoenie nachal'nykh matematicheskikh poniatii pri raznykh vidakh materializatsii ob'ektov i orudii deistvia [The acquisition of elementary math concepts under different types of representation of objects and tools]. *Voprosy Psikhologii, 1,* 47–56.

Salvia, J., & Ysseldyke, J. E. (1981). *Assessment in special and remedial education.* Boston, MA: Houghton Mifflin Company.

Samuels, M. (2000). Assessment of post-secondary students with learning difficulties: Using dynamic assessment in a problem solving process. In C. S. Lidz & J. G. Elliott (Eds.), *Dynamic assessment: Prevailing models and applications* (pp. 521–542). Greenwich, CT: Elsevier-JAI.

Samuels, M., & Scholten, T. (1993). A model for the assessment of adults encountering learning difficulties. *International Journal of Cognitive Education and Mediated Learning, 3,* 13–151.

Samuels, M., Tzuriel, D., & Malloy-Miller, T. (1989). Dynamic assessment of children with learning difficulties. In R. T. Brown and M. Chazan (Eds.), *Learning difficulties and emotional problems* (pp. 145–166). Calgary, Alberta: Detselig Enterprises.

Sasaki, M. (1996). *Second language proficiency, foreign language aptitude, and intelligence.* Baltimore: Peter Lang.

Sawyer, M. (1992). Language aptitude and language experience: Are they related? *The Language Programs of the International University of Japan Working Papers, 3,* 27–45.

Sawyer, M., & Ranta, L. (1999). Aptitude, individual differences, and instructional design. In P. Robinson (Ed.), *Cognition and second language instruction* (pp. 424–469). New York: Cambridge University Press.

Schlatter, C., & Büchel, F. P. (2000). Detecting reasoning abilities of persons with moderate mental retardation: The Analogical Reasoning Learning Test (ARLT). In C. S. Lidz & J. G. Elliott (Eds.), *Dynamic assessment: Prevailing models and applications* (pp. 155–186). Greenwich, CT: Elsevier-JAI.

Schlee, J. (1985). Förderdiagnostik – Eine bessere Konzeption? [Treatment-oriented assessment – a better scheme?] In R. S. Jäger, R. Horn, & K. Ingenkamp (Eds.) *Tests and trends* (pp. 82–208). Weinheim: Beltz.

Schmidt, L. (1971). Testing-the-limits in Leistungsuerhalten: Moglichkeiten and Grenzen. In E. Duhm (Ed.), *Praxis der Klinischen Psychologie. Bond II.* Gottingen: Hogrefe.

Schmidt-McCollam, K. M. (1998). Latent trait and latent class models. In G. M. Marcoulides (Ed.), *Modern Methods for Business Research* (pp. 23–46). Hillsdale, NJ: Erlbaum.

Schon, D. A. (1983). *The reflective practitioner.* New York: Basic Books.

Schöttke, H., Bartram, M., & Wiedl, K. H. (1993). Psychometric implications of learning potential testing: A typological approach. In J. H. M. Hamers, K. Sijtsma, & A. J. J. M. Ruijssenaars (Eds.), *Learning potential testing* (pp. 153–173). Amsterdam: Swets & Zeitlinger.

Serpell, R. (1993). *The significance of schooling: Life journeys in an African society.* New York: Cambridge University Press.

Serpell, R. (2000). Intelligence and culture. In R. J. Sternberg (Ed.), *Handbook of intelligence* (pp. 549–580). New York: Cambridge University Press.

Sewell, T. E. (1979). Intelligence and learning tasks as predictors of scholastic achievement in black and white first-grade children. *Journal of School Psychology, 17,* 325–332.

Sewell, T. E. (1987). Dynamic assessment as a nondiscriminatory procedure. In C. S. Lidz (Ed.), *Dynamic assessment: An interactional approach to evaluating learning potential* (pp. 426–443). New York: Guilford.

Shochet, I. M. (1992). A dynamic testing for undergraduate admission: The inverse relationship between modifiability and predictability. In H. C. Haywood & D. Tzuriel (Eds.), *Interactive testing* (pp. 332–355). New York: Springer-Verlag.

Siegel, L. S. (1971). The sequence of development of certain number concepts in preschool children. *Developmental Psychology, 5,* 357–361.

Siegel, L. S. (1989). IQ is irrelevant to the definition of learning disabilities. *Journal of Learning Disabilities, 22,* 469–478.

Sijtsma, K. (1993). Classical and modern test theory with an eye toward learning potential testing. In J. H. M. Hamers, K. Sijtsma, & A. J. J. M. Ruijssenaars (Eds.), *Learning potential testing* (pp. 117–133). Amsterdam: Swets & Zeitlinger.

Silva, J. M., & White, L. A. (1993). Relation of cognitive aptitudes to success in foreign language training. *Military Psychology, 5,* 79–93.

Silverman, H., & Waksman, M. (1992). Assessing the learning potential of penitentiary inmates: An application of Feuerstein's Learning Potential Testing Device. In H. C. Haywood & D. Tzuriel (Eds.), *Interactive testing* (pp. 356–374). New York: Springer-Verlag.

Skehan, P. (1989). *Individual differences in second-language learning.* London: Edward Arnold.

Skehan, P. (1990). The relationship between native and foreign language learning ability: Educational and linguistic factors. In H. Dechert (Ed.), *Current trends in European second language acquisition research* (pp. 83–106). Clevedon, UK: Multilingual Matters.

Skehan, P. (1998). *A cognitive approach to language learning.* Oxford: Oxford University Press.

Slosson, R. (1971). *Slosson Intelligence Test.* East Aurora, NY: Slosson Educational Publications.

Snow, R. E. (1990). Progress and propaganda in learning testing. *Contemporary Psychology, 35,* 1134–1136.

Sparks, R. L., Ganschow, L., Fluharty, K., & Little, S. (1995). An exploratory study on the effects of Latin on the native language skills and foreign language aptitude of students with and without disabilities. *The Classical Journal, 91,* 165–184.

Sparks, R. L., Ganschow, L., & Patton, J. (1995). Prediction of performance in first-year foreign language courses: Connections between native language and foreign language learning. *Journal of Educational Psychology, 87,* 638–655.

Spearman, C. A. (1927). *The abilities of man.* London: Macmillan.

Spector, J. E. (1992). Predicting progress in beginning reading: Dynamic testing of phonemic awareness. *Journal of Educational Psychology, 84,* 353–363.

Speece, D. L., Cooper, D. H., & Kibler, J. M. (1990). Dynamic testing, individual differences, and academic achievement. *Learning and Individual Differences, 2,* 113–127.

Spirova, L. F., & Letvinova, A. V. (1988). Differentsirovannyi podkhod k proiavleniiam narushenia pis'ma i chtenia u uchachshikhsia obshcheobrazovatel'nykh shkol [Differentiative approaches to the manifestation of writing and reading problems in school-aged children]. *Defectologiia, 5,* 4–9.

Spolsky, B. (1995). *Measured words.* Oxford : Oxford University Press.

Sternberg, R. J. (1977). *Intelligence, information processing and analogical reasoning: The componential analysis of human abilities.* Hillsdale, NJ: Erlbaum.

Sternberg, R. J. (1985). *Beyond IQ: A triarchic theory of human intelligence.* New York: Cambridge University Press.

Sternberg, R. J. (1986). *Intelligence applied.* Orlando, FL: Harcourt Brace College Publishers.

Sternberg, R. J. (1987). Most vocabulary is learned in context. In M. McKeown (Ed.), *The nature of vocabulary acquisition* (pp. 89–105). Hillsdale, NJ: Erlbaum.

Sternberg, R. J. (1988). *The triarchic mind: A new theory of human intelligence.* New York: Viking.

Sternberg, R. J. (1990). *Metaphors of mind.* New York: Cambridge University Press.

Sternberg, R. J. (1994a). Cognitive conceptions of expertise. *International Journal of Expert Systems: Research and Application, 7,* 1–12.

Sternberg, R. J. (Ed.) (1994b). *Encyclopedia of human intelligence.* New York: Macmillan.

Sternberg, R. J. (1996). Myths, countermyths, and truths about human intelligence. *Educational Researcher, 25,* 11–16.

Sternberg, R. J. (1997a). *Successful intelligence.* New York: Plume.

Sternberg, R. J. (1997b). *Thinking styles.* New York: Cambridge University Press.

Sternberg, R. J. (1998a). Abilities are forms of developing expertise. *Educational Researcher, 27,* 11–20.

Sternberg, R. J. (1998b). A balance theory of wisdom. *Review of General Psychology, 2,* 347–365.

Sternberg, R. J. (1999a). Human intelligence: A case study of how more and more research can lead us to know less and less about a psychological phenomenon, until finally we know much less than we did before we started doing research. In E. Tulving (Ed.), *Memory, consciousness, and the brain: The Tallinn Conference* (pp. 363–373). Philadelphia, PA: Psychology Press.

Sternberg, R. J. (1999b). Intelligence as developing expertise. *Contemporary Educational Psychology, 24,* 259–375.

Sternberg, R. J. (1999c). The theory of successful intelligence. *Review of General Psychology, 3,* 292–316.

Sternberg, R. J. (Ed.) (2000). *Handbook of intelligence.* New York: Cambridge University Press.

Sternberg, R. J., Castejón, J. L., Prieto, M. D., & Hautamäki, J., & Grigorenko, E. L. (2001). Confirmatory factor analysis of the Sternberg Triarchic Abilities Test (multiple-choice items) in three international samples: An empirical test of the triarchic theory of intelligence. *European Journal of Psychological Assessment.*

Sternberg, R. J., Ferrari, M., Clinkenbeard, P. R., & Grigorenko, E. L. (1996). Identification, instruction, and assessment of gifted children: A construct validation of a triarchic model. *Gifted Child Quarterly, 40,* 129–137.

Sternberg, R. J., Forsythe, G. B., Hedlund, J., Horvath, J., Snook, S. Williams, W. M. Wagner, R. K., & Grigorenko, E. L. (2000). *Practical intelligence in everyday life.* New York: Cambridge University Press.

Sternberg, R. J., & Grigorenko, E. L. (1997, Fall). The cognitive costs of physical and mental ill health: Applying the psychology of the developed world to the problems of the developing world. *Eye on Psi Chi, 2,* 20–27.

Sternberg, R. J., & Grigorenko, E. L. (1998). Measuring common sense for the work place. Unpublished manuscript.

Sternberg, R. J., & Grigorenko, E. L. (2000). *Teaching for successful intelligence.* Arlington Heights, IL: Skylight.

Sternberg, R. J., Grigorenko, E. L., Ferrari, M., & Clinkenbeard, P. (1999). A triarchic analysis of an aptitude-treatment interaction. *European Journal of Psychological Assessment, 15,* 1–11.

Sternberg, R. J., Grigorenko, E. L., & Nokes, C. (1997). Effects of children's ill health on cognitive development. In M. E. Young (Ed.) *Early child development programs: Investing in our children's future* (pp. 85–125). Amsterdam: Elsevier.

Sternberg, R. J. Grigorenko, E. L., Ngorosho, D., Tantufuye, E., Mbise, A., Nokes, C., Jukes, M., & Bundy, D. A. (in press). Assessing Intelligence Potential in Rural Tanzania School Children. *Intelligence.*

Sternberg, R. J., & Horrath, J. A. (Eds.) (1999). *Tacit knowledge in professional practice.* Mahwah, N.J.: Erlbaum.

Sternberg, R. J., & Kaufman J. C. (1998). Human abilities. *Annual Review of Psychology, 49,* 479–502.

Sternberg, R. J., & Lubart, T. I. (1995). *Defying the crowd: Cultivating creativity in a culture of conformity.* New York: Free Press.

Sternberg, R. J., & Lubart, T. I. (1996). Investing in creativity. *American Psychologist, 51,* 677–688.

Sternberg, R. J., Nokes, K., Geissler, P. W., Prince, R., Okatcha, F., Bundy, D. A., & Grigorenko, E. L. (2001). The relationship between academic and practical intelligence: A case study in Kenya. *Intelligence.*

Sternberg, R. J., Powell, C., McGrane, P. A., & McGregor, S. (1997). Effects of a parasitic infection on cognitive functioning. *Journal of Experimental Psychology: Applied, 3,* 67–76.

Sternberg, R. J., & Rifkin, B. (1979). The development of analogical reasoning processes. *Journal of Experimental Child Psychology, 27,* 195–232.

Sternberg, R. J., & Spear-Swerling, L. (1996). *Teaching for thinking.* Washington, DC: APA Books.

Sternberg, R. J., Torff, B., & Grigorenko, E. L. (1998a). Teaching for successful intelligence raises school achievement. *Phi Delta Kappan, 79,* 667–669.

Sternberg, R. J., Torff, B., & Grigorenko, E. L. (1998b). Teaching triarchically improves school achievement. *Journal of Educational Psychology, 90,* 1–11.

Sternberg, R. J., Wagner, R. K., & Okagaki, L. (1993). Practical intelligence: The nature and role of tacit knowledge in work and at school. In H. Reese & J. Puckett (Eds.), *Advances in lifespan development* (pp. 205–227). Hillsdale, NJ: Lawrence Erlbaum Associates.

Sternberg, R. J., Wagner, R. K., Williams, W. M., & Horvath, J. A. (1995). Testing common sense. *American Psychologist, 50,* 912–927.

Swanson, H. L. (1984a). A multidirectional model for assessing learning disabled students' intelligence. *Learning Disability Quarterly, 5,* 316–326.

Swanson, H. L. (1984b). Process assessment of intelligence in learning disabled and mentally retarded children: A multidirectional model. *Educational Psychologist, 19*, 149–162.

Swanson, H. L. (1988). A multidirectional model for assessing learning disabled students' intelligence: An information-processing framework. *Learning Disability Quarterly, 11*, 233–247.

Swanson, H. L. (1992). Generality and modifiability of working memory among skilled and less skilled readers. *Journal of Educational Psychology, 84*, 473–488.

Swanson, H. L. (1993). Working memory in learning disability subtypes. *Journal of Experimental Child Psychology, 56*, 87–114.

Swanson, H. L. (1994). The role of working memory and dynamic assessment in the classification of children with learning disabilities. *Learning Disabilities Research and Practice, 9*, 190–202.

Swanson, H. L. (1995a). Effects of dynamic testing on the classification of learning disabilities: The predictive and discriminant validity of the Swanson Cognitive Processing Test. *Journal of Psychoeducational Testing, 1*, 204–229.

Swanson, H. L. (1995b). Using the cognitive processing test to assess ability: Development of a dynamic assessment measure. *School Psychology Review, 24*, 672–693.

Swanson, H. L. (2000). Swanson Cognitive Processing Test: Review and applications. In C. S. Lidz & J. G. Elliott (Eds.), *Dynamic assessment: Prevailing models and applications* (pp. 71–107). Greenwich, CT: Elsevier-JAI.

Talyzina, N. F. (Ed.) (1995). *Formirovanie priemov matematicheskogo myshlenia* [The formation of mathematical thinking skills]. Moskva: Ventana-Graf.

Terman, L. M. (1970). *Concept Mastery Test.* New York: Psychological Corporation.

Tharp, R. G., & Gallimore, R. (1988). *Rousing minds to life: teaching, learning and schooling in social context.* Cambridge: Cambridge University Press.

Thelen, E. (1992). Development as a dynamic system. *Current Directions in Psychological Science, 1*, 189–193.

Thelen, E., & Smith, L. B. (1994). *A dynamic systems approach to the development of cognitions and action.* Cambridge, MA: Bradford Books, MIT.

Thelen, E., & Smith, L. B. (1998). Dynamic systems theories. In W. Damon (Series Ed.) & R. M. Lerner (Vol. Ed.), *Handbook of child psychology: Vol. 1. Theoretical models of human development* (5th ed.). New York: Wiley.

Thom, R. (1975). *Structural stability and morphogenesis.* Reading, MA: Benjamin.

Thomas, H. (1989). A binomial mixture model for classification performance: A commentary on Waxman, Chambers, Yntema, and Gelman. *Journal of Experimental Child Psychology, 48*, 423–430.

Thomas, H., & Lohaus, A. (1993). Modeling growth and individual differences in spatial tasks. *Monographs of the Society for Research in Child Development, 58*, (9, Serial No. 237).

Thomas, H., & Turner, G. F. W. (1991). Individual differences and development in water-level task performance. *Journal of Experimental Child Psychology, 51*, 171–194.

Thorndike, E. L. (1924). *An introduction to the theory of mental and social measurement.* New York: Wiley.

Throne, J. M., & Farb, J. (1978). Can mental retardation be reversed? *British Journal of Mental Subnormality, 24,* 63–73.

Tzuriel, D. (1992). The dynamic testing approach: A reply to Frisby and Braden. *The Journal of Special Education, 26,* 302–324.

Tzuriel, D. (1995). *Dynamic-interactive testing: The legacy of L. S. Vygotsky and current developments.* Unpublished manuscript.

Tzuriel, D. (1997a). The relation between parent-child MLE interactions and children's cognitive modifiability. In A. Kozulin (Ed.), *The ontogeny of cognitive modifiability* (pp. 157–180). Jerusalem: International Center for the Enhancement of Cognitive Modifiability.

Tzuriel, D. (1997b). A novel dynamic assessment approach for young children: major dimensions and current research. *Educational and Child Psychology, 14,* 83–108.

Tzuriel, D. (1998). *Cognitive modifiability: Dynamic assessment of learning potential* (in Hebrew). Tel Aviv, Israel: Sifriat Poalim.

Tzuriel, D. (2000). The Cognitive Modifiability Battery (CBM): Assessment and intervention. In C. S. Lidz & J. G. Elliott (Eds.), *Dynamic assessment: Prevailing models and applications* (pp. 375–406). Greenwich, CT: Elsevier-JAI.

Tzuriel, D. (in press). Parent-child mediated learning interactions as determinants of cognitive modifiability: Recent research and future directions. *Genetic, Social, and General Psychology Monographs.*

Tzuriel, D., & Caspi, N. (1992). Dynamic testing of cognitive modifiability in deaf and hearing preschool children. *Journal of Special Education, 26,* 235–252.

Tzuriel, D., & Feuerstein, R. (1992). Dynamic group testing for prescriptive teaching: Differential effects of treatment. In H. C. Haywood & D. Tzuriel (Eds.), *Interactive testing* (pp. 187–206). New York: Springer-Verlag.

Tzuriel, D. & Haywood, H. C. (1992). The development of interactive-dynamic approaches for assessment of learning potential. In H. C. Haywood & D. Tzuriel (Eds.), *Interactive assessment* (pp. 3–37). New York: Springer-Verlag.

Tzuriel, D., Kaniel, S., Kanner, E., & H. C. Haywood (1999). Effects of the "Bright Start" program in kindergarten on transfer and academic achievement. *Early Childhood Research Quarterly, 14,* 111–141.

Tzuriel, D., Kaniel, S., Zeliger, M., Friedman, A., & Haywood, H. C. (1998). Effects of the "Bright Start" program in kindergarten on teachers' use of mediation and children's cognitve modifiability. *Early Child Development and Care, 143,* 1–20.

Tzuriel, D., & Kaufman, R. (in press). Mediated learning and cognitive modifiability: dynamic assessment of young Ethiopian immigrants children to Israel. *Journal of Cross-Cultural Psychology.*

Tzuriel, D., & Klein, P. S. (1985). Analogical thinking modifiability in disadvantaged, regular, special education, and mentally retarded children. *Journal of Abnormal Child Psychology, 13,* 539–552.

Tzuriel, D., & Klein, P. S. (1987). Assessing the young child: Children's analogical thinking modifiability. In C. S. Lidz (Ed.), *Dynamic assessment: An interactional approach to evaluating learning potential* (pp. 268–282). New York: Guilford.

Tzuriel, D., & Samuels, M. T. (2000). Dynamic assessment of learning potential: Inter-rater reliability of deficient cognitive functions, types of mediation, and non-intellective factors. *Journal of Cognitive Education and Psychology, 1*, 2–23.

Tzuriel, D., & Weiss, S. (1998). Cognitive modifiability as a function of mother-child mediated learning strategies, mothers' acceptance-rejection, and children's personality. *Early Development and Parenting, 7*, 79–99.

van der Maas, H. L. J., & Molenaar, P. M. C. (1992). Stagewise cognitive development: An application of catastrophe theory. *Psychological Review, 99*, 395–417.

van Geert, P. (1987). The structure of Gal'perin's model of the formation of mental acts. *Human Development, 30*, 355–381.

van Geert, P. (1991). A dynamic systems model of cognitive and language growth. *Psychological Review, 98*, 3–53.

van Geert, P. (1993). A dynamic systems model of cognitive growth: competition and support under limited resource conditions. In L. B. Smith & E. Thelen (Eds.), *A dynamic systems approach to development. Applications* (pp. 265–331). Cambridge, MA: MIT Press.

van Geert, P. (1994). *Dynamic systems of development: change between complexity and chaos.* New York: Prentice Hall/Harvester Wheatsheaf.

van Geert, P. (1995). Dimensions of change: a semantic and mathematical analysis of learning and development. *Human Development, 38*, 322–331.

van Geert, P. (1997). Nonlinear dymanics and the explanation of mental and behavior development. *Journal of Mind & Behavior, 18*, 269–290.

van Geert, P. (1998). A dynamic system model of basic developmental mechanisms: Piaget, Vygotsky, and beyond. *Psychological Review, 105*, 634–677.

van Geert, P. (2000). The dynamics of general developmental mechanisms: from Piaget and Vygotsky to dynamic systems models. *Current Directions in Psychological Science, 9*, 64–68.

Vaught, S. & Haywood, H. C. (1990). Interjudge reliability in dynamic assessment. *The Thinking Teacher, 5*, 2–6.

Verster, J. M. (1973). Test administrators manual for deductive reasoning test. Johannesburg, South Africa: National Institute for Personnel Research.

Vlasova, T. A. (1972). New advances in Soviet defectology. *Soviet Education, 14*, 20–39.

Vlasova, T. A., & Pevsner, M. S. (1971). *Deti s vremennoi otstalost'iu razvitia* [*Children with temporary retardation in development*]. Moskva: Pedagogika.

Vye, N. J., Burns, M. S., Delclos, V. R., & Bransford, J. D. (1987). A comprehensive approach to assessing intellectually handicapped children. In C. S. Lidz (Ed.), *Dynamic assessment: An interactional approach to evaluating learning potential* (pp. 327–359). New York: Guilford.

Vygotsky, L. S. (1962). *Thought and language.* Cambridge, MA: MIT Press. (Original work published in 1934).

Vygotsky, L. S. (1978). *Mind in society: The development of higher psychological processes.* Cambridge, MA: Harvard University Press.

Vygotsky, L. S. (1983). Istoriia ravitiia vyshikh psikhicheskikh funktsy [A history of the development of the higher mental functions] (Original work written in 1931). In *The collected works of L. S. Vygotsky. Vol. 3.* Moskva: Pedagogika.

Vygotsky, L. S. (1987). *The collected works of L. S. Vygotsky. Vol. 1.* New York: Plenum.

Wagner, R. K., & Sternberg, R. J. (1987). Executive control in reading comprehension. In B. K. Britton & S. M. Glynn (Eds.), *Executive control processes in reading* (pp. 1–21). Hillsdale, NJ: Erlbaum.

Wechsler, D. (1974). *Manual for the Wechsler Intelligence Scale for Children – Revised.* New York: Psychological Corporation.

Wertsch, J. V. (1991). A sociocultural approach to socially shared cognition. In L. B. Resnick, J. M. Levine, & S. D. Teasley (Eds.), *Perspectives on socially shared cognition.* (pp. 85–100). Washington, DC: American Psychological Association.

Wertsch, J. V., & Tulviste, P. (1992). L. S. Vygotsky and contemporary developmental psychology. *Developmental Psychology, 28,* 548–557.

Wesche, M., Edwards, H., & Wells, W. (1982). Foreign language aptitude and intelligence. *Applied Psycholinguistics, 3,* 127–140.

Wiedl, K. H., & Carlson, J. S. (1976). The factorial structure of the Raven Coloured Progressive Matrices Test. *Educational and Psychological Measurement, 36,* 1015–1019.

Wiedl, K. H., Guthke, J., & Wingenfeld, S. (1995). Dynamic assessment in Europe: historical perspectives. In J. S. Carlson (Ed.), *Advances in cognition and educational practice* (Vol. 3, pp. 33–82). Greenwich, CT: JAI Press.

Wilson, M. (1989). Saltus: a psychometric model of discontinuity in cognitive development. *Psychological Bulletin, 105,* 276–289.

Wimmers, R. H., Beek, P. J., Savelsbergh, G. J. P., & Hopkins, B. (1998). Developmental changes in action: Theoretical and methodological issues. *British Journal of Developmental Psychology, 16,* 45–63.

Wober, M. (1974). Towards an understanding of the Kiganda concept of intelligence. In J. W. Berry & P. R. Dasen (Eds.), *Culture and cognition: Readings in cross-cultural psychology* (pp. 261–80). London: Methuen.

Wohtwill, J. F. (1960). A study of the development of number concept by scalogram analysis. *Developmental Psychology, 97,* 345–377.

Wright, B. D., & Stone, M. H. (1979). *Best test design.* Chicago: MESA.

Wurtz, R. G., Sewell, T., & Manni, J. L. (1985). The relationship of estimated learning potential to performance on a learning task and achievement. *Psychology in the Schools, 22,* 293–302.

Index

Page references to tables are followed by "t" (e.g., 24t)